AF428472

Persuade

and

Grow Rich

A streetsmart course for small businesses to convert NOs into YESes

Volume I-XII

VIBHOR ASRI

Table of Contents

VOLUME - I

Hey Pal,

Welcome to the first 12 volumes of my course, "Persuade and Grow Rich"!

As you know by the name, this course will talk about Persuasion, Sales, and Wealth.

For me, all these three terms are inter-related.

How?

Wealth cannot be created unless you sell something to someone.

It can be your products.

Your services.

And even yourself.

But to sell effectively requires the skill of persuasion.

So, what is exactly Persuasion?

In a very simple language, Persuasion is the art of getting others to take action, and this art is based on the science of human behaviour.

No, it's not about any kind of action. It's about the action that **you want** others to take.

Technically, Persuasion is different from the art of Convincing.

Convincing is getting others to AGREE on your views.

But, as I said, Persuasion is getting others to TAKE ACTION on your requests.

The Agreement is weak in comparison with Action.

It's a bit easy to make people agree on your views. But it's difficult to make people act on your views.

Why?

First of all, there is some inertia involved when you ask someone to take action.

Second, you could face some skepticism and resistance from the people whom you want to persuade.

Like...

Why should they follow your advice?

Why should they act on your instructions?

Why should they buy your products?

Third, it requires more commitment, more involvement from these people if they want to act on your requests. And it's in our nature that we try to avoid commitments as much as possible.

That's why I found Persuasion extremely challenging.

But remember bigger the challenge, the bigger the rewards.

If the challenge is not big then everyone would be doing this.

Around 1/3 rd of salespeople quit their job, simply because they cannot deal with the continuous pressure to bring sales every day... every month... every quarter... every year... They cannot deal with the rejection, which is part and parcel of the business.

Surviving in this profession requires your creative approach... out-of-box thinking... sharpening your skills.

In short, mastering the game of Persuasion.

And this is what my aim is.

To guide you on how to become a Master Persuader, so that you can sell more.

In the beginning, you have to learn this skill consciously. But gradually, you will become a NATURAL.

It's just like any kind of sport.

For example, Cricket:

When a newbie starts learning to bat, he has to learn everything very consciously.

He has to know his strengths and weaknesses.

He has to understand the pitch.

He has to notice the weather.

He has to learn how to grip the bat.

He has to observe his body posture.

He has to see the condition of the ball.

He has to research the opposite team's strengths and weaknesses.

He has to think about the bowler's form.

He has to guess what will be his next ball.

He has to see the field placements.

And many other things... which are beyond my knowledge.

But gradually, this new player starts playing his strokes by simultaneously observing all these things subconsciously.

This is what makes a difference between a batsman playing on streets and a batsman playing in international matches.

It's about how one learned the game.

So, I want you to be an international player in the game of persuasion.

Sales is an extremely lucrative profession.

If you know your game, you can get rewards very fast.

Unfortunately, over the years, it has earned a bad reputation.

Some of the reasons are that mediocre salespeople are selling desperately, unethically, and with a lack of persuasion.

The fact is, since selling doesn't require any formal education, anyone can enter into the sales profession.

No limitations. No barriers. No examinations. No entry costs.

One can switch to the sales profession anytime.

But contrary to easy entry, surviving and thriving is quite difficult, unless one knows this game.

It happened to me as well.

I was an accidental salesman.

This means I was unintentionally moved into the sales. It was not my childhood dream to become a salesman. In fact, I wanted to become an engineer, though I was not a great science student.

After completing my engineering, I joined a company as a tech executive.

My job was to give demonstrations and trainings on CAD softwares.

But one day, one of my colleagues who was in sales, left the company. And I was asked to handle the selling part for a few days till they get a new Salesman.

Since then, I have never got a chance to leave the sales.

It was a roller-coaster ride for me, many ups and downs.

But one thing I knew right from the beginning. The best salespeople are doing something different from the rest of the mediocre salespeople.

To find out what it is, and then to learn, practice, apply, and teach has become the mission of my life.

That's how I'm here today.

I'll teach you what I found.

But learning, practicing, applying is in your control.

I hope you will do your BEST.

Once you start improving your skill of Persuasion, I urge you to sell more, earn more, and become rich one day.

Becoming rich is a vague term.

It all depends on one's financial blueprint how much money you want to make every day, every month, every year, ultimately adding to your net worth.

Becoming Rich depends on how big your vision is.

Have you seen 'The Founder' movie?

It's based on the life of Ray Kroc, the founder of McDonald's.

Actually, Ray Kroc was not the founder.

It was two brothers who started this business: Richard and Maurice McDonald.

They owned a restaurant, which after running it
successfully for 11 years, decided to improve.

They wanted to make food faster, sell it cheaper, without
worrying about replacing cooks.

They adopted the mass production idea from the
automobile assembly line and redesigned their restaurant.

So that burgers can be made on order and delivered within
minutes to save customer's time.

These two brothers were excellent in their craft, but not so
visionary.

It was Ray Kroc who saw the opportunity in this business
and sold its franchise all over America.

He applied his creative ideas, out-of-box thinking,
persuasion skills in selling McDonald's franchise. And he
did all this after the age of 50. When Ray Kroc died, he was
one of the richest men in America.

So, it all depends on your vision.

It doesn't matter where you start.

What matters is where you want to see yourself in the next
10... 20... 30 years.

That's why, in this volume, I'll talk about the most
important character in the whole process of Persuasion.

YOU.

Let me recommend two books, *The Law of Success* and *Think and Grow Rich*, written by Napolean Hill.

One of the richest men in the early 1900s, Andrew Carnegie assigned this project to Napolean Hill to interview wealthy people in America to find out their secrets behind their success.

He wrote these books based on that research.

There are some books and even movies that had a huge impact on the public.

I consider *Think and Grow Rich* as one of them.

Earlier, people used to assume that most rich people inherited their money. The rich were rich because of 'old' money.

But this book changed the whole concept of becoming rich.

As the title suggests, becoming rich depends on your MINDSET. Mastering your money has more to do with psychology and mindset than anything else.

So, if you control the process of your thinking, you can see yourself becoming rich, year by year.

When you read this book, you'll find some characteristics of rich people, which make them different from others.

But what I found the most important are the first two.

1) Burning Desire

2) Faith

No matter how skilled you already are, how much educated you already are, how much visionary you already are, if you don't have a Burning Desire to achieve your goals, you're not going to achieve them.

And if you have Burning Desire, but don't have Faith in you, again, it's very unlikely that you're going to achieve your goals.

So, it all starts with your mindset.

Once you control your process of thinking, Persuasion could be 10 times more effective.

Because this time, you are determined that you're going to achieve your goals no matter what comes in life.

Creating Your Standards

There is another way, which could psychologically help you to achieve your goals.

It's called - Creating Your Standards.

Now I have seen some people make long term as well short term goals.

Long term means where you want to see yourself in the next 10 years. How much money you want to make. Or if you're in a job, you may want to become President in your company.

Short term means you want to increase your income by 30-50% next year. You want to double your clients in two years. You want to go to Europe with your family on vacation next month.

All of these are OK. I have no problem with your goals.

However, I just want you to increase your level of INTENSITY to achieve these goals.

How?

By creating and strictly maintaining NEW STANDARDS in your daily life.

Let me show you what I mean by helping you to make some standards for you.

Suppose you used to travel in second class in trains.

New Standard: From next time onwards, travel ONLY in the first class, no matter what.

Suppose you generally travel in ordinary buses.

New Standard: Travel in a luxury AC bus.

Suppose you're planning to buy a new car, standard version.

New Standard: Buy the top version –sports model or automatic gears or ABS—whatever suits you in that segment.

Suppose you're living in a 1 BHK apartment.

New Standard: Shift to 2 BHK apartment in a good locality. If you're living on rent, then I don't think it would be so difficult.

Suppose your kid studies in an average school.

New standard: Shift your kid to a better school, which has more facilities.

Suppose you eat in a decent nearby restaurant.

New Standard: Start eating in a 5-star restaurant. At least you can try once a month.

Suppose you wear locally tailored clothes.

New Standard: Start wearing famous branded clothes.

These are just some ideas. There are hundreds of ways you can improve your living standards.

Also, if you have noticed, most of these new standards are just ONE STEP ABOVE your current living standards.

Now I know what you're thinking...

"How is it possible Vibhor, with my current salary or limited income?"

And this is exactly my point.

These new standards are created to build internal pressure inside your mind.

Because, by raising your standards, you have actually raised your expenses.

And now you have to make more money to cover up these expenses, which is possible ONLY if you do more hard work... if you sell more... if you become more creative in your approach... if you apply out-of-box thinking in your business...

Just see the difference:

On one side, you made passive long-term and short-term goals, which you may forget or dump after some time.

But on the other side, you've already increased your expenses. **Now you have no other choice except to sell more and make more money.**

This is a kind of reverse psychology.

Many people dream of a higher standard of living IF they had more money.

But here, we have already started living a higher standard with the same income, that's why there is internal pressure for us to make extra money.

However, I don't want to change all your existing standards.

I want you to start with at least one or two.

It all depends on an individual capacity, how much pressure one can handle.

And for God's sake, please DON'T take any debt for paying these extra expenses.

Because the whole purpose of this exercise is to focus on your CASHFLOW.

Building Belief

Creating new standards also depends upon the level of BELIEF you have in yourself and your products and services.

If you don't love what you're selling or if you don't enjoy your work environment, then also it could be difficult for you to do this exercise.

That's why it's better to go slow and see the results.

It will also help you in gaining confidence to take bigger risks.

Now coming to BELIEF, I've always considered it more important than creating your standards.

Why?

To know the reason, I want you to see again the examples of new standards that I discussed with you on the last page.

Tell me frankly; how much are you confident that you can maintain these new standards? Particularly...

If you're starting your business from scratch.

If you're just a newbie in the profession of Sales.

If you've lost your job.

Or if you are sitting quite comfortably and secured in your current position.

You see, it all depends on your belief, how much risk you're able to take no matter what happens tomorrow.

Take the case of Columbus.

He had a super strong belief in himself that one day he would find Asia.

Take the example of Mahatma Gandhi.

He had a super strong belief that his non-violence approach would bring freedom to India.

Mark my words; without self-belief, you cannot think BIG.

Belief is not a magic pill that once you take, you'll get whatever you want.

Belief helps you to keep standing by your ideas, standards, goals, even in the case of adversaries.

Belief helps you create your destiny as per your dreams.

It's the backbone of your lifestyle.

Now you might be thinking you don't have too much belief in yourself.

No problem.

I don't consider it a God gift.

You have to build your belief just like you created your new standards a few minutes back.

You see, our life is shaped by our society.

Most of the things we chose in life are because of the influence of our family, friends, relatives, authorities.

I decided to take science in school and later went for Engineering because most of my cousins were doing the same thing.

No, I don't blame my family for this. Parents want the best for their children and want to provide a secure life.

But Engineering was not my passion. In fact, at that time, I was not even aware of my passion.

That's why I feel jealous of those guys who knew their passion when they were quite young.

Sachin Tendulkar, Tiger Woods, Bill Gates, Warren Buffett, Lata Mangeshkar, all these people knew since their young age what they want to do in life.

I recommend one more book: *Outliers* by Malcolm Gladwell.

In that book, the author talks about the lives of some successful people who became outliers in their respective fields – the people who are the best, the brightest, the most famous, and the most successful.

What I found interesting in the book is a **10,000-hour rule** - one of the factors responsible for their success.

This rule says it takes 10,000 hours of practice to achieve mastery in a particular task.

That's why some outliers became successful at an early age as they devoted many hours in their passion since their childhood.

Well, it doesn't mean that you should stop working on it after 10,000 hours. But, at least you're much ahead of your competitors, who have started late.

Now, coming back to how to develop your beliefs.

As I mentioned earlier, I don't believe too much in gifted talents. I believe in developing talent until you become a master in it.

Building super-strong self-belief requires your creative approach.

The more creative you are, the better you may get the results.

And for that, you need to practice to grow your creative muscles.

Suppose you're an average salesman in your company. Just doing enough every month to save your job.

But somewhere inside your mind, you desire to become the top salesman in your company.

After all, who doesn't want to live a better life, to get more respect in the company as well as in the family? And most importantly, to earn more commissions?

But your belief system is not ready to accept it's possible.

Why?

Because your belief system doesn't have references to consider.

Your belief system has seen what kind of work you do every day.

Your belief system has seen your average results.

Your belief system knows what others think of you behind your back.

Your belief system knows what kind of excuses you give, every time you lose sales.

Your belief system knows why you have never tried for a better position.

Your belief system knows that somehow you have compromised with your current standards, blaming the system, education, family, company, boss, even your market.

In short, your belief system has accepted that you're just a mediocre salesman.

So, what need to do now?

How can you change your old beliefs?

The solution is... Start doubting your old beliefs.

Start questioning old beliefs.

You need to challenge your belief system that you're not an ordinary salesman. In fact, you're better than others.

But how?

You need to provide reference legs to support your idea that you're already one of the best salesmen in your company.

But what is a reference leg? And how to find these reference legs?

The reference leg is proof that supports your idea. Just like the legs of the table support the top.

It's simple arithmetic.

The more the numbers of legs, and the greater the thickness of each leg... the lesser the probability that your idea will fall.

Here, the thickness of the leg means the level of emotional intensity.

So, what is the easiest way to find your references?

It's your personal experiences.

You need to dig deep into your past to find out some deals that you closed, which were not easy.

The sales you made without any colleague's help.

The biggest order you ever got.

The biggest commission paycheque you ever got.

The awards you got in the company for your performance.

The unexpected promotion you got because of some exceptional work.

Taking the family for dinner at a high-class restaurant because of closing an important deal.

Dealing with some tough customer who was not ready to give the order.

The more emotional it is, the better it is. Because higher emotional intensity will increase the thickness of your reference legs.

So, keep digging your past and write down all your best moments in sales.

Remember, the more experiences you have, and more importantly, the more emotional they are, the faster and stronger you will develop your new beliefs.

But what if you're just born in the ruthless world of sales?

What if you don't have any good experiences in sales?

What if you remember only painful experiences?

No worries!

You're not the first person who is facing this.

Everyone has gone through the same phase.

Everyone started at zero.

Everyone faced some bad experiences. It's the part of life.

That's why the senior-most people in any organization are so proud of their years and years of experience.

There is no doubt that they have more experience. They have dealt with more people as compared to others in the organization. They have seen more successes and failures than you.

But, ultimately, what matters is who achieves his goals... Who becomes rich enough to live a life of his choice...

Bill Gates became a billionaire at the age of 31. Mark Zuckerberg became a billionaire at the age of 23. Whereas, many seniors can't even afford their retirement.

So, it's not a matter of counting your years of experience.

It's the matter of how FAST you can achieve your success by focussing on the right strategies.

Let's assume you have not done a single sale in your life. So, how can you build your belief that you're one of the best salesmen in your company?

Now here comes your creative part.

You have to visualize yourself that you're already one of the best.

How?

By cheating your subconscious mind.

Cheating Your Subconscious Mind

The human mind is divided into three levels: conscious, subconscious, and unconscious.

Let me explain the difference between conscious and subconscious through a simple example.

Suppose you don't know how to drive a car.

But one day, you decide to learn driving.

In the first few days of your driving session, you feel a bit uncomfortable.

Because you find it's not easy to control steering, clutch, accelerator, brakes, and gears simultaneously.

It's too much pressure on your mind and body. Your conscious mind is trying its best to learn.

You do mistakes and then correct them.

Again do some mistakes, and then again correct them. And it keeps going until you perfect your driving skills.

And what happens when you master the driving skill?

You can drive your car comfortably, using both your hands and legs simultaneously while looking at the front, back, and sides at the same time. And you do all this while listening to the radio and talking with others sitting in your car.

But how's this become possible?

Because now, your subconscious mind has taken full control of driving.

So, it's your subconscious mind that performs almost all your activities daily.

Consider yourself as a robot; and subconscious mind like a chip inside your body, which is programmed to perform your daily tasks.

That's why never underestimate the power of the subconscious mind.

But what about your conscious mind? What is its role in your brain?

Your conscious mind is basically the gatekeeper of your subconscious mind. This means it has the power to choose what to send inside your subconscious mind and what not to send.

In short, your conscious mind has the power of the present.

It has the power of choice.

What to see and what not to see.

What to listen and what not to listen.

What to say and what not to say.

So, once you decide **consciously** what messages you want to send to the subconscious mind, start feeding those messages to your subconscious mind continuously.

Gradually your subconscious mind will start accepting and believing those messages no matter if it's true or false.

By now, I hope you got my point.

You can cheat your subconscious mind by making it believe your lies.

One of the ways to do this is through visualization.

What is visualization?

In a simple language, it's a powerful way to implant the false images in your mind.

This mental practice can get you closer to where you want to be in life, and it can prepare you for success.

Let me share a famous example of Natan Sharansky, a computer specialist who spent 9 years in prison in the USSR after being accused of spying for the US.

Sharansky has a lot of experience with mental practices. While in lonely imprisonment, he played himself in mental chess, saying: "I might as well use the opportunity to become the world champion!"

Astonishingly, in 1996, Sharansky beat world champion chess player Garry Kasparov.

So, what you need to do in visualization?

Here, you have to do two things simultaneously. You have to add positive images in your mind, and you have to remove negative images from your mind.

It's not as easy as writing down your emotional experiences to build belief.

Moreover, these images are weak because they are not your real experiences.

Still, if you practice your visualization exercise every day, within a few weeks, your subconscious mind will start accepting these false images.

Let me show you one of the exercises on how to do it.

Suppose, recently, your boss yelled at you in front of others. And you're not able to forget this painful experience.

On the other side, you've dreamed of receiving the award for the best performer of the month. You want your colleagues cheering for you.

Here's what to do...

Put the negative experience image in front of your eyes imagining that you're watching a movie in the theatre. You can see your boss, anger on his face, your boss cabin, table, chairs, laptop, and other colleagues.

Keep this negative image coloured and bright with the size of the theatre screen.

On the other side, put your positive image on the palm of your right hand.

Here, you can see your boss's office, with the whole staff applauding you while you're receiving an award from your boss.

Keep this positive image black & white with size so small that it can easily fit on your right-hand palm.

Now you have to do two things simultaneously.

First, start reducing the size of your negative image. Simultaneously, remove colours from the image, making it a dull, blurred, fade image.

Second, start moving your positive image from your right-hand palm to front of your eyes. And while doing this, make this image bigger and brighter along with adding colours.

Ultimately, your negative image should become so small that you can't even see it, whereas your positive image should be now the size of the theatre screen.

So, you have replaced your negative experience with one of your positive expectations.

I know it's not so easy, and it may take weeks to see some results, but you should be happy that you have started working on your creative muscles.

If you think it's too much for you, then the best strategy is to divide it into smaller parts and master each part one-by-one.

You can start with a recent negative experience first that had shattered you.

Let me share my story of how visualization saved my sales career...

During the beginning of my sales career, I used to sell CAD softwares.

One day I had an appointment with the Dean of one engineering college.

He was a retired military man. Since I waited outside his office for a long time, so he apologised for that and started telling me about his busy schedule.

And in return, I said, "I understand sir, you're a busy chap."

It was just a slip of the tongue that I called him "chap". Due to my college time habits.

But it made him furious. He was extremely annoyed and told me to leave immediately otherwise he would complain to my boss.

I felt devastated. I never had such kind of experience before. I was shivering while returning home.

I decided that the sales profession was not for me.

Fortunately, that time I had already developed my habit of reading self-help books.

While going through some of the books, I found one good exercise on how to deal with a negative experience.

So, what I did exactly was I converted that scary experience into a funny scene.

How?

I imagined I'm sitting in a theatre, watching that particular scene when I was at the Dean's office.

Now to make it funny, I added some hilarious stuff to that scene.

I changed that office into a kind of small kids' classroom.

I put some funny clothes on the Dean.

I changed his face into a clown, telling me how busy he was as he had to entertain everyone.

And the moment I spoke the word "chap," I changed his yelling into a silly song.

I made him stand up, start dancing and singing the song:

"You called me chap, chap, chap, chap, chap..."

"You called me chap, chap, chap, chap, chap..."

Also added some funny music in this scene.

It was not a one day exercise. It took me many days.

Gradually, the intensity of the painful experience was reduced.

And now I remember it as a funny incident.

The point is, **this exercise saved my sales career**.

Try this exercise if you had some very bad experience recently, which is haunting you all the time.

While doing this exercise, don't try to be a perfectionist. Just be creative.

Remember, every situation is different. I never say to follow exactly what I say. There are no rules in this game.

You need to apply your common sense as per the situation. You need to apply your creativity to see what suits you best.

Another way to cheat your subconscious mind is to start using **auto-suggestions** where you're implanting your ideas through words instead of images. I mean repeating words and phrases which give you positive energy and motivation to perform best.

Your subconscious mind is like a genie.

Whatever commands you give, it will start accepting them. But it will take some time because these are not real experiences. The reality is much stronger as compared to your dreams.

I'm sure you must have noticed that it's not easy to remember your dreams, but you can immediately recollect your experiences even from your childhood. Because those things actually happened in your life. They are stored somewhere in your unconscious mind.

However, using visualization and auto-suggestion, you can start creating your new image.

You can write your own story.

You can build your destiny.

Okay, let's summarize what you have done till now.

You have kicked out your old standards and created your new standards.

You have kicked out your old beliefs, which were stopping you to take challenges.

You have built your new beliefs so that you can live with these new standards. You're never going to compromise, no matter what happens.

In short, you have burned your boats to go back to your ordinary life.

I must congratulate you. You have already started learning the science and art of persuasion to sell and grow rich.

Incorporate Persuasion In Your Daily Life

There's a famous management principle called the Pareto Principle. It was named after Italian economist Vilfredo Pareto.

This principle is also known as the *80/20 rule* or the *law of the vital few*.

The Pareto principle states that, for many events, roughly 80% of the effects come from 20% of the causes.

The Pareto principle has become a popular maxim.

Some common examples of the Pareto principle are:

80% of wealth is owned by 20% of people.

80% of the matches are won by 20% of players.

80% of the work is completed by 20% of the team.

80% of sales come from 20% of clients.

80% of sales come from 20% of products.

80% of sales come from 20% of salespeople.

Gotcha!

Have you realized the value of the top 20% salespeople?

Who doesn't want to hire these killers?

I sincerely want you to be part of that list.

For this, you need to know what these champions of champions are doing differently from others.

How are they persuading their prospects to win sales?

For me, it's not just a game of tactics. It's the matter of transforming oneself into a super-salesman.

It's about how to think like a Master Persuader... How to perform like a Master Persuader...

It's the matter of adopting principles of persuasion in life and living by them every day.

There's an old saying in hunting:

"You eat what you kill."

The same thing applies to Sales.

What you earn today is because of what you sell today.

In short, if you don't sell, you'll not make money.

That's why you need to adopt selling as a part of your lifestyle.

One of the common questions people ask me is how to start incorporating persuasion in their daily life.

And my answer is: Start practicing by persuading your near and dear ones. Of course, these people are your easy targets. But this is the easiest way to start with.

You can persuade your colleagues to buy you lunch today.

You can persuade your parents to allow you to go on an adventurous trip.

You can persuade your cousin to help you with your current project.

You can persuade your husband to go shopping today.

You can persuade your wife to let you watch a cricket match today.

You can persuade your boss to give you an important project.

You can persuade your friends to go to a movie tonight.

If you observe consciously, you will find there are hundreds of opportunities in front of you where you can apply the principles and techniques of persuasion.

One of my ex-bosses told me a long time back that most of the time, opportunities are lying very near to us. We just need X-ray eyes to see them.

So, you need to begin with persuading your friends and family and then gradually move towards persuading your existing customers and prospects.

The biggest challenge is persuading the strangers who have never heard of you and your products & services.

Don't worry! It will take some time.

The better you become in persuasion, the more you start challenging yourself.

But how you'll know that you're getting better in persuasion?

Simple! By measuring your results every day.

You need to keep checking how many times people have agreed and acted on your requests.

In short, you need to **quantify your results** whenever you apply any technique of persuasion.

This will help you in checking your progress.

It will also help you in building confidence in your abilities.

Remember, I told you about reference legs to support your belief?

So, whenever you win, you add one more experience as a reference leg, no matter how small that win is.

One more important point.

You see, persuasion skill has one major drawback.

It can be used by good people.

And it can be used by bad people.

For example, Con artists who manipulate others for frauds, Ponzi schemes. They understand human behaviour quite well. They easily lure others into their trap.

That's why it's very important to stick with your ethics while applying persuasion techniques. Don't bring it a bad name.

Persuasion is meant for WIN/WIN deals.

If it's a WIN/LOSE deal, then it's a problem.

And if it's a LOSE/WIN deal, then again it's a problem.

But to make it a WIN/WIN deal, you should know about your customer, your target market.

That's why next month I'll talk about the other important character in the process of Persuasion, your customer.

Who Is The No. 1 Enemy Of A Salesperson?

Before I end this letter, I want to share an interesting experience with you.

A long time back, when I was selling softwares, I got the chance to attend one sales training.

The trainer asked all the participants: "What do you think is the no. 1 enemy of a salesperson?"

For a few seconds, there was a deep silence in the entire class.

And then answers started coming one by one.

One participant said: "High price."

The second participant said: "A skeptical or uneducated customer."

The third said: "Low-quality products and poor service."

Even one said: "the customer's wife."

And like these, there were a bunch of answers in the next 5-10 minutes.

After listening to all these answers carefully, the trainer gave his opinion.

He said: "I think it's the Internet."

That answer made me think about my future.

At that time, I was in Direct Selling. I mean selling one-to-one.

Generally, face-to-face selling is perfect for high-ticket items because it involves multiple meetings sometimes. Here, being a salesperson, you play the role of a consultant while dealing with customers.

You listen to your customer's problems, objections, and requirements, and provide the best solution to them.

But I started realising the power of the internet.

There are many advantages to selling on the internet.

The internet is open 24 hours, unlike any office or a retail shop.

The internet works 365 days without taking any sick leaves.

The internet doesn't have an attitude problem.

People can buy from any part of the world.

And the feature I like the most about the internet is that it's transparent.

Nowadays, many things sell online without any salesperson's help.

Online retail is a perfect example.

Even high-ticket items can be sold online if your website and sales page are super-effective.

That's why, after that training, I started studying advertising and internet marketing.

Why advertising?

Because advertising is multiplied salesmanship.

You can sell your products to the hundreds and thousands of people with a single advertisement.

What I found during my research, the great advertisers of the last century used the same principles of persuasion very effectively to sell on TV, Radio, and print magazines.

And now, Internet Marketers are using these principles and techniques of persuasion to sell online.

But there is one disadvantage also by selling online as compared to selling face-to-face.

In personal selling, you have the advantage to see customer's reactions to your proposal. Your customer can discuss all the objections with you at the meeting.

You can mould your presentation as per your audience's mood.

You can answer all their concerns in front of them.

But in Advertising and Internet Marketing, you're selling to the masses.

So, you need to imagine your target market as much accurate as possible.

You need to presume your target market's fears, pains, needs, desires.

The point is, the better you know your customer, the more you can sell them no matter what kind of business you're involved in... no matter what way you market your products and services...

Whether it's personal selling... advertising... internet marketing... or even merchandising...

You cannot afford to ignore studying your customer.

In the next volume, I'll talk about your customer.

VOLUME - II

In this volume, I'll talk about your customer - the human creature that is going to buy whatever you sell at a price that makes you some profit to live a life that you always want.

But do you think this is the reason your customer buys from you?

Well, I don't think so.

Your customer is as selfish as you.

He buys only for his own reasons.

Your customer doesn't care if you're struggling to meet your ends.

Your customer doesn't care if you're not able to pay your loans.

Your customer doesn't care if you're not able to pay your monthly bills.

Your customer doesn't care if you want to win the award of the best salesman in your company.

Your customer doesn't care if you want to go with your family to Europe on vacation.

In short, your customer is not at all interested in your life. He is interested in only solving problems in his life... fulfil his needs and wants.

But it doesn't mean your customer will automatically come to you, even if you're selling groceries (still, most of us go to the bazaar to buy groceries and other basic things, but time is changing).

It's your job to reach your customer... physically... online... TV... radio... or through any other media.

You see, most of the time customer is not even aware of his problems until you make him realise his pains.

And if he knows his problems, then maybe he is not aware of solutions in the market.

And if he knows there are solutions available in the market, then maybe he is not aware that you have the best solution to his pains.

But it's not just about pains. Your customer wants someone to fulfil his daily needs and lifelong desires.

There is a BIG difference between Need and Desire.

Need is the basic thing without which a person cannot live.

For example,

You need food to eat.

You need shelter to live.

You need clothes to wear.

You need a vehicle to commute.

So, according to your financial capacity, you spend money on these basic things.

Whereas, the Desire is what you want in life.

Let me explain this with some examples...

You need food to eat. You buy groceries from the market, prepare food at home, and eat along with your family. This is your daily routine.

But you desire to eat expensive food at 5-star restaurants. Try different cuisines. Drink wines and mocktails.

You need a 1 bedroom house to live with your small family.

But you desire to live in a 3 bedroom house in a posh society... where you can avail facilities like 24-hour power backup, swimming pool, gym, club, secured parking, and children's playground.

You need paracetamol to treat pain and fever.

But you have to take expensive protein shakes and supplements if you desire for bigger and stronger muscles.

The same way you desire for famous designer clothes, luxury cars, the latest gadgets, expensive cell phones, laptops, 3-D video games, vacations abroad, etc, etc, etc.

There is no limit to one's desires.

Sometimes advertisements tell us how people think. Like this famous slogan coined for Pepsi "Ye Dil Maange More," means This Heart Desires More.

Now the question comes where you think salesmanship requires the most?

Selling NEEDS or selling WANTS?

The answer is quite easy. It's WANTS.

Why?

It's because people are well aware of their basic needs and daily use items to fulfil them.

They are aware of brands available in the market. They are aware of shops and online stores where they can buy these items.

So, you being a marketer of daily use items, don't need to put extra effort into educating them.

However, you need to tell your customer why your product is better than your competitor, no matter you're selling NEEDS or you're selling WANTS.

You need to position your brand in your customer's mind.

You need to find out your ideal market – the people who qualified best for your products and services.

You need to find out weaknesses in your competitors' products.

You need to break the loyalty of your competitor's customers.

You need to create a **Unique Selling Proposition (USP)** for your company and products.

What is USP?

This term was developed by television advertising pioneer and author of a classic book *Reality in Advertising*, Rosser Reeves, in the early 1940s.

And now, USP has become an important topic to be covered in every marketing book.

In a simple language, USP means how your product is different from others. The unique point which helps in selling your product to your target market. The quality that makes you different from your competitor.

USP can be a unique feature developed by your organization.

USP can be a specific benefit only for your target market.

USP can be a bold guarantee which nobody else can dare to give.

USP can be your lucrative offer, which none of your potential customers can refuse.

USP can be your expertise in a niche area.

USP can be your big claim, which nobody else can dare to counter.

USP can be your years of experience, like being the oldest in your market.

USP can be your extraordinary service that keeps your customers completely satisfied.

Some of the famous examples of USP are:

Domino's Pizza – You get fresh, hot pizza delivered to your door in 30 minutes or less, or it's free.

M&Ms – The milk chocolate melts in your mouth, not in your hand...

Raymond – The Complete Man.

Hutch – Wherever you go, our network will follow.

DeBeers – A diamond is forever.

Universal Studios Theme Park – A unique theme park based on the entertainment industry, particularly, movies and television.

Maggi – Ready in 2 minutes.

Sometimes, the company's USP gets so occupied in the public mind that people used to call the entire product or industry by that company's name.

For example:

You might have noticed that still many people say *Bisleri* instead of mineral water.

Also, people say *Google it* instead of search online.

Some credit goes to advertisements, which play a big role in positioning the USP and company/product's name in our mind.

I remember one of the famous headlines of Rolls Royce ad.

"At 60 miles an hour, the loudest noise in this new Rolls-Royce comes from the electric clock"

What a great way to differentiate Rolls-Royce from other cars.

Similarly, in the 1960s, there was a famous print ad campaign for Volkswagen Beetle when it was launched in the USA.

That campaign made the Beetle one of the world's most popular cars. The multiple ads run in that campaign helped in positioning the unique points of the Beetle car in the reader's mind.

Here are some of the headlines:

1. "Think small"

2. "Lemon"

3. "Do you earn too much to afford one?"

4. "It makes your house look bigger."

5. "$1.02 a pound."

6. "It's ugly, but it gets you there."

7. "And if you run out of gas, it's easy to push."

8. "Why is our nose so stubby?"

9. "Who in the world seals the bottom? Volkswagen"

10. "The only water a Volkswagen needs is the water you wash it with."

11. "Why you should open a window before you close the door of a Volkswagen?"

12. "Our number one salesman."

Also, I remember one IBM phrase that immediately differentiated IBM from other computers:

"Nobody ever got fired for buying IBM."

I saw one ad in a Hindi newspaper some years back. I don't remember exactly the headline, but it was something like this:

"Swaad masaalo me hota hai, naaki sabzi me"

In English, it means:

"Taste is in spices, not in vegetables."

It's a good way to show the value of Indian spices. However, the ad didn't show the USP of the company or its products. Any spices company in the world can use the same headline.

That's why USP is very important to position your product or service in your customer's mind, especially in a competitive market.

Positioning helps you capture some space in your customer's minds.

But it's not an easy job.

I read somewhere that an average man or woman encounters 1,500 to 2,000 advertisements daily without even realizing consciously.

They see ads when they watch TV, read newspapers, magazines.

They see ads on billboards, posters on their daily commute.

They listen to ads on the radio.

And of course, whenever they are online, they see ads on Facebook, Google, and other websites.

So, imagine how difficult it is to take the attention of your prospect, even for a few seconds.

The more people get busy, the tougher it becomes to attract new customers.

And if you're a small business owner, then you need to be more effective because you're competing with big brands that spent crores in the advertising to buy a plot in your customer's mind.

However, the competition is less if you're first in the market with a new concept or a new product.

Then your challenge is to sell the unaware market who have never seen such an idea before.

Here, you need to prove your business model to your market.

You need to demonstrate your invention to your market.

Earlier designers, architects, and the draftsmen used to make drawings on paper and board since there was no CAD software in India.

In the 1980s-90s, when companies started selling CAD softwares to these designers, their initial response was we don't need these softwares.

One of the reasons was these softwares were quite expensive.

Second, the designers were reluctant to work on computers.

So, how salespeople sold these expensive CAD softwares?

By simply showing them that the designers can delete, undo, copy, cut, paste, duplicate any part of the drawing whenever and wherever they want, which was impossible to do on paper.

In this way, marketers created the demand for these softwares among designers.

Later, when CAD softwares started facing competition with each other, they have to come up with their own USP to get inside the customer's mind.

However, it's not just your company or products that need USP. You need to create your own USP, which your customers remember while dealing with you.

In fact, your USP should be so powerful that your target market treats you like a celebrity.

How?

By positioning your unique trait, style, achievement, expertise in the minds of your customer.

People remember celebrities for their unique image.

For example:

People call Amitabh Bachhan the Angry Young Man.

People call Sachin Tendulkar the Master Blaster.

People call A.R.Rahman the Mozart of Madras.

People call Oprah Winfrey the Queen of All Media.

People call Azim Premji the Czar of the Indian IT industry.

People call David Ogilvy the Father of Advertising.

Of course, these are famous names that are known for their achievements.

However, it doesn't mean you should also wait for your big achievements.

You can create your USP in any niche area where you're different from others, and which ultimately helps you in selling.

But don't waste time on building a brand for yourself if it's not sellable.

Keep in mind; you're always selling yourself first, then your company, and then your company's products.

Now, coming back to the point I mentioned at the beginning of this volume.

Don't expect your prospect will come to you even if they are well aware of their needs and desires.

It's your job to reach your market and persuade them to buy your products.

Now, you might be wondering people go to stores to buy their daily items. People search online about what they want to buy. And sometimes you receive inquiries from people whom you've never pitched your service.

Of course, people go to stores to buy their daily need items. They visit websites to order online. And sometimes they directly come to you to buy your products.

But don't take it as a surprise.

People have already bought these products in their minds before going to stores.

How?

People have already seen your advertisements.

People have already bought the brand name in their minds.

People have already compared your product with others in their minds.

People have already seen your website.

People have already heard about you and your services from their friends.

People have already seen your reviews online.

People have already got referrals from their circle of influence.

The store is just the final place to close the deal. People have already bought you or your products in their minds.

That's why knowing your customers is extremely important.

The better you know your customer, the more you can sell them, again and again.

Understanding your market will help you in many ways.

You will come to know what your market is looking for. What problems they are facing every day.

And as a manufacturer or product developer, you can come up with a product or service which can solve your customer's problems.

And not just one customer's problems. Your product should solve the problems of thousands or even millions of people.

So, you need to understand your customer whether you're a manufacturer or self-employed... whether you're selling products to the masses or you're selling your customized services to your clients.

In fact, you need to build a profile of your ideal customer.

It will help you to understand your market so that you can put your energy and resources efficiently to get the results fast and at less cost.

But how to build your customer profile?

By dividing your target market into three major categories:

1) Geographic profile

2) Demographic profile

3) Psychographic profile

Let's talk about the Geographic profile first...

Geographic Profile

Geographic profile means where your prospect lives. If you want to target your local market, then it's easy for you to meet these people, understand their culture, their likes and dislikes, their language.

If you're starting small and have limited resources, then this is perhaps the easiest way to start with.

You know the area.

You know the market.

You hire local people.

You advertise in local newspapers and even online.

You can buy raw material and deliver the products fast.

You can easily build your brand in your local market.

The point is you should build a good marketing system and reputation that whenever someone is looking for your type of products, he should buy from only you.

Let me give you one of the best examples of how to become a leader in your local market.

Joe Girard is considered as the greatest automobile salesman in the world. He sold more than 12,000 Chevrolet cars and trucks for a Dealership in the US in a total of 15 consecutive years.

He averaged more than 5 cars and trucks sold every day he worked, and he has been called the world's "Greatest Car Salesman" by the Guinness Book of World Records.

In 1963, Joe Girard joined Chevrolet dealership as a Salesman. Before joining this car dealership, he had never sold any automobile in his entire life.

He knew nothing about cars and trucks. He joined the dealership because he had no other option left when he came to know from his wife that there was no food for children.

It was a Do-or-Die situation for Joe Girard. He had already witnessed flop businesses.

At the age of 35, he was penniless. His family was starving. He had no idea what to do.

When he received a commission on selling the first car, his eyes were sparkled to see $10. That $10 was the most precious thing for him that day because that money brought him groceries for his family.

Since that day, he never forgot one simple arithmetic equation:

"Selling cars would bring him money, and that money would bring food to his family."

Joe Girard became an aggressive salesman.

He wanted to sell as many cars as possible.

He had tasted the success.

He was exploring new strategies on how he could sell more cars every day.

He knew that the more prospects if he could meet inside the car showroom, the more chances of selling cars.

But at the same time, he started facing opposition from his colleagues who were also selling cars in the same dealership.

The dealership wanted every salesperson should get an equal chance to meet new prospects.

So Joe Girard faced competition not only from other brands, not only from other dealerships of Chevrolet but even from his own dealership staff.

He realized he could not sell more cars due to this policy.

But Joe was ambitious. He wanted to sell more cars so that he could earn more money because he had seen the extreme pain of living without money. He wanted to get everything for his family.

So, he started exploring out-of-box thinking.

He developed such a good marketing system for himself that every prospect wanted to deal with only and only Joe Girard.

Most of the time, prospects entered inside the showroom looking for Joe Girard.

Since the dealership didn't want to lose the sales, so they had no other choice than letting Joe get the deal.

And the rest is history.

So, what did Joe Girard do that every prospect wanted to deal only with him?

The secret was his creative methods of Prospecting.

What is Prospecting?

Prospecting is the process of looking for new customers. It's one of the most important parts of the entire sales process.

In fact, the entire conventional Sales process can be divided into three major parts:

1) Prospecting

2) Presenting

3) Closing

Joe Girard was so good at prospecting that people wanted to buy only from him.

One of his theories was the **Law of 250**.

According to Joe Girard, everyone knows 250 people in his or her life important enough to invite to the wedding and the funeral.

This means if you see 50 people in a week, and only 2 of them are unhappy with the way you treat them, at the end of the year, there will be around **26,000 people** who are influenced by these guys to not buy from you.

2 X 250 X 52 = 26,000.

Another secret to Joe's success was getting customers to like him.

So what he did that his customers liked him a lot?

Each month he sent each of his customers and prospects a holiday greeting card containing a personal message.

The holiday greeting changed from month to month as per the occasion, but the message printed on the face of the card never varied.

It reads, **"I Like You."**

Another famous method of Joe Girard was working with people who have strong social connections due to their profession or hobbies.

You can easily find such people in your surroundings.

For example:

Local Politicians / Union Leaders

Barbers

Waiters

Receptionists

Medical Representatives

Loan approvers in Banks, Finance companies

Doctors

Taxi Drivers

Chemists

Marriage Bureaus

Cable Operators

Petrol Pumps & Gas Stations attendants

NGO workers

So, if someone was looking for a new car, and came in contact with any such influencers, that person got inclined to buy from Joe Girard. And in return, Joe gave incentives to these people on each sale.

Joe used to call these people his birddogs. And they included even his existing customers.

Like these, there were many smart ways through which Joe Girard spread his name all over the town.

If you're a car or insurance salesman or a medical representative or a business owner running your own store, restaurant, institute, etc. you should read Joe Girard's books.

You should study his unconventional techniques in selling, especially prospecting.

The point is, you should know your local market as much as possible.

And if you're selling in a limited area, your sole objective should be:

Get your name in front of your prospects whenever you can - and get it into their Circle of Influence.

For this, you need to build your **Marketing Arsenal** – I mean, in how many ways you can put your name in front of your prospects and even existing customers so that they never forget you.

It's very important because we're living in a world where there is so much clutter. Here are some of the things that you can include in your Marketing Arsenal according to your financial capability:

Calendar with your/your company name

Business Cards

Stationary

Personal Letters

Telephone Marketing

Toll – Free Number

Classified Ads

Local Cable TV Ads

Street Banners

Social Media Posts/Ads

Posters

Direct Mail

Newspapers/Magazine Ads

Local Radio Ads

Website – Even if you don't have your own business and you sell for others in a limited area, then also I suggest you should have your own website. It's very useful in showing your USP to others.

Email List – Just like the website, you should also build your email list. Consider this as your business asset.

Email Signature

Pay per Click Ads on different websites

Brochures

Catalogs

Infomercials

Seminars

Demonstrations

Business Directories

Google Ads

Circle of Influence

Don't ignore your prospect's **Circle of Influence**. They are the people who influence your prospect's decisions. For example, spouse, friends, relatives, business partners, colleagues.

If the husband is the head of the family, then the wife is the NECK of the family. She has the power to move the head up & down to say yes OR move left & right to say no.

Another benefit is you will start getting referrals from these people.

A referral is worth 10 times a cold call.

This means that it takes 1/10 the time, energy, and resources to close a sale with a referral than it takes to start cold-calling and find new prospects.

The truth is the highest-paid salespeople work on the basis of referrals mostly. In the case of Joe Girard, out of 10 sales, 6 were from existing customers.

It's the daily task of top salespeople to ask for referrals from everyone, and everywhere they go, even on holidays.

They have developed so many sources of referrals that they leave it on junior salespeople to do cold calls.

Demographic Profile

The second way to categorize your market is through their Demography.

You can target your market according to their age. For example:

Children

Teens

Young (20s to 30s)

Middle Age (40s to 50s)

Old or Retired (60+)

You can target your market according to their occupation. For example:

Employee

Self-employed

Business Owner

Investor

Housewives

You can target your market according to how society defines them. For example:

Parents

Religion

Country

Language

Health status (suffering from any disease)

Net worth (Income group)

Education

Food (Veg/Non-Veg)

However, all these are basically a general way of categorizing through demography. Now I'll go into more detail…

You can target your market according to their job profile.

Here are some examples:

Big Boss

Big Boss are the people who run the organization – profit, non-profit, political party, government, society, club, university, etc.

For example:

Business Owners

CEOs, CFOs

Directors

School/College Principals

Entrepreneurs

Deans

Ministers

Bureaucrats

Head of Department

Team Captain

Some of their major characteristics are:

They are logical in their decision-making approach.

They are extrovert.

They are dominating and fast-paced.

They are task-oriented. Getting things done is their priority.

They are In-Charge of projects.

They are impatient. Want results at any cost.

They don't waste time on details.

They are self-confident and independent.

They are strong-willed.

They like challenges.

They decide quickly.

They make decisions with whatever facts are available.

They are easier to convince.

They want you to present your proposal quickly, convincingly, directly coming to point.

They want you to speak more quickly.

They want you to stick to the most important points of discussion.

Generally, most of their time is spent in meetings, conferences, events, networking.

They are visionary.

To meet the organization's goals is their main objective.

They want you to tell them what your product does or what your idea is and how it will help them in achieving their goals or solving their biggest problems. But they want you to be brief and hit the key points.

Analytical

Analytical are the people who are someway engaged in analysis in their day-to-day job.

For example:

Engineers

Scientists

Town Planners

Doctors

Judges

Accountants

Detectives

Auditors

Draftsmen

Lawyers

Coaches

Investors

Researchers

Bankers

Professors

Statisticians

Some of their major characteristics are:

They are logical.

They are introvert.

They are slower-paced.

They are consistent.

They are methodical.

They are good with numbers.

They are good at analysis.

They believe in processes, systems.

They are a perfectionist.

They are good at problem-solving.

They do an in-depth investigation.

They speak less, but whatever they say could have deep meaning.

They prefer to work alone.

They believe in following directions and rules.

They don't hurt others' feelings.

They are short of giving praise.

They don't make decisions from instinct.

They need proof, facts, details, thorough explanation, and as much documentation as you can gather to make decisions.

They need time to think about your proposal and can't be pressured into making a decision immediately.

Cordial

Cordial are the people who are good-natured and easy to get along with.

For example:

Housewives

Chefs

Dancers, Musicians

Primary School Teachers

Hotel/Restaurant Managers and Waiters

Shopkeepers

Architects

Authors

Spiritual/Yoga Gurus

Flight Attendants

Interior Designers

Art Painters

Carpenters, Plumbers, Electricians

Fashion Designers

Massage therapists

Some of their major characteristics are:

They are emotional.

They love to feel the situation.

They are introvert.

They are relaxed, casual.

They love relationships.

They are great listeners.

They are kind, considerate, and supportive and agree with your points.

They are good counselors.

They don't take the risk.

They can't say no or yes easily.

They are slow to make decisions.

They don't like arguments or fights.

They are loyal and dependable.

They don't want you to be aggressive, excitable, and too enthusiastic in your sales presentations and follow-ups.

Instead, they want you to be as gentle as much as possible.

They need constant reassurance that they are making a
good decision.

They want you to build rapport and relationship with them.
Then only they will be convinced of your sincerity.

Social Butterfly

Social Butterfly are the people who love meeting and talking to more and more people every day.

For example:

Celebrities

Receptionists

Hair Stylists

Customer-service executives

Salesmen

Actors, Stand-up Artists, Comedians

Radio Jockeys

Tele-Callers

TV Anchors

Journalists

Politicians

Travelers

Some of their major characteristics are:

They are emotional.

They love to feel the situation.

They are extrovert, enthusiastic, and friendly.

They enjoy being the centre of attention.

They enjoy relationships.

They are talkative, can talk on the phone all day.

They like being with people.

They love entertainment.

They are party animals.

They are fun-loving.

They are optimistic about life.

They are quite active in social media.

They are not good with details.

They go with their intuition.

They are flighty, going in all directions.

To convince them is not difficult but time-consuming.

They consider your proposal only if you have offered the same to the other members of their group.

They need recognition.

They want you to acknowledge their self-worth.

They want you to show them who else uses your product.

They want you to keep your presentation super-exciting, positive, and enthusiastic with NO boring facts and figures.

In my next volume, I'll cover the Psychographic profile.

Out of three categories, this one is the most important.

It's because the Psychographic profile tells you who your ideal customers are and why they are going to buy again and again from you if you meet all their requirements.

So, we will dig deep inside your customer's mind.

Remember, the more you know your customer, the more effective your communication will be while dealing with them.

And gradually, your communication will become so persuasive that your customers start feeling like they are talking to their mirror, even if they have never met you once in life.

Whom do you think people love the most?

Themselves, of course!

That's why they are always seduced towards their mirror image.

VOLUME - III

In the last volume, I talked about the Geographic and Demographic profile of your customers.

The Geographic profile could be as simple as selling to people in your neighbourhood. Or it could be as complex as selling to people of the entire nation.

Similarly, the Demographic profile of your customers could be as simple as selling to people of different ages, languages, communities. Or it could be as complex as selling based on how people communicate, work, make decisions according to their educational background and occupation.

And now, in this volume, I'll talk about the Psychographic profile of your customer.

You see, our customers have complex personalities just like you and me.

Hundreds and thousands of thoughts are going on here and there.

I read that each day the average person has about 50,000 thoughts.

That's why it's impossible to find out what the other person is thinking. Which means we can't predict whether someone will buy our product or not.

But we can make guesses based on how similar kinds of people have behaved in the past.

Therefore, it's very important to know the factors that are involved in shaping our personalities, such as our childhood experiences, beliefs, values, the Circle of Influence, and even the profession we chose.

In short, we need to build the profile of our customers based on how they think and process information in their minds according to their personality and past behaviours.

The big advantage of building the psychographic profile is that it helps us to understand our target customers not just of our town, but of the entire world.

Therefore, working on a Psychographic profile could do wonders for you if you want to market your products across the globe.

Have you watched movies from different countries? Like American, Chinese, French, Korean, Spanish, etc. Their languages are different. Their cultures are different. **But their emotions are the same.**

Psychographic Profile

If you ask me how to tie up the particular advantages of your product and service with the personal motivation of the greatest number of people, my answer will be to start building their psychographic profile.

To create a Psychographic profile of your ideal customer is the smart way to reach and capture your global target market.

These are the people who will not only buy your products immediately; in fact, they will remain your lifetime customers if you keep fulfilling their requirements.

They will become your customers irrespective of age, gender, occupation, languages, geographic boundaries, currency & taxes.

To build a Psychographic profile, you need to know how your customer thinks.

So, let's decode your customer's mind.

Indifferent Buyers

Indifferent Buyers are around 5% of the total population.

They are never going to buy anything, no matter how good it is.

They are pessimistic, cynical, depressed.

They have a lot of problems in their personal and professional life.

They waste salesperson's time.

Their general reaction to your sales pitch is that it's too expensive.

Instead of tiring yourself out with them, free yourself as politely as you can and leave. Go and talk to someone else who will be more likely to buy.

Proactive Buyers

Proactive Buyers are exactly the opposite of the Indifferent Buyers.

They also represent around 5% of the market.

They are positive, pleasant, a pleasure to deal with. They are full of enthusiasm.

They know precisely what they want.

They know exactly the features and benefits they are looking for, and at what price they are willing to buy.

They will take your products and services immediately with few or no questions. Most of the time, they have already researched your products. (That's why it's very important to build your **Marketing Arsenal**, mentioned in the Volume-2).

It's better to sell them exactly what they say they want. Don't sell them something else or something different.

Don't change the specifications.

While giving additional information, don't divert their mind towards any other product.

Visual

They represent things in their minds with pictures.

They prefer to look at pictures, diagrams, charts, videos, graphs, colours, shapes, forms, audiovisual.

They remember things, past incidents in the form of pictures.

They don't forget the faces of people.

Their attention can be easily diverted towards people's looks, dresses, jewelry, accessories, and colour & design of cars, buildings, furniture, etc.

They speak rapidly.

They enjoy theatre, art galleries, museums, and window shopping.

They are good at spelling because they memorize words in the form of pictures.

Their confidence increases when they look good.

They would prefer to be shown a presentation than have something explained to them.

They evaluate others based on their appearance.

They love watching television, movies.

Their home, office, and car must be kept clean and shinning.

They enjoy watching people wherever they go.

They prefer visualization exercises to build their beliefs.

They do traveling mostly for sight scenes.

They often remember what someone looked like, but not the person's name.

They enjoy photography.

They enjoy speakers more if they use visual aids.

Generally, 35% of people in the world are visuals.

Some of the common professions they chose: Art Painter, Movie Director, Actor, Architect, Interior Designer, Fashion Designer, CAD Designer, Professional Photographer.

They use words like see, view, light, picture, look, show, bright, clear, illustrate, highlight, watch in their conversation, and writing.

Auditory

They represent things in their minds with spoken words.

They speak moderately and rhythmically.

They love to listen to music.

They are aware of what voices sound like on the phone, as well as face-to-face.

They can easily identify anyone's voice if they have heard them before. For example: the singer's voice on the radio, the speaker's voice on the phone.

They would prefer an oral test than a written test.

They have a good speaking voice.

They pay attention to each word while others speak.

They think they can resolve problems more quickly when they talk out loud.

They try to determine sincerity by the sound of a person's voice.

They would prefer listening to DVDs, audiobooks, and podcasts than reading books.

They prefer autosuggestions to build their beliefs.

They love to live in quiet places where they cannot be easily distracted.

They can hear even the slightest noise that their car makes.

Others tell them that they are easy to talk to.

You'll often find them humming or singing to the music.

They would like to have an idea explained to them instead of reading it.

They look for quiet areas in the office and public places.

They love the telephone. They get more business on the phone because they love to hear themselves and others talk.

Generally, 25% of people in the world are auditory.

Some of the common professions they chose: Telesales, Musician, Singer, Motivational Speaker, Journalist, Radio Jockey, Office Secretary, Politician, Standup Comedian.

They tend to use words like hear, tone, sounds good, listen, in tune, say, tell, ring, speak, express, mention, accent, resonate, ask, in their conversation, and writing.

Kinesthetic

They represent things in their minds with feelings and sensations.

They speak slowly. Their breathing is deep and slow.

They are calm in their communication.

Instead of singing, they feel compelled to dance to good music.

They love to do exercise, walking, cycling, swimming.

They answer tough questions with their gut feelings.

They enjoy being touched, getting a body massage.

They want to hold or touch things as they are being explained.

They like shaking hands with others. The way others shake hands with Kinesthetic people gives a strong impression about those guys.

They like to participate in activities rather than watch. They like outdoor activities. They enjoy going for long drives, visiting theme parks, doing water sports.

They like reading novels, stories.

They spend more time in the bath as compared to other family members.

They like driving luxury cars that make them feel comfortable.

They tend to touch people when talking. They like patting people on their shoulders and back.

It's a bit difficult for them to remember the looks and names of people whom they met a long time back.

They like to make things with their hands.

They evaluate others based on how they feel about them.

They prefer doing the workout in the gym instead of watching TV or listening to songs.

Being comfortable in dresses is much more important to them than how they look.

Generally, 40% of the population is Kinesthetic.

Some of the common professions they chose: Writer, Hair Stylist, Chef, Yoga Teacher, Traveler, Athlete, Therapist, Novelist, Dancer, Martial Artist.

They frequently use words like comfortable, feel, grab, touch, hold, contact, handle, rub, grasp, suffer, pressure in their daily conversation.

If you're selling products that involve some kinds of fragrance, taste, and touch, Kinesthetic could be your preferred market.

Master All The Three Modes

Remember, if someone is a Visual personality, it doesn't mean he is not Auditory and Kinesthetic.

Similarly, if someone is an Auditory or a Kinesthetic personality, it doesn't mean she is not Visual.

The point is, everyone is partially Visual, Auditory, and Kinesthetic. But they have **one preferred mode** of understanding, learning, and communicating with others.

However, I have seen people who have two preferred modes instead of one. This means they can equally represent things in their minds in Visual and Auditory, or Auditory and Kinesthetic, or Visual and Kinesthetic forms.

And some rare people are excellent in all three modes of communication.

Do you think its natural talent?

Absolutely not.

Although these people started with one preferred mode of communication, they overcame their limitations, learned, practiced, mastered all the three modes so that they can persuade all kinds of people.

In the upcoming volumes, I'll keep sharing creative ways on how to develop new products, marketing offers &

strategies, and how to communicate and present your proposal to Visual, Auditory, and Kinesthetic people.

If you are not communicating with your prospects in their preferred mode of communication, you're losing a big chunk of the market. Most of the time, the problem is not in your product; it's in your communication.

Also, I have seen one of the reasons people fail in their job is because they are in the wrong profession.

Imagine a person who is passionate about singing is doing a designing job.

Or a person who loves doing martial arts for hours and hours is in telesales.

The disgusting part is the people who fail in their jobs lose their self-esteem. They start considering themselves losers.

Instead of blaming themselves, these people should study their personalities and choose their profession accordingly.

For example:

If someone is an Engineer and extremely visual, he can choose CAD designing as his career instead of working in a manufacturing plant.

Or if someone is a lawyer and extremely kinesthetic, she can do well in writing crime novels where a lot of imagination is required instead of arguing cases in the court.

If people start choosing work according to their personalities, then that work will not remain work for them; it will become fun for them.

It could also help in hiring the right people. These people are self-motivated who don't need constant supervision.

Values And Lifestyle

Another way to categorize people is according to their **values and lifestyle**.

This psychographic profile was designed for American citizens in the 1970s. But you'll find it amazing how it fits perfect everywhere in the world.

That is the biggest advantage of building a psychographic profile. You can target your prospective customers anywhere in the world if you know the thinking pattern of your ideal customer.

Many advertising agencies use psychographic profiles based on values and lifestyles for creating persuasive advertisements to appeal to their target market.

You can use this profile for creating new products and selling them fast and more by targeting the right people.

Belonger

They represent conservative, old-fashioned people.

They belong to the old school. This means they keep doing things the way they have done in the past.

Most of them are now 45+ years old and belong to the middle and lower-middle class.

They have a strong need to belong and to be included in family, community.

They are traditional, religious.

They are deeply connected with their families. They want both their parents and children to live together with them.

They are extremely patriotic.

They are very proud of their culture.

They hate changes. They don't like too much modernisation in society.

They drive economical cars (proven model) of domestic brands.

They dress conservatively.

Many of them still do blue-collar jobs. They are hardworking and disciplined in whatever they do.

They have a strong work ethic.

They want their children to live a secure life.

They save money entire life. They keep their money in local financial institutions, banks, post office.

They strongly believe in unity and community.

They prefer communicating in their mother tongue.

They keep talking about their olden days when everything was in abundance.

They want their children and locals to get a job first instead of outsiders.

They don't like challenges, changing jobs, financial risks.

They're very much involved in their society and don't want to bring a bad name. They want their children to get better education and jobs than anyone else in their relations and neighbourhood.

They prefer traditional medicines and home remedies.

Although they are not rich or successful, they want to associate themselves with their country's achievements and other successful people.

For example: When their home team wins some important match, they celebrate by saying "WE WIN". But when the same team loses a match, they say "THEY LOSE".

Once a Belonger becomes a customer of your business, he will try his best to encourage others in his community to buy from you.

If you're selling traditional services, local & economical products, alternate health products, domestic brand products, mutual funds, local bank saving schemes, insurance, this could be your preferred market.

Emulator

To emulate means a strong desire to equal or surpass the successful people.

Emulators are 16 – 35 years old.

They want to become successful, just like their favourite rich and famous guys.

They try to be like other successful people, but they lack vision, originality, creativity, initiative, persistence skills.

They seek material success. They want to have beautiful cars, big houses, a huge fan following.

They don't believe in work ethics. Instead, they look for shortcuts to achieve success.

They are attracted to extremely confident people.

But they get demotivated when they face setbacks or feel a lack of confidence.

Emulators desperately want what others have. They want to possess all luxuries, name and fame, just like the rich and famous.

They have a powerful sex drive.

They are extremely conscious of their outward appearance.

They are attracted to products that could improve their appearance and attractiveness.

Emulators neither save money nor do they invest their money.

They are dependent on their month to month paycheque. Whatever money they earn is spent on their lifestyle, especially on their outward appearance.

They want the best of everything, like their ideals. But since they can't afford the best things, so they compromise with knock-offs and imitations.

Most of their purchasing is through credit cards.

You can see Emulators wearing stylish watches, shoes, trousers, bracelets, jewellery, sunglasses.

They live in a nice rented house, buy an expensive mobile phone, and drive a car, which is, of course, out of their budget and bought on loan.

To Emulators, everything revolves around their sex appeal.

If you're selling expensive, stylish products, which if you could relate to sex appeal creatively, then Emulators could be your preferred market.

Achiever

These are the people who are already successful.

Their no.1 desire is to be unique, different from others. They buy things that separate them from the masses.

Whether it's sports, music, art, business, politics, they want to stay best.

They are self-made, rich, and famous in their respective industries.

They wear the signature clothing of top-class fashion designers.

Since they are already super successful in their ventures, they have absolute confidence in themselves.

Their nightmare is to become a part of the crowd. They are leaders, not followers.

They don't like to waste their time in petty matters.

They have a huge fan following. They like people talking about them.

They enjoy the attention when the media follow their tweets and posts.

They want to publish their biographies. They want someone to make movies based on their life.

They want the best and top quality products. If any particular product is not available in the local market, they will get it from anywhere in the world, no matter how much cost is involved.

Their houses are designed by top architects.

Although they are no short of money, they don't want to spend time and money on useless things. They will pay for value, quality, and results.

In fact, they don't like wasting their money. They are buying expensive unique things because they want to relish the rewards of hard work they have done to become super successful.

Socially Conscious

They are highly educated people.

They want to be a part of intelligent groups who are concerned about their surroundings.

They are outdoors-oriented. They don't like sitting idle at home after retirement or on weekends (if they're working).

They are too much concerned about the environment.

They are extrovert and outspoken.

They love debating on social issues. They want to bring awareness in the society about the biggest challenges the world is facing.

They watch the news daily. They are worried about the increase in crimes in their neighbourhoods, and they complain about the lack of moral values in the young generation.

They are too much concerned about war, nuclear issues, violence, and even cybercrimes.

They want everyone to support the old, homeless, handicaps, sick people, and animals.

They enjoy volunteering in social activities right from their school days.

Some of them start their own non-profit organizations.

They never compromise with their integrity and moral values.

They think they are on a mission and want to make a difference by contributing to society.

They believe it is their duty and responsibility to keep fighting against the bureaucratic system.

They are very skeptical. They don't easily trust government agencies, bureaucrats, authorities, rich and famous.

When you pitch them your products and services, they try to collect all the information about you.

They are frugal with their money. They are always looking for the best discount deals and keep collecting coupons from newspapers and magazines.

Society Conscious people are the hardest to sell. They may interrogate you and your staff.

Need Driven

They live at the poverty level.

They are welfare recipients.

They survive on government assistance.

Integrated

These people are Achievers who also become Socially Conscious.

They want to make a difference in the world through their philanthropy efforts.

They want to leave a legacy behind them.

They want people to remember them even after hundreds of years for their contribution to society.

But they are also committed to making unlimited income along with their philanthropic work.

For them, success is measured by achieving their goals on both sides of their life.

Do Our Customers Work Like Robots?

Another way to know about your customers is by knowing their **Meta Programs**.

Do you remember I talked about the conscious and the subconscious mind in the Volume-1? I told you to never underestimate the power of the subconscious mind.

Most of the decisions we make in our daily life are done by our subconscious mind.

In fact, we all are in someway robots who are programmed to do daily tasks.

Our customers are also not from any different planet. They are programmed like us that help them decide what to buy and what not to buy.

These programs help them in filtering the communication that they receive every day. What to accept, what to reject, what to twist, and what to delete forever.

The good news is we can try to predict our customers' behaviours and actions if we know how they are programmed.

And if we know our customer's behaviour, we can mould our communication accordingly.

Meta Programs

Meta Programs are the filters that tell us how people process information in order to be convinced, make decisions.

These programs are based on how our minds are conditioned right from our childhood.

These programs are generalizations that are stored in our brain based on our past experiences, and information (original, accurate, or distorted, or even some parts deleted) that we keep getting from everywhere.

These stored programs continuously filter all the messages we receive so that we can make the right decision for our well being.

That's why one of the most effective ways to persuade people is to use the same 'Programming' that they process information with.

Here are some of the Meta Programs:

Moving Towards Pleasure vs. Moving Away From Pain

Whatever we do in life is based on two kinds of basic human motivations:

a)   The desire to gain

b)   The desire to avoid the loss

In short, we either want to gain pleasure or we want to avoid loss.

Moving Towards Pleasure

Some people are always attracted to pleasure in life instead of worrying about their existing tough conditions.

They want to live a comfortable life.

They want to attain things easily.

They want to make more and more money for spending on their lifestyle, saving for their retirement, or giving to others.

They want to feel proud of their accomplishments and possessions.

They want to advance in their business. They want better jobs. They want success in their new ventures.

They want to be their own boss.

They want to be first in everything.

They want rewards for merit.

They want to influence others.

They want people to know how they win by overcoming obstacles and competition.

They want to look stylish.

They want more leisure. They love to travel with their family and friends. They want to experience happiness and enjoyment through entertainment, food, drink, mingling with friends.

They want to spend time on their hobbies, like playing music, games, going to movies, reading books, attending seminars on self-development.

They want to save their precious time at any cost. Time is money for them. They want to get everything fast.

They want to get whatever they want without any effort.

Convenience is vital for them in their busy life.

They want to be healthy. They want more strength, energy, endurance.

They want to live longer.

They want to become famous through their attractive personality or their achievements.

They want security in old age. They want to live an independent life even when they are old. They don't want to depend on others.

They want all luxuries that they can't afford today but have always dreamed about since their childhood.

They want to be a leader in their community or industry. They want people to follow them.

They want themselves and their surroundings to be neat and clean.

They want to be creative.

They want to feel superior and seek praise from others for their intelligence, judgment, knowledge.

They want to gratify their never-ending curiosity.

They want to satisfy their appetites with delicious food and drinks.

They want to have all the beautiful possessions in the world.

They want to attract the opposite sex through their appearance, beauty, style, physical build, fragrance, cleanliness.

They want others to appreciate their beauty.

They want to be unique in whatever they do.

They want respect from others for their generosity.

They want to model successful people.

They want to take advantage of opportunities.

They want to be good parents.

They want to be sociable. They want to keep moving in better circles. They want social acceptance wherever they go by keeping themselves up-to-date.

They want to collect rare things.

They want to make lots of friends.

They want to express their personalities and thoughts.

They want to be efficient in whatever work they do.

They want to win others' affection.

They want to improve themselves mentally. They want to be up-to-date in their skills and knowledge.

They want to be recognized as authorities.

They want to do things well.

Moving Away From Pain

Similarly, many people just want to avoid pain. They want to move away from their poor conditions, misery as far as possible. They are so much occupied by fears, worries, hardships, struggles, anxieties that they have never thought of pleasure in life.

They don't want to be dominated by others.

They don't like criticisms.

They don't want to lose their possessions.

They don't want physical pain.

They don't want to lose their reputation.

They don't want to lose their hard-earned money.

They don't want to get involved in any kind of trouble.

They don't want to depend on their children, relatives, or government assistance after retirement.

They don't want to live and die in poverty.

They don't want to die.

They don't want to lose their near and dear ones.

They don't want to face any kind of rejection.

They don't want to fail.

Big Picture vs. Specific

Big Picture

Some people are convinced by how big your vision is.

They want to see an overview of your entire project.

They are more interested in your 'in a nutshell' communication.

These people want to know the major benefits of your products and services.

People who are in a senior position like Director, Top-level executives, CEO, Minister, Dean come under this category.

Once you tell them the biggest advantage, then only they want to know more about your services.

When you're pitching these people, you need to start with your biggest claims.

For example:

- Our product/service can reduce your overall cost by 25%.

- Our product/service can increase your sales by 35%.

·   90% of students of our coaching institute clear the entrance examination in the first attempt.

·   Our software is used by over 1 million people.

·   We are going to build the largest mall in our city.

·   We are the largest manufacturer of this component in our country.

·   Our App has 4 unique features that make it different from any other available in the market.

In short, Big picture is your BIG IDEA, expressed in the fewest possible words, which immediately takes the attention of others.

Here are some book titles and advertising headlines which clearly show the big idea to attract their target market:

Think and Grow Rich

How to Retire at 40 instead of 60

The Four Hour Workweek

Get Rich Slowly

How to Win Friends and Influence People

One Stock Crorepati

The Lazy Man's Ways to Riches

Good to Great

The Power of Positive Thinking

Should every corporation buy its president a Rolls-Royce?

The Rs. 1 Lakh Retirement Secret

The Great Vitamin Hoax

The Deaf Now Hear Whispers

The Bitcoin Insider Code

The University of the Night

The Magic of Thinking Big

Specific

Some people are convinced by how much detail you provide for your products and services. Just showing Big Picture is not enough for them.

They want to know specifics like the type of material, weight, size, volume, price of each component, taxes, delivery, time of completion of the project.

They want to know how your services will affect different areas of their life or business.

Professionals like engineers, technicians, researches, doctors, investors, lawyers, accountants come under this category.

Your sales pitch should cover all the details if you want to convince and sell them FAST.

For example:

- We reduce the operational cost of your production department through these three different ways. Let me explain all these one by one.

- Please find below the specifications of all our best-selling laptops. Let me know what suits you best.

- Here are all the topics that we cover in our course.

In the 1950s, David Ogilvy, popularly known as Father of Advertising, wrote a print advertisement for Rolls Royce car, which became one of the most famous automobile ads of all time.

The ad was written in such a way that it could appeal to all those who wanted to know more about the car. These people wanted to know what made this car so different and special.

Here are some sentences from that classic ad:

- Every Rolls Royce engine is run for seven hours at full throttle before installation, and each car is test-driven for hundreds of miles over varying road surfaces.

- The finished car spends a week in the final test-shop, being fine-tuned. Here it is subjected to 98 separate ordeals. For example, the engineers use a stethoscope to listen for axle-whine.

- The coachwork is given five coats of primer paint, and hand rubbed between each coat, before nine coats of finishing paint go on.

- There are three separate systems of power brakes, two hydraulic and one mechanical. Damage to one system will not affect the others.

- You can get such optional extras as an Espresso coffee-making machine, a dictating machine, a bed, hot and cold water for washing, an electronic razor or a telephone.

Can you see how effective these sentences are?

Can you compare this ad with what some dumb marketers do today?

They try to make ads entertaining, funny, too much emotional, meaningless, and sometimes completely BS.

And other times, they do nothing but simply put the name of the brand in front of us.

A few years back, I visited a premium car dealership in Delhi and asked a salesman, "What's the difference between your car and others? Why it's so expensive?" And he said, "Simple! Because it's (brand name)".

Do you think it's so simple to sell a premium product by just emphasizing on the brand name? And if it's really so simple, then why do we need salespeople who don't even know how to answer queries of prospective customers?

Of course, the giant companies have huge budgets that they can blindly spend on useless ads. Unfortunately, the situation is not the same for small business owners who can't afford to spend their money without any accountability.

I strongly recommend reading David Ogilvy's book *Ogilvy on Advertising,* even if you have nothing to do with advertising.

David Ogilvy is considered one of the greatest persuaders of all time.

Ogilvy started his career as an apprentice chef in a hotel in Paris. But after a year, he went to Scotland selling cooking stoves, door-to-door. Later he joined an advertising agency in London.

But it was George Gallup's *Academic Research Institute* in America, which influenced Ogilvy's thinking, emphasizing meticulous research methods and sticking to reality.

Trained at the Gallup research organization, Ogilvy attributed the success of his campaigns to meticulous research into consumer habits.

Ogilvy created some great campaigns like Come to Britain, Come to France, Come to the United States, and Come to Puerto Rico, which helped these countries in becoming a popular tourist destination.

Some of his clients were Rolls Royce, Mercedes, Shell, IBM, American Express, Sears Roebuck.

Ogilvy increased sales of Mercedes-Benz car by 4 times (from 10,000 to 40,000) in just one year. At that time, Mercedes was not so popular in the United States.

One of his greatest successes was "Only Dove is one-quarter moisturizing cream." (Do you remember I talked about how important it is to create USP in the Volume-2?) This campaign helped Dove become the top-selling soap in the United States.

Today the same advertising agency, founded by Ogilvy in 1948, is present in 83 countries. It's considered one of the top agencies in the world.

Ogilvy, who started as an apprentice chef, became so successful in advertising because he always studied his market. He knew the hot buttons of people.

And that's what you should do.

Salesmanship has nothing to with your educational background. You don't need a world-class MBA to become a great marketer.

The point is, whether you're a manufacturer, an advertiser, a salesperson, a politician, a freelancer, a movie director, or a celebrity, you should keep studying your target customer.

The more you know about your customers, the lesser the gap will be between you and them.

From now onwards, I want you to start calling yourself **Sales Detective**.

Immediate vs. Length Of Time vs. Multiple Times

Immediate

Some people are convinced within the first meeting. For them, the first impression means a lot.

They automatically assume your product/service is good if you deliver a strong presentation.

Dealing with such kind of customers is every salesperson's dream.

Length of Time

Some people are convinced only after you have spent some time with them.

It could be days, weeks, months, or even years.

This is very common in the normal business world. Many people get promotions or better opportunities only when they have years of experience in a particular job or business.

However, it doesn't mean their performance was exceptional in all those years.

On one side, still, many people in our society are influenced by someone's period of experience.

On the other side, there are ambitious and aggressive people who want to deal with those smart guys who have achieved success in a relatively short period.

Multiple Times

Some people are convinced only if you've visited them or presented your product multiple times.

For example,

They need to see the advertisement multiple times before they make their decision to buy that product.

They need to meet the salesperson multiple times before they decide to buy from him.

They want to conduct multiple interviews before they hire a candidate.

They want to see multiple houses or the same house multiple times before they finalize it.

They want to test drive even their favourite car multiple times before they book it.

Work Alone vs. Work With Team

Work Alone

Some people prefer to work alone.

They make all decisions themselves.

They prefer jobs where they don't need to depend on others. If they are not able to find such jobs they become freelancers.

Instead of being a jack of all trades, they prefer to be an expert in one area.

For example: author, lawyer, surgeon, photographer, blogger, designer, chef, musician, architect.

Work With Team

Some people like to work with a team.

If you apply for a job in their company, then almost everyone in their team will take your interview.

One of their major tasks is to coordinate with different departments.

They like conducting daily meetings.

The whole team will study your business proposal and collectively make a decision.

Working alone is a nightmare for them.

Internal Frame vs. External Reference Or Data

Internal Frame

Some people make decisions based on their guts, intelligence, knowledge, judgment.

They don't need someone's approval on how they are living their life.

Their judgment pattern is located internally.

These people know inside themselves that they're doing a good job or they're making a mistake.

Most of their decisions are based on what is important to them.

They live an independent life, not easily influenced by their family and friends.

Once they understand your proposal, they act fast.

Don't get confused about this category with *Work Alone* meta program. It's not at all necessary that the Internal Frame people should work alone. They can be the chairperson of a big company, politician, team leader, a movie director.

The point is, they don't need any reference or help from others in deciding what is right or wrong. And they don't hesitate in making decisions that might be not liked by their family, friends, colleagues.

External Reference or Data

These people are dependent on other people, data, evidence, social proof, testimonials, the authority to make every decision, no matter how big or small it is.

They take a lot of time in making buying decisions.

They need constant feedback from advisors, partners, friends, colleagues, teachers to know they are doing a good job.

While presenting your proposal, show them testimonials, statistics, charts, or any reference from their Circle of Influence.

Don't ignore the External Frame people's Circle of Influence. They are highly influenced by their spouse, friends, relatives, business partners, colleagues.

Their Circle of Influence enjoys a great power to turn the case against you or in your favour.

Balanced

Some people take a balanced approach. Means they use both internal and external frame in making decisions.

For these people, your proposal should carry both points, that is, how your products and services meet the most important needs of the prospect along with testimonials, proofs, references, statistics.

In the next volume, I'll talk about some more Meta Programs, and **one of my favourite ways to get inside your customer's mind**. If you master this technique, it could do wonders for you.

Remember, we need to match our customers' beliefs, values, lifestyle, attitude, meta-programs if we are to be completely effective in the persuasion process.

And the only way we can do this is by collecting as much information about them as possible.

In the next volume, I'll also talk about what details you need to collect about your customers so that it becomes a bit easy for you to determine your customers' programming.

Some people ask me how much information they need to collect about their customers. And my typical answer is: Just more than what your competitors collect.

So, if you want to stay ahead of your competition, you need to know more about your customers.

VOLUME - IV

In the previous volume, I discussed some Meta Programs with you.

Meta Programs are the filters that tell us how people process information in their minds to communicate, do their daily work, make decisions, and take action.

These programs are based on how our minds are conditioned right from our childhood.

What is the role of Meta Programs in Persuasion?

One of the most effective ways to persuade people is to use the same 'Programming' that they process information with.

In this hyper-competitive age, the more we know about our customers, the easier it becomes to compete with giant organizations that are too much occupied in their day-to-day operations.

However, we need to remember that the purpose of using this information is to ethically persuade our prospects to buy our products and services since we strongly believe they can improve our customers' lives.

Here are some more Meta Programs:

Extrovert vs. Introvert

Extrovert

Some people are very expressive. They can easily share their feelings and emotions with others.

They discuss almost everything with their family, friends, and colleagues.

They are talkative and like those professions where they can meet more and more people every day.

Many times they don't even think before they speak.

Introvert

Some people are unable to express their feelings with others. Instead, they prefer keeping their thoughts with themselves.

They are open to only a limited number of people.

They like professions where they can spend maximum time only with them.

Since they keep emotions with themselves, they are hard to crack.

They enjoy doing boring tasks.

They think too much while speaking.

In the sales meeting, you need to use open-ended questions to find out their unspoken objections. (Refer my premium guide: *Become A Master of Closing Sales*)

Match vs. Mismatch

Match

Some people, while considering you, your product, your proposal, look for **similarities**.

They will match what you're saying in your presentation to what they already know.

These people, in order to understand the world, will look at the similarities.

It makes them feel comfortable that they are dealing with familiar things.

They will judge you according to their known parameters.

There are two kinds of *Match* people:

1)   *Mild Match*

2)   *Extreme Match*

When you present your proposal to *Mild Match* people, first, they will look for all similarities between your services and what they already know or experienced or have.

After that, they will start looking for differences, like how your products and services are superior/better/newer to what already available in the market.

Whereas when you present your proposal to *Extreme Match* people, they will look ONLY for similarities and delete everything else that is different.

Mismatch

These people, while analyzing your products & services, will look for **differences**.

They will look for all the ways how your solution is different from everything they have ever seen before.

On the positive side, some *Mismatch* people are attracted to new designs, features, ideas, innovations, fashion, updates, and improvements in existing products. They are bored with existing things and are looking for totally new products which can bring a massive change in their life.

On the negative side, some *Mismatch* people will look for what is wrong, abnormal, asymmetrical, or out of place in your products and services.

Again, like *Match* people, there are two kinds of *Mismatch* people:

1) *Mild Mismatch*

2) *Extreme Mismatch*

When you present your proposal to the *Mild Mismatch* people, they will look for the differences first, and then the similarities.

They are excited to know how your product is better than existing products available in the market or already used by them. But at the same time, they don't want to miss any old features.

When you present your proposal to the *Extreme Mismatch* people, they will not entertain any of the old designs.

They are looking for new creative ideas, innovative products which can bring revolution in the world.

Cost vs. Convenience

Cost

Many people are cost-oriented. They get excited by how much money they can save using your products and service.

Instead of paying the full amount, they opt for installments.

Discount offers appeal to them a lot.

Convenience

Some people value their time and convenience instead of saving money.

For them, time is the most precious thing which, once gone, cannot come back. They want to save their time, energy, and efforts even if they have to pay some extra money.

Because of their busy schedule, these people are always looking for such products and services, which can make their life simpler, better, more comfortable.

Necessity vs. Possibility

Necessity

Some people don't take action unless they've reached their threshold pain.

Necessity people act only when they realize there is no other choice left with them.

They don't want to adopt changes until it becomes necessary. It's no wonder that sometimes it reaches to a Do or Die situation.

Their life is governed by limits. They resist changing the rules.

Most of these guys are mechanical in nature. They ignore creative ideas prevailing social and economic issues until they realize if they further delay, it could even affect them and their families.

Possibility

These people are proactive… dreamers… inventors… who want to make the world a better place to live.

Their life is motivated by their desires, and not by pain.

They are always looking for better opportunities, never satisfied with their current job, possessions.

They want to see all the possible options available in the market to get the best deal.

Possibility customers want to explore how many ways the product can fulfill their desires.

If *Possibility* people are product developers, marketers, entrepreneurs, or from the creative industry, they come up with crazy ideas, others have never thought before.

Past vs. Present vs. Future

Past

Some people refer to their past experiences while processing new information.

For example, if they had bad experiences while dealing with some individuals of a particular area, society, industry, even country, they start considering everyone from that group to be bad.

In some commercial complexes, you'll find that many offices are having a board hanging outside their gate, where it's written: "Salespeople are not allowed". The reason is, these companies had some bad experience while dealing with salespeople that used to do cold calls in such commercial complexes.

On the contrary, if people had a good experience while dealing with some companies in the past, they will consider buying from them again.

And if in case they are buying a new product from an unfamiliar company, they will look for a proven track record.

Present

These people are not bothered about the past.

Their concern is to solve the present problems that they are facing. They will immediately buy from you if you provide them the solution to their problems.

These people always look for innovative products which can make their present conditions better.

If you're an entrepreneur, you must target these people.

They don't need any past track record or references from others. Just **demonstrate** how your product can solve their problems, and they will buy from you.

But your demonstration should be extremely powerful.

There is a famous old example of how Otis demonstrated the new automatic braking system, which could stop the elevator from falling if cables suddenly break.

At that time, people were extremely afraid of using elevators because of deadly accidents.

When Otis developed this new braking system, he announced everywhere about his achievement. But nobody believed him.

Otis was extremely disappointed that in spite of such a great innovation, people were still afraid of riding in elevators.

Then one day, he got one idea.

Otis himself demonstrated the capability of his automatic braking system in front of the public in New York, where he rode in an open-sided elevator and then had his assistant cut the rope cable with an axe.

The elevator dropped a few inches and then stopped securely.

This demonstration made headlines across America. The public lost its fear of riding in elevators. Only the condition was they should be OTIS elevators.

After this demonstration, developers all across the world started making buildings more than four stories high because people no longer feared elevators.

Future

These people are more interested in the future benefits of your products and services.

For example, instead of buying a small house in a congested city, they would prefer a large house on the outskirts, where they can spend good quality time with their children and grandchildren after retirement.

Instead of buying petrol or diesel cars, they buy electric cars because they believe the electric vehicle is the future.

Instead of choosing civil or criminal law, they choose cyber law because they think cyber law could have a huge demand in the future.

Instead of doing marketing in conventional ways, they focus on developing internet marketing skills because they believe the internet will play a huge role in growing business.

If you're selling softwares, then don't forget to pitch them upcoming versions with all the latest features.

Dissociated Thinker vs. Associated Feeler

Dissociated Thinker

Some people easily detach themselves from feeling about what's going on in their or other people's life.

They don't get involved emotionally in the past, present, or future circumstances.

They don't get bothered by good and bad feelings.

They don't try to understand the pains and pleasures of other family members, friends, colleagues, customers.

On the negative side, *Dissociated Thinkers* are considered as self-centered, selfish, shrewd, ruthless, disciplined, cold, the people who have no heart.

But on the positive side, *Dissociated Thinkers* are considered hard-core professionals with high integrity.

They are practical. They don't get emotional easily.

They don't lose focus even in tough situations.

They are dependable on secret assignments.

Dissociated Thinkers don't consider their clients and staff as friends. They only maintain a professional relationship, just like how doctors treat their patients.

In short, *Dissociated Thinkers* are not carried away by other people's emotions, not even by their own emotions.

On the contrary, there are some people for whom it's not easy to detach from problems which are haunting them day and night.

They live in worries, anxiety, fears… even suffer from phobias.

There is a technique called *Dissociation* in NLP (Neuro-Linguistic Programming), which could help these people to live a life free of worries, painful memories.

Here's how you can apply the *Dissociation* technique using your creativity to distance yourself from some horrific episode, which keeps spoiling your mood.

I want you to recall one of your most painful experiences, which is still bothering you a lot and easily make you upset at any moment.

Have you ever thought why this memory is bothering you so much?

The reason is you have strongly associated yourself with that incident because it was extremely emotional for you.

Still, you can clearly see all the things that happened at that time. You can feel yourself present in that situation, watching, listening, talking, and expressing everything that happened to you at that moment.

Now I want you to dissociate yourself from that scene.

How?

Instead of feeling that you're present in that painful situation, I want you to imagine yourself sitting in a theatre where you're watching that scene, just like an actor who is watching his movie.

So, basically, you have shifted your focus from performing in that scene to watching that scene from outside.

Now, you can do many things with that scene to lower its impact on your mind.

You can rewind and forward that scene as many times as you want.

You can fade colours, brightness. You can make it black & white.

You can reduce the size of that scene to a dot.

You can change sounds, words, dresses, interiors, location… whatever you want.

In this way, you're trying to emotionally dissociate yourself from that situation.

Now I want you to follow one more step.

You need to use your creative muscles and imagine again that this time you're watching yourself sitting INSIDE theatre watching your scene.

The objective is to move more and more away from that scene so that it stops affecting you deeply.

There is a famous proverb – "Out of sight, out of mind." That's what we're trying to do here.

Dissociation is a powerful technique used in NLP, which could help you in lowering the intensity of painful experiences in your mind.

Neuro-Linguistic Programming (NLP) is the science and art of modeling other people in order to produce similar behavior & results in the self or other people.

It is generally used in personal development, communication, and even psychotherapy (in treating problems like depression and phobias).

NLP was created by *Richard Bandler* and *John Grinder* in the 1970s. They claim that NLP methodology can model the skills of exceptional people allowing anyone to acquire those skills.

I would suggest reading some NLP books to learn more about such techniques and exercises if you want to overcome your fears and anxiety.

But apply your imagination to make these exercises more interesting instead of simply following rules. I always believe Creativity is the biggest asset we all have if we know how to use it for our well-being.

Associated Feeler

Associated Feelers get easily distracted by their own or other people's feelings.

They associate themselves with what's going on in other people's lives.

They try to understand the pains and pleasures of other family members, friends, colleagues, customers.

They get emotional easily and might lose focus in their work.

Associated Feelers treat everyone they meet like their friends. They love to give friendly advice to others, including their clients.

It's important to note that, to become a good marketer, you need to associate yourself with the feelings of your customers. You need to understand deeply what's going on in their life, what are their problems, fears, ambitions which keep them awake the whole night.

In short, you need to get inside your customer's head.

Here's one powerful technique on how to get inside your customer's head that I learned from one of my close friends. It's called...

Method Marketing

If you watch movies, you've probably heard 'Method Acting' where an actor prepares for his role by getting deep into the skin of the character he is playing.

In this way, the actor tries to understand his character **by becoming exactly like him**.

'Method Acting' was introduced by *Konstantin Stanislavski*, who was the founder and teacher at the Moscow Art Theatre.

He was widely recognized as an outstanding character actor and got fame for his 'system' of actor training, preparation, and rehearsal technique.

Stanislavski said that **great acting makes the audience forget it is something artificial.**

But it was *Lee Strasberg* who got ideas from Stanislavski and popularized 'Method Acting'.

He was the director of non-profit *Actors Studio* in New York City, considered "the nation's most prestigious acting school."

Strasberg is often considered as the father of method acting in America.

He trained many famous actors, including Marilyn Monroe, Al Pacino, and Robert De Niro.

There are many Hollywood and Bollywood actors who adopted 'Method Acting' in their work like Marlon Brando, Dilip Kumar, Heath Ledger, Aamir Khan, Kamal Haasan, Daniel Day-Lewis, Christian Bale, Irrfan Khan, Jim Carrey, Leonardo DiCaprio, Nawazuddin Siddiqui.

If you want to see how effective 'Method Acting' is, don't forget to watch movies like The Godfather, Taxi Driver, The Dark Knight, Dangal, Raging Bull.

The idea behind 'Method Acting' is when you watch an arresting movie; you forget that you are watching something fictional. You willingly stop disbelieving that you're watching a fictional story.

Similarly, the idea behind 'Method Marketing' is that when you're communicating with your prospect, even though he knows you're there to sell him, but he suddenly forgets about it and just focuses on what you're talking about.

This happens because you've already practiced in getting inside your prospect's head, which helps you to behave and communicate in a manner that directly hits your prospect's hot buttons.

So, whatever you say or show to your prospect triggers an emotional response in your prospect's mind that makes him want to forget about the selling process and just focus on your story.

The question comes, why your prospect is so much engaged in your story that he forgets everything else, even that whatever you're showing is nothing but a sales message?

It is because no one before you has shown him so clearly, in so detail, his daily frustrations, struggles, childhood dreams, pains, likes and dislikes.

In short, your prospect is hypnotized by your presentation, which is basically his story told by you.

The question is how to become a great Method Marketer.

Here's the process shared by one of my close friends how he used to write Advertisements and Sales Letters for the health market.

One of his projects was to write an ad copy for people who are suffering from arthritis.

This was the first time he was writing for the arthritis market. So, he did some homework.

For example:

My friend started reading some books on arthritis.

He studied deeply how an arthritis patient feels the whole day.

He started spending some time with arthritis patients in his surroundings.

He even bought a cane and walked like an arthritis patient.

He started following the same routine, diet, exercise, dos and don'ts that arthritis patients have to follow during their treatment.

The point is, you need to start behaving like your target customer the whole day.

This is not an easy task. It requires a lot of practice.

The more you behave like your customer, the faster you start feeling like your customer.

And for this, you need to involve your all 5 senses.

Start watching what your customers watch.

Start listening to what your customers listen to.

Start using words, phrases, jargon, slang that are generally used by your customers.

Start eating, shopping, dressing like your customer.

*Caution: Acting like your customer is NOT meant to impress your customers. It is done for your own knowledge so that you can FEEL like how your customer feels day and night.

Unless you put yourself in your customers' shoes, you can't bring the right product at the right price at the right time.

Just take the example of *Henry Ford*, who developed and manufactured the first automobile that many middle-class Americans could afford.

His introduction of the Model T automobile in 1908 revolutionized transportation and American industry.

The car was very simple to drive and easy and cheap to repair.

By 1918, half of all cars in the United States were Model Ts.

With the mass production of inexpensive goods coupled with high wages for workers, Ford converted the automobile from an expensive curiosity into a practical conveyance.

Born in a farmer's family, Ford didn't know anything about the automobile and how to run a business until he started working as an Engineer in the Edison Electric Illuminating Company.

Later, when he started manufacturing automobiles, he constantly wanted to improve his automobiles, instead of putting them to market.

Ford wasn't interested in just making another luxury automobile that only rich people could afford. He wanted to sell an automobile that an average person could afford.

His genius was taking existing ideas and making them radically better.

Before building the Model T, Henry Ford conducted extensive research on who would buy it, how much they could afford to pay, and what they would want and need in a car.

By the time the Model T was introduced, Ford already knew he had a large market of potential buyers, what features would make the buy, and what to charge them.

Ford believed in offering his customers solutions to problems they didn't even know they had.

One of his famous quotes was:

"If I had simply asked people what they wanted, they would have asked me for faster horses!"

If you're an entrepreneur, a marketer, a product developer, you need to memorize this quote forever.

Remember, knowing your target market goes much deeper than simply knowing what they say they want.

Many times, people don't even know what they want. And if they have the slightest idea, they don't know how to express.

It's our job to find out values, beliefs, hidden desires, pains, and fears of our target market so that we can come up with the most suitable products and services and present them effectively to our prospects.

And it's not just about creating the right products and services... we need to keep testing which offers work best for our market... what to say and what not to say that could turn NOs into YESes... what changes need to be done in our environment, communication, body language, and techniques that could influence our customer's behaviour.

Take an example of *Paco Underhill...*

Paco Underhill is an internationally acclaimed author, an environmental psychologist who helps his retail clients in growing their business based on his research about **how our surroundings influence our behaviour**.

In short, he observes consumer behaviour in a particular environment, makes changes to that environment, and measures the changes in sales.

His team uses high-end equipments, cameras, and a piece of paper they called *track sheet*. The trackers, who always carry this track sheet in their hand, quietly make their way through stores following shoppers and noting everything they do.

When a shopper enters the shop, the tracker sticks with that person as long as he or she is in the store, and records on the track sheet almost everything the shopper does.

Paco Underhill and his team study many aspects of human behaviour like how consumers shop with their hands, how people move in stores, how different people shop (like men, women, children, older people), how people make payments, etc.

I recommend you to read his famous book *Why We Buy: The Science of Shopping*, where he tells about the importance of analyzing the behaviour of people when they are shopping.

In the book, which is the result of many years of field research conducted by Paco Underhill and his team, he advises **how retailers should arrange the setup based on how people behave inside the store.** He offers plenty of advice based on real-life observation.

For example:

- Since shoppers have only two hands, shopping baskets must be always available to them throughout the store, so that impulse shopping keeps going on even after two items are selected.

- If there is a coffee shop like Starbucks near to your store, make sure your carts have cupholders.

- **The possibility to hold and touch a product will greatly influence the buying decision.**

- A woman accompanied by another woman will shop longer than one who's alone, but a woman with a man will stay in the store for the shortest time of all.

- Paco Underhill talks about how important touch is. His observations showed that towels were, on average, touched by six different shoppers before being purchased.

- **He found there is a direct correlation between the time a customer remains in a store and the amount he will purchase.**

- The higher the *interception rate* (contacts with employees), the higher the chance of purchase.

Paco Underhill talks about the area where shoppers first enter the store, which is commonly known by retailers as the *decompression zone*. It's a transition area needed by shoppers to adjust to your store environment. Since shoppers need time to transition from where they have just come to where they are now, shoppers don't notice what's in this area. That's why this area needs to be kept clear of signage, merchandise, salespeople so that shoppers can transition quickly and easily. Otherwise, people, after entering your store, may walk straight back out again.

In the 1980s, a marketing professor, *Ronald E. Milliman*, explored **how the tempo of the store's background music can influence the pace of the shopper and sales volume**.

When fast-music is played, shoppers walk more quickly through the shop. This gives people less time to make impulsive purchases.

On the other hand, slow music has the opposite effect. It slows customers down as they shop, and people purchase more during their visit.

So, you can see how people behave subconsciously while shopping. I can bet if you ask buyers why they behave in such ways; they might not have proper answers.

That's why experienced salespeople keep telling us: "Don't believe in what customer says, believe in what customer does."

So, start studying and applying 'Method Marketing' if you want to win the hearts of your target market, just like Method Actors practice and perform on the screen to win the hearts of their audience.

The opposite of 'Method Marketing' is **5-Senses Selling**, where instead of modeling customers, you are setting up a condition to engage all 5 senses of customers in your dealing with them.

For example, in the test drive of a new car, prospects get the opportunity to see the car even from inside… listen to the sound of the engine, music… touch car seats, dashboard, steering wheel, gear shift knob… smell the fragrance of a new car… and also, prospects can eat & drink while driving.

In this way, the 5-Senses technique can be easily applied in selling automobiles, houses, furniture, pulling people to movie theatres, theme parks, etc.

Unfortunately, still, many businesses do not use this technique, thinking that their products & services do not require people to involve all 5 senses in buying their products.

5-Senses Selling could be very effective if businesses know how to apply some creativity in engaging customers' senses whenever they get a chance: Pre-Sales – Presentation - Post-Sales.

For example, if you're selling industrial, pharmaceutical, or engineering products, you can apply your creativity in the packaging of products by making it look attractive and nice to touch, which sends signals to your clients that they are dealing with a professional company who knows what their customers like.

You can also add a special fragrance in your packaging, products, office, which again helps in building a **unique image** of your company in your client's mind.

Don't ignore the power of smell even it has nothing to do with your products. Out of all the 5 senses, olfaction is the only one that travels directly to the forebrain without going to the thalamus.

Singapore Airlines has created its own fragrance as its **scent brand**. This fragrance is called *Stefan Floridian Waters*. It is pumped throughout the flight cabin space, blended it into their hot towels and pillows, even worn by flight attendants as perfume.

Similarly, new Rolls Royce cars emit a scent called "Old Rolls" from under their seats.

So, you can also try something unique (but affordable), which can trigger any or all senses of your customers.

The problem is every person is different in some way or the other. So you can't spend time studying each of your customers.

Then how to find the most suitable feature for your customers that you could add in your existing product or service, which ultimately helps in building your company's unique image in the mind of your customers?

And the answer is… start building a profile of your target market.

I have already shared some personality traits with you. Now you need to find out what are the most common traits among your customers.

Make a list of all traits. You need to check whether most of your customers are extremely or moderately Visual, Auditory, or Kinesthetic.

You need to check whether most of your customers are Analytical, Social Butterfly, Cordial, or the Big Boss.

You need to check the common age, gender, occupation, industry, habits of your target market.

You need to find out the most common Meta Programs used by your customers… to check whether your target market comes into the category of…

- Moving Towards Pleasure or Moving Away from Pain

- Big Picture or Specifics

- Immediate, Length of Time, Multiple Times

- Work Alone or With Team

- Internal Frame or External Reference

- Extrovert or Introvert

- Match or Mismatch

- Cost or Convenience

- Necessity or Possibility

- Past, Present or Future

- Dissociated Thinker or Associated Feeler

Along with these traits, you also need to start observing your customers and study them as much as possible.

In the last volume, I urged you to start calling yourself "Sales Detective" because, in the profession of Selling, one of your daily tasks is to find out more and more information about your customers.

*Caution: To find out more information about your customer does NOT mean that you stalk your customer.

You can collect information through various ways like:

- Surveys

- Interviews

- Blogs

- Articles in magazines

- Questionnaires

- Podcasts

- Observing body language in meetings

- Testing different advertising methods and analysing responses

- Books and research reports on psychology, human behaviour

- Newspapers, trade publications, website, social media

- Office colleagues, suppliers, friends...

But apart from personality traits, what else can you know about your customer?

Well, there is no limit on what you want to know about your customers. However, it should NOT affect his or her privacy.

Here are a few things you can learn about your customers that could help you in creating better products & services, communicating effectively with your market, and providing a delightful customer experience in order to get **repeated sales**:

- Can you describe your ideal customer in one sentence?

- What is the date of birth and anniversary of your customer?

- Is your customer an employee/self-employed/business owner?

- What is your customer's background?

- From which part of the country or world does your customer belong?

- What kind of education your customer had?

- Does your customer have any expertise? If yes, in which particular area?

- What are the hobbies and interests of your customers?

- What is the business/job background of your customer? Can you make a list of all your customer's previous employments?

- What is the current designation of your customer if he is working somewhere?

- Is your customer the decision-maker or influencer?

- What kind of image your customer has inside the office? How others in the organisation treat your customers?

- What is the income level of your customer?

- Does your customer consider himself successful? If not, why?

- Has your customer won any awards?

- What are your customer's favourite memories of which she is proud of?

- What is the long-term goal of your customer? Where does she want to see herself after 10... 20... 30 years?

- Is your customer visionary, or is she more involved in day-to-day operations?

- What is your customer's biggest pain at the moment?

- What are the short-term personal goals of your customer?

- Does your customer have any club membership? If yes, in which particular club?

- What are your customer's favourite topics of discussion? Does your customer like to talk about Politics/Movies/Sports?

- Does your customer involve in social activities?

- What is your customer's major source of income? Does she have more than one source of income? If her expenses double tomorrow, would she be able to meet them without going into debt?

- What are the sensitive things that customer doesn't want to discuss with you?

- Where does your customer often go for lunch or dinner? What is the favourite food of your customers? Does your customer drink or smoke?

- What are the favourite vacation places for your customers?

- Why your customer chose you over your competitors?

- What is your customer's Circle of Influence?

- What are your customer's priorities?

- What your customers exactly want from your products and services?

These questions may help you to develop a profile of your ideal customer. You can create a checklist and add more questions like these.

If you start learning all you can about the customer, you'll find topics for catching their attention, face-to-face meetings, emails, advertisements, which can open doors for you and your company.

Moreover, it could help you in bringing repeated sales from the same customer, which is the backbone of every great business.

Let me explain with an example of how one could use such kind of information to get repeated sales.

Suppose you need to travel to some other city on a business trip for 3 days next week.

You booked the hotel online based on customer reviews.

Within a few hours of booking, you get a call directly from the hotel. You find it a bit surprising as generally you never expect a call from the hotel.

The manager of the hotel says thanks to you for choosing their hotel and requests you to fill one short form to understand your preferences so that they can make arrangements before you check-in.

The form consists of 15 simple questions that need to be answered in only 1-2 words.

You agree to provide information considering it just a small formality. Also, you're a bit curious to know how this information could make your stay better in this hotel.

Next week when you reach the hotel and check-in your room, you start getting little surprises which you've never expected.

For example:

You're welcomed with your favourite fresh fruit juice.

The room is perfumed with your favourite fragrance.

The TV is already set to your favourite news channel.

You find your favourite brand tea bags near the electric kettle.

On the study table, you find one latest book by your favourite author.

Also, you find a notebook and a pen of your favourite colour on the same study table.

Near the intercom, you find a menu of only vegetarian food.

In the refrigerator, you find your favourite beer.

In the morning, at exactly 6:30 am you receive your favourite newspaper.

In the bathroom, you find soap and shampoo of your favourite fragrance.

These are just a fraction of examples. There is no limit on how this hotel can customize the room to make it more personal to you.

The point is, although these are little things which you barely notice consciously, they are hitting your hot buttons.

You find all these things happening continuously during your stay in the hotel. In fact, the longer you stay, the more opportunities the hotel staff gets to know you personally so that they can make your experience more delightful whenever you visit again.

How?

By keeping a record of everything inside their system.

Now my question is: would you like to stay in the same hotel during your next business trip?

Gotcha!

Personalization helps in reducing customer turnover.

Personalization helps in converting a new customer into a loyal one.

Personalization helps small businesses to compete with big competitors.

Even giant tech companies know the importance of personalization.

Netflix recommends movies based on what you've watched before.

Facebook suggests groups based on what pages you've liked and the groups you've joined.

Amazon recommends products based on what've you bought in the past.

Of course, they have advanced technologies like Artificial Intelligence… But it doesn't mean we can't be innovative in our small business if we have limited resources.

We are living in an era where progressive companies keep bringing innovative solutions beyond customer's expectations.

That's what we all need to do if we want more sales than our competitors. We need to raise the expectation level of our customers.

However, once a customer sets expectations from us, our job is not to disappoint him in the future. In fact, we should always try to give more than his expectations if we want repeated sales.

Remember, without repeat sales - no business can survive for a long time.

So, you can see that the *5-Senses* technique can be used to customize whole settings to make it more personal for the customer. All this is done on the basis of the information provided by the customer.

One of the biggest advantages of personalization is you can charge more than your competitors who are still doing conventional things in their business.

Just take the example of buying a Rolls-Royce car, where customers have a choice to configure their car.

More than 90% of all Rolls-Royce vehicles sold are personalized. For Rolls-Royce, **the future is customization.**

However, the *5-Senses* technique can be used oppositely, in businesses where you focus on selling to masses instead of a few individuals.

In this case, you need to build your business on the principle of **standardization**, just like you see in franchise businesses.

If you've gone to some franchise store, I'm sure you must have noticed how everything they do is standardized so that the whole business is least dependent on people working there.

The franchise model is one of the most successful business models, where the objective is to build a **system-dependent business** first, and then sell its franchise to others.

Let me recommend a great book, *E-Myth*, by Michael E. Gerber, which tells how to turn a messy business into an organized firm.

In fact, as per my own experience, this book not just helps in building a systematized business; it also helps us in becoming more professional.

Nowadays, people no more want to deal with unorganized businesses and executives. They want to deal with professional companies who know how to deal with their customers.

In building a franchise business, little things play a huge role in creating your unique identity in the mind of customers. Therefore, if you apply the *5-Senses* technique in all these little things, then wherever your customers go, **they will find the same unique experience.**

The good news is, if you own a small business, you can adopt this franchise business philosophy in your operations.

I mean, whether you're running a restaurant, dealership, software company, or you're self-employed, you can create your own unique image in your customer's mind by implementing standardization in your business.

And for this, you need to target all the 5 senses of your customers... so that they can easily differentiate you from your competitors inside their minds.

Here are some ideas on how you could try standardization in following things/processes based on your financial capacity:

- Manufacturing, packaging, delivery process

- Colour, perfume, taste

- Office interiors, stationery, uniform, vehicles

- Logo, website, business cards, contact number, customer service response time

- Email format, font size, signoff in all communications

- Script used by salespeople and telemarketers.

In short, everything could be standardized so that your customers feel they are dealing with a professional company.

There is a famous quote of Tom Watson, the founder of IBM:

"I realized that for IBM to become a great company, it had to act like a great company long before it ever became one."

Watson had a picture in his mind about how the company would look and be when it was finally done.

So, you can see that how you can apply *5-Senses Selling* creatively not only in customizing your products and services to make them more personal for your customers but also in making your company look exclusive and professional to them. In this way, you're building a unique brand.

However, never forget that whatever changes you're adopting in your business should be based on what you know about your target market.

Have you ever thought why the McDonald's sign is red and yellow?

In the next volume, I'll talk about how emotions win our rational thinking process.

Also, I'll share some examples of the potent technique, based on one of the principles of Persuasion, which could turn a normal casual situation into a desperate one, even to such an extent that it becomes a now or never opportunity for us.

Plus, I'll share a proven process that one could follow to achieve mastery in any skill.

VOLUME - V

Today is the best time to go through your bank statement for the last 3 years.

Check how much you were earning...

3 years back...

2 years back...

1 year back...

Calculate how much increase in income you got every year.

Now you need to ask yourself...

Is the increase in a particular year has matched your goal of that year?

Are you satisfied with your last 3 years' total income?

If NOT, what are the reasons?

Are these reasons within your control or not?

If YES, then what strategy are you going to follow this year, so that you don't get disappointed again?

Remember, if you're not growing, you're dying.

There is a famous quote by a professional speaker Reid Buckley which I always keep near to me...

"If you are not continually learning and upgrading your skills, somewhere, someone else is, and when you meet that person, you will lose."

To become a top salesperson requires mastering skills like:

- Decoding the customer's mind

- Observing people and situations

- Rapport building

- Persuasion principles and techniques

- Seduction

- Communication skills (both verbal and non-verbal)

- Mind games and psychological warfare

- Attracting new customers and turning them into life-long customers (prospecting, presenting, closing, building relationship)

- Advertising and copywriting (both direct response and image building)

- Dealing with objections

- Breaking loyalty of competitor's customers

- Indirect hypnosis

- Negotiation tactics

- Internet marketing (including social media)

- And many more...

Each of these areas can be further divided into small skills which need to be mastered to move ahead of others...

Many people quit this game when they face obstacles. The reason is, they are looking for shortcuts to reach the top. But when they fail, they move back to the start.

Mastering every relevant skill is the difference between the top and mediocre salespeople.

Of course, these skills cannot be learned and mastered in one day.

Mastering a new skill requires focus, perseverance, continuous learning, and practicing on the field, which many people find impossible.

It's a step-by-step process. All you have to do is to follow the right process to condition your mind to learn that skill.

Even if you master a single persuasion technique, it could help you in increasing your sales and beating your competitors (if they don't know how to counter your technique).

Neuro-Linguistic Programming (NLP) offers a useful Four Step model of how the mind learns. It can be served as a useful calibration tool to measure your progress in mastering the skill.

According to NLP, there are four stages of learning and mastering a new skill:

Four Stages of Learning and Mastering a Skill

1. Unconscious Incompetence

2. Conscious Incompetence

3. Conscious Competence

4. Unconscious Competence

Stage 1

Unconscious Incompetence

It is the stage when you're not even aware that you don't know a particular skill OR when you are doing something wrong, and you don't know you are doing it wrong.

Many people are so much occupied in their daily life that they don't even bother to know they lack a particular skill-set to achieve their goals.

Stage 2

Conscious Incompetence

Now you have consciously accepted that you don't know a particular skill-set OR there is something wrong in your process, however, you haven't yet fixed the problem.

This is the first breakthrough in achieving mastery because, at last, you have recognized and accepted your previous mistakes.

Very few people have so much courage to accept their limitations.

Stage 3

Conscious Competence

Now, after learning new strategies and going through a rigorous training program, you have consciously learned the right way to do it.

You are doing it correctly with focused attention. But the moment you lose your awareness, you again start making mistakes.

This is the most difficult stage because you have to do self-assessment frequently about how you review yourself in the perfection of that particular skill learned so far.

For self-assessment, you need to critique yourself harshly. Rate yourself 1 to 10 in each area, with 1 being completely deficient, 5 being average, and 10 being perfect in the skill.

If you are learning some complex skills, try to break the whole process into small steps and consciously practice each step. If you still find learning difficult, try to break it into further smaller steps.

Stage 4

Unconscious Competence

Once you have consciously practiced the third stage of learning and reviewed yourself thoroughly on that skill, you have to no longer think about making mistakes... your mind is now conditioned to perform your tasks correctly.

Your mind has learned to follow the entire process in an organized way.

This is the stage when people start calling you a NATURAL in your game.

This is the stage where you enjoy the fruits of your hard work.

You will start getting better results in your tasks. You will start taking bigger challenges.

People will start following you. Some of your colleagues and friends will adore you, and others will envy you.

Some people will think you are born talented, but it's only you who knows how you've transformed yourself from unskilled to a perfectionist.

You are not alone who has gone through all this work to become the best of the best. It happened to every master in the world, whether it's Muhammad Ali or Bruce Lee... Charlie Chaplin or Michael Jackson... Tiger Woods or

Sachin Tendulkar... Shakespeare or Stephen King... Bill Gates or Warren Buffett...

But the question is if this process is the same for everyone, then why only a few people become masters in their respective fields?

The answer lies in these two factors:

1) **Pain**

2) **Pleasure**

Pain and pleasure play an important role in learning a new skill. Some people are motivated by pain and others are motivated by pleasure to learn and master a skill.

It depends on individual to individual what kicks us most.

For example,

If the lifestyle of legends inspires us to become like them, then *Pleasure* is the factor that is motivating us to learn and master a skill just like our ideals, no matter if it costs us blood, sweat, and tears.

Whereas if we have never thought of learning a new skill but faced some kind of bad situation in life which forced us to learn an important skill in order to avoid that awful situation again, then its *Pain* factor which is motivating us to learn that particular skill.

Here's how these four stages of learning come into play when you have never thought of learning a particular skill or procrastinated learning in the future.

Imagine that you are just 21 years old. One day you are going with your uncle and cousin to meet your relatives who live in another state.

Your uncle is driving the car, and you and your cousin are talking about college life.

Suddenly your uncle feels severe pain in the chest because of which he starts losing control of the car but somehow manages to stop the car instantly.

Your uncle needs immediate medical attention, but you are still 50 km away from the city.

And the worst part is, both you and your cousin, who is two years younger than you, don't know how to drive the car.

You have regularly watched your father driving the car. So you think you can also drive, but the moment you take hold of the steering wheel and try to move the car forward, immediately you realize that it's not that easy as you thought.

This is the first stage of learning known as UNCONSCIOUS INCOMPETENCE when you first time realize that you lack an important skill.

Somehow you manage to take the help of local people and rush to the hospital in another vehicle for immediate treatment.

On that day, for the first time, both you and your cousin realize the importance of driving because of the **intense pain** you both have gone through.

(*Note: In sales, when we find that our prospect is quite casual or procrastinating the buying decision, being a Master Persuader, it's our job to create intense pain in our prospect's mind so that he could realize what he is going to miss if he doesn't buy our products and services today.)

And you decide to start learning driving from the very next day.

When you begin taking classes, you realize how difficult it is to drive, park, reverse, balance the car. You feel very uncomfortable.

This stage is known as CONSCIOUS INCOMPETENCE when you understand how hard it is to learn a skill.

Within the next few days, you started learning bit by bit with full concentration, focusing all energy and time in learning and mastering each and every detail.

This stage of learning is called CONSCIOUS COMPETENCE because you're alert all the time while performing a task.

For example, let's divide the driving process into a few basic steps.

- Balancing the steering wheel while driving.

- Applying and removing clutch while changing gears.

- Changing gears from neutral to 1st to 2nd to 3rd and so on as you pick up the speed.

- Reverse gear driving.

- Parking the car at the exact position.

- And most important, applying brakes at the right time.

So you have to practice all these steps **consciously** in order to drive smoothly.

In a matter of a few days, you will be able to rate yourself in each step of driving skills.

And finally, after one month, you are driving comfortably. Your hands and legs are moving simultaneously while listening to music, watching outside scenery, following traffic rules, and talking to your friends about college life.

This is the final stage of learning, known as UNCONSCIOUS COMPETENCE.

But wait!!

Do you know what happens when, after some time, you try to take part in a car race?

Again you realize that you are UNCONSCIOUS INCOMPETENT.

Even though you have learned to drive the car but you find that you stand nowhere in front of other expert drivers who know how to drive in tough conditions.

The same thing happens in business development when after losing a crucial deal to our competitors, we realize we're missing an important skill.

Ideas Implementation – Quantification - Internalization

(The Secret Recipe of Achieving *Conscious Competence*)

I'm sure you know, out of these four stages, which is the most difficult one?

It's the third stage, 'Conscious Competence,' because you have to work on yourself continuously to learn a new skill.

You have to consciously learn every single thing which could help you in getting better and better in your skill until you reach a level where others start calling you a perfectionist... master... genius...

But there are some questions which you need to keep in mind when you're at this stage, like:

- How will you know you're getting better in your skill?

- How will you know where you're lacking in your skill? I mean, which are your weak areas?

- What changes need to be done to get better in your skill?

- And once you know what is working for you... what to avoid and what to follow... then how much time will it take to master that part and move ahead?

The answers to these questions lie in a secret formula I call **Ideas Implementation – Quantification – Internalization**.

Ideas Implementation means what changes you need to do on yourself so that you can become better in your skill **OR** what changes you need to make in your business to get better results.

For this, you need to be creative in coming up with new ideas.

I firmly believe to be creative in whatever we do is the most important skill we can acquire to live a life of our choice.

Sadly, our education system teaches us how to be more competitive. And the same thing we follow throughout our lives in our job or business.

If we were taught how to be creative right from the initial years of school, we could have produced so many things to make this world a much better place to live.

No problem, it's better to be late than never.

So, right from today, I urge you to come up with new ideas in whatever you do. Ideas can be both at the strategic as well as tactical level.

This is the first step in your *Conscious Competence* process.

But the question comes: how will you know that whatever changes you are bringing in your work is actually helping you to become better in your craft?

For this, you need to QUANTIFY every idea that you're incorporating in yourself or your business.

Let me explain with some examples...

Being a hard-core sales guy my examples are related to changes that you could adopt on yourself or your business and then measure the effectiveness of each change in terms of **increase in sales**.

But you should use this formula in all other departments and wherever possible to become more effective.

- What is an increase in sales when your organization's objective is changed from selling cheaper products to premium quality items and services OR vice-versa?

- What is an increase in sales when you start targeting a niche market instead of the masses OR vice-versa?

- What is an increase in sales when you target a different age group?

- What is an increase in sales when you change your advertising strategy from image building to direct response OR vice-versa?

- What is the increase in profit if you choose a direct-to-consumer model instead of hiring the middlemen OR vice-versa?

- What is an increase in profit when you move from local to international or vice-versa?

- What is an increase in sales by changing the voice or face in your marketing communications?

- What is an increase in sales by using doom and gloom in your marketing communication instead of talking about a bright future OR vice-versa?

- What is an increase in sales by appearing on podcasts instead of TV and radio OR vice-versa?

- What is an increase in sales when you create irresistible offers?

- What is an increase in sales when you change the bonus you're offering with your premium service?

- What is an increase in votes in elections when you change your image from *diplomatic* to *politically incorrect* OR vice-versa?

- What is an increase in sales when you change your focus to achieving monthly targets instead of quarterly OR vice-versa?

- What is an increase in sales when you fire *yellow salespeople* and hire *green salespeople* OR vice-versa?

- What is an increase in sales if you do sales calls before vs. after lunch… Mon-Friday vs. Saturday… inside vs. outside office… face-to-face vs. telephone?

- What is an increase in sales when you target all the 5 senses of your customers?

- What is an increase in sales when you add one more persuasion technique in your arsenal?

- What is an increase in sales when you instruct salespeople to wear a uniform instead of casuals or vice-versa?

- What is an increase in sales when you use pictures and videos in your sales presentation?

- What is an increase in sales when you ask salespeople to do three sales meetings instead of two every day?

- What is an increase in sales if you do outbound marketing instead of inbound OR vice-versa?

- What is an increase in sales when you adopt direct mail and print advertising along with internet marketing?

- What is an increase in sales by providing some valuable information instead of entertainment in advertising OR vice-versa?

- What is an increase in sales when you start writing long copy in your advertisements, website, and emails?

- What is an increase in sales if you write short headlines instead of long ones OR vice-versa?

- What is an increase in sales when you change your website design and content?

- What is an increase in sales when you change the format of a sales letter from text to video OR vice-versa?

- What is an increase in sales when you chose dynamic ads instead of static ads on your website OR vice-versa?

- What is an increase in sales if you add exit popup instead of entry popup on your website OR vice-versa?

- What is an increase in sales when you start building your email list?

- What is an increase in sales when you start using two links instead of one link in your marketing emails OR vice-versa?

- What is an increase in sales when you work on improving the open and click-through rate of your emails?

- What is an increase in leads/sales when you increase mediums through which people respond to your ads? For example: toll-free number, Whatsapp, Facebook, etc.

- What is an increase in sales when you start delivering products directly to home?

- What is an increase in repeat sales when you reduce the delivery/service time to half?

- What is an increase in profit when you use new technologies in processing orders?

So, you can see that ideas can be strategic, like selling expensive premium quality products instead of cheap stuff.

And ideas can be tactical like asking "Anything else?" by waiter immediately after he receives an order from the customer.

Likewise, in a store, instead of saying, "How can I help you?" you say, "Is this the first time you are visiting our store?" If the person says yes, you say, "We have a special offer for new visitors. Would you like to know about it?"And if the person says no, you say, "We have a special offer for our existing customers. Would you like to know about it?"

Like these, there are hundreds of ways you can apply small or big ideas and quantify the results. And when you start getting better results, then your job is to simply adopt these changes in yourself or your business. It's called **Internalization,** which involves your daily practice.

Of course, adopting small changes does not require too much effort. But the question is: how much practice you need to do to achieve mastery in a complex skill?

In one of the earlier volumes, I recommended one book: *Outliers* by Malcolm Gladwell.

In that book, the author talked about the lives of some successful people who became outliers in their respective fields – the people who are the best, the brightest, the most famous, and the most successful.

One of the things that I found interesting in the book is a **10,000-hour rule** - one of the factors responsible for their success.

According to this rule, it takes 10,000 hours of practice to achieve mastery in a particular task.

That's why some outliers became successful at an early age as they devoted many hours in their passion since their childhood.

However, it doesn't mean that you should stop working on it after 10,000 hours. But, at least you're much ahead of your competitors, who started late.

I have seen many young people are confused about what skill they need to upgrade regularly.

My suggestion is, start each day by asking yourself, "What one task that only I do will make the greatest difference in my job or business? What one skill that I learn and practice daily will help me the most to double or triple my income in the next 1-2 years?"

Whatever your answer is, work on that skill every day.

Being a salesperson, I realized a long time back that, for me, the most important skill to learn and master is Persuasion. I outsourced other work so that I can fully focus on mastering this skill.

It's not easy when you're in a job where you have to do multiple things, like making reports, attending useless meetings, etc.

And it's not at all easy when you're running your own business where you have to manage so many things along with sales & marketing.

However, one should remember that the future belongs to experts and not to jack of all trades. So you need to be ruthless about your time management. I mean, you need to devote your maximum time to one particular skill, which is ultimately going to make you rich.

In my case, it was the word *Persuasion* that changed my life completely. To learn and master principles and techniques of Persuasion became my sole purpose, and I have dedicated my life to this wonderful skill.

And now, it's your time to become a Persuasion practitioner.

But before I start talking about the principles and techniques of Persuasion, you need to understand how our mind process information and how emotions dominate our thinking process.

How Emotions Win Over Logic?

A long time back, I read a very tragic story in a classic book ***Emotional Intelligence*** written by famous psychologist Daniel Goleman.

The story was about a 14-year-old girl Matilda Crabtree who died accidentally while playing a joke with her parents.

One day Matilda was out with friends, and her parents thought that she was going to stay with friends that night. When Matilda's parents came home late at night, they heard some noises as they entered the house.

Matilda's father reached for his pistol and went into her bedroom to investigate.

To surprise her father when Matilda jumped out of a closet and yelled "Boo!" her father shot her in the neck. Matilda died 12 hours later.

Fear that compelled him to protect his family from danger led Matilda's father to shoot before he could know what he was shooting at, even before he could recognize her voice.

This tragic story tells us how emotions can paralyze our thinking process sometimes.

I strongly recommend reading this book to understand the importance of Emotional Quotient (EQ) over Intelligence Quotient (IQ).

There are three important parts of our brain which play a crucial role in how we process every single bit of information that we receive through our frontal lobes (5 senses).

1)   Thalamus – It filters the message based on how important, relevant, or urgent it is and then send it to Visual Cortex.

2)   Visual Cortex – It is the thinking part of our brain.

3)   Amygdala – It is the emotional part of our brain.

So, whatever you see, listen, read, smell, or touch, every bit of information that our senses receive is processed through these three departments of the brain.

In one of the previous volumes, I mentioned that we are exposed to 1500 – 2000 advertisements every day.

But how many of these ads do we remember and buy something?

It's very few.

So, what's the reason why we don't take action on each ad... request... email... or any other kind of message?

The reason is most of these messages are filtered out by Thalamus.

And why Thalamus does this?

It's because, according to the program stored inside Thalamus, these messages are not so significant, relevant, urgent, or from any important person.

So, when visual signals first go from the retina to the Thalamus, it filters out useless messages continuously to keep the functioning of other departments as simple as possible.

However, important messages then go to Visual Cortex, which is the thinking part of the brain.

In Visual Cortex, the messages are analyzed and assessed for meaning and appropriate response.

If that response is emotional, a signal goes to the Amygdala, our emotional/irrational brain, to activate emotional centers. At that time, our heart rate and blood pressure increase. And large muscles prepare for quick action.

And finally, we take action.

So, this is how the three departments of our brain process every information non-stop.

But there is some twist in this process...

If the message is very emotional, some portion of the original signal goes straight from the Thalamus to the

Amygdala in a quicker transmission in order to produce a faster response.

And if Amygdala finds that message as a threat, fear, or something which requires immediate action, it raises alarm inside the brain.

The architecture of the brain has given the Amygdala a privileged position to hijack the brain.

It takes over the rational brain and triggers an emotional response before other parts have fully understood what is happening. This can lead that person to react emotionally, irrationally, and even violently.

This is popularly known as **Fight or Flight response**.

For example, when we see a snake on the road, the message is directly passed from Thalamus to Amygdala because our brain is programmed that the snake is an extremely dangerous and life-threatening species.

The moment Amygdala finds there is some threat to life, it reacts instantaneously, sending a message of crisis to all parts of the brain. And then, we either try to kill the snake. Or run away from that place as fast as we can.

In this *Fight or Flight reaction*, the Visual Cortex, our thinking/rational brain doesn't get a chance to understand what is happening, so that it could decide what the correct thing is to do. And then send instructions to Amygdala to take appropriate action.

The point is, if the message carries too much emotional intensity, Amygdala hijacks the rational part of the brain to take fast action.

This whole process is called **Emotional Hijacking** by Daniel Goleman in his awesome book *Emotional Intelligence.*

Emotional Hijacking is the situations in which people are so overwhelmed by their feelings that they become out of control... act without any concerns... do not think about what they are doing and what will be the consequences of their actions.

That's why we should never underestimate the power of Emotions.

Advantages of Emotion Over Logic

As rational human beings, we like to think that logic drives most of our buying decisions. But the fact is, in most selling situations, **people buy on emotion and justify with fact**.

People may be convinced by reason, but they are moved by emotion.

Emotions have huge advantages over logic, like:

- Emotion-arousing arguments lead people to drop their natural defenses and distract them from the persuader's real intention to convince. For example, religious and political speeches convert listeners into followers.

- Emotion requires less effort than logic for influencing people. During a logical presentation, people have to put a lot more cognitive effort while weighing the pros and cons as compared to the effort they put during an emotional pitch.

- Emotion-based pitches are generally more interesting and memorable. For example, people find stories interesting because of inherent drama; they easily remember characters in the story and recall the story effortlessly. Whereas, people find it difficult to remember hard-core facts and figures. Ask yourself, how many algebraic formulas do you still remember that were taught you in school? I think very few. But you may still remember stories that you read or listened to that time. Likewise, in selling, prospects may forget all the data and features of your products and service within 24 hours, but they remember the stories you tell for weeks, months, and even years.

- Emotion-based arguments that use pictures, music, slogans are much easier to recall than factual evidence. For example, most of the advertisements that you see on TV never talk about boring facts. Instead, they try to entertain you mindlessly.

- Emotion seems to lead more quickly to behaviour change than logic does. For example: By just smile and politeness, you can convert a cold stranger into a warm friend.

You can't ignore the power of emotions even in highly practical professions like the *judiciary*, which considers only facts and proofs.

Take the example of a high profile criminal case *OJ Simpson vs. State of California*, which is popularly known as the "Trial of the Century."

On October 3, 1995, over 100 million people watched Simpson receive an acquittal verdict for the murders of his ex-wife, Nicole Brown Simpson, and her friend, Ronald Goldman.

The defendant OJ Simpson, who was a former football player and a famous celebrity, hired a team of high-profile defense lawyers (at the time dubbed "The Dream Team").

His lawyers used influence & persuasion tactics, propaganda, whatever required to win this case in spite of the unprecedented amount of media coverage and solid evidence against Simpson.

After 11 months of exhausting court proceedings and conflicting testimonies, Simpson was not found guilty of the crimes, sending shockwaves across the nation. It remains an unsolved case to date.

There are many books and documentaries made on the OJ Simpson case, which you can easily find online.

This case was the battle between Logic and Emotion. On one side, the prosecution was confident about the solid evidence against Simpson. On the other side, Simpson was shown as the victim of racism and false evidence.

There were many interesting aspects in this case, but two things which I think made a huge impact on the decision was OJ Simpson's dramatic demonstration of wearing gloves and his defense attorney Johnnie Cochran's closing argument.

A pair of bloody gloves was key evidence in the murders. One was found at the scene of killings, and the other was found at Simpson's home. DNA results showed genetic material consistent with both victims and Simpson.

But during the trial Simpson, successfully demonstrated how the gloves didn't fit by restlessly moving around, pulling, and tugging. This was the big turning point of the case.

To take advantage of this demonstration, the defense attorney told the jury in his closing argument, "If it doesn't fit, you must acquit." It was one of the most memorable moments of the trial.

The point is, in this world of **clutter**, whatever messages we're communicating with our family, friends, colleagues, customers, and authorities should be **extremely effective** if we want a fast and positive response.

We Respond the Effective Messages in Two Ways

Thoughtful Communication (Direct)

- *Thoughtful* is a direct form of communication.

- It's also known Central route of communication.

- When we are thoughtful, we listen hard and attentively to what the salesperson is saying; we weigh the pros and cons of each argument.

- We critique the message for logic and consistency, and if we don't like what we hear, we raise objections and ask questions for more information.

- When we are in the thoughtful mode, the persuasiveness of the message is determined by the merits of the case.

- When we receive the message, we actively think about the message and rationally analyze all the points, facts, and evidence presented.

Mindless Communication (Indirect)

- *Mindless* is an indirect form of communication.

- It's also known as the Peripheral route of communication.

- The busier the people, the lesser the efforts they want to put in making decisions. The reason is they don't have time, energy, or ability to concentrate properly on each message. Responding mindlessly helps them to keep their anxiety level in control.

- People make mindless decisions based on their **mental shortcuts**, instincts, and Pre-Programming instead of relying on facts, logic, and evidence.

- When we respond to messages mindlessly, our brains are locked on some kind of automatic mechanism. We spend little time processing the content.

- Our mind activates a decision trigger, which tells us to say yes or no. These triggers are largely emotionally driven.

To become effective in Persuasion, one should use both ways of communication in order to get the best results.

For example, when we do sales arguments, we should also use peripheral ways of communication to support our pitch.

One of the ways is setting up an environment in such a way that the message receiver starts perceiving you and your message very valuable.

Let me share one of the potent techniques where a normal person can be turned into desperate for other products and services.

It reduces the negotiating power of other parties, whether they are buyers or sellers.

Here's how this technique is used in the recruitment process…

Suppose you are looking for a new job. Although you're not facing any problem in your current job, you keep exploring better opportunities.

So, one day you get a call for an interview from a company, and you reach their office as per scheduled date and time.

Since you already have a decent job and salary, so there is nothing desperate at your end.

You are behaving quite normally, reading a magazine while waiting for your interview.

Within a few minutes, since you reached their office, you see one more applicant entering your room and sitting next to you.

You find it quite normal thinking that the company might have called a few more applicants along with you.

But what you find surprising that within 30 minutes after you entered the office, more than 15 people are present in the same room who have applied for the same job.

Some of them looked more experienced than you.

Two of them are wearing their company uniform, which immediately tells you that they have come from bigger companies than yours.

And after having a short chat with 3-4 guys, you come to know they have come from different parts of the city, which are quite far from this location.

Although you still don't know too much about this company, exact job profile, pay structure, etc., suddenly you start finding this company and job quite attractive.

The value of this company and job is automatically increased in your mind.

Your approach toward this job is no more casual.

The more you see people in the room contesting for the same job, the more you're becoming desperate to get this job.

And the more you're becoming desperate, the lesser will be your efforts to negotiate.

You may start thinking that there is definitely something special that you don't know which has caused so many people to apply for this job.

So, you decide you will not talk too much about your expectations and will accept their offer without any conditions.

This happens when you give the SAME appointment time to everyone. The simultaneous scheduling creates an atmosphere for <u>competition for a limited resource</u>.

Another common example of the *same appointment time* technique is inviting at least 2-3 prospective buyers to show your house or car.

When there was only one buyer, he was casually assessing the car's pros and cons. But as soon as the second buyer shows up, the whole situation changes dramatically.

The moment the second buyer comes to see the same car, the anxiety starts growing on the first buyer's face. The availability of a car suddenly becomes limited by the presence of the other.

Moreover, the first prospective buyer's desire to buy a car as per his terms and conditions is suddenly threatened. And it's not just limited to the first buyer. The second buyer is also equally agitated by the combination of **rivalry & restricted availability**.

Whether the buyer finds the product useful or not has become a secondary issue.

To possess the product has become the primary concern.

A sudden competition from other buyers has greatly affected one's desire to have a car in the sense of possessing it.

A casual situation has become a **now-or-never limited-time-only** opportunity. The prospective buyers have to rush to decide on a car, which has now become a **contested resource**.

This technique of influence is known as ***Competition for a Scarce Resource***, where a normal opportunity, person, product, or service is turned into a prized possession, thereby making it highly valuable in the minds of other people.

This technique is based on the principle of human behaviour. All of us are competitive by nature. Not only do we want the same item more when it is scarce, but we also want it most when we compete for it.

We don't want to lose to our rivals. We turned from uncertain to obsessive whenever we encounter the powerful construction of **Scarcity plus rivalry**.

The feeling of competing for scarce resources can motivate us to do anything to possess those scarce resources.

Just like the *Fight or Flight* situation, *Competition for a Scarce Resource* blocks our ability to think. When we find that what we want could be taken by our rivals, a physical agitation sets in; the blood boils up, emotions rise to the peak, the logic goes right out of the window.

There are many ways this technique is used in our personal and professional life. Sometimes accidentally, other times intentionally.

For example, you will find the same technique used in a *Triangle Love* situation where the lover is competing with a rival for the love of the beloved.

When you come to know that your friend is also interested in your love, then suddenly that normal, casual relationship turns into an intense rivalry.

You will find the same technique used in *Auction*, where an intense environment is created to build pressure in the mind of buyers.

Participants bid openly against one another, with each subsequent bid required to be higher than the previous bid.

In this way, participants lose control of them and buy a product at an extremely high price, which they might have never done in normal trading.

You will find the same technique used in *entrance examinations*, where young students spend months and even years to crack the exam.

You will find the same technique used by real estate agents when *you're looking for a new house*.

Suppose you want to shift in a locality, which is near to your office... and for this, you've approached to some agents. Your priority is a furnished house.

One Sunday morning, you get a call from an agent to see one vacant unfurnished flat in the afternoon. Although you're not interested in an unfurnished house, you decide to make a casual visit since you've nothing important to do in that afternoon.

You reach that place and find two other parties already there to see the same house. Now without uttering a single word, the real estate agent has created the value of that unfurnished house in your mind by showing a direct competition in front of you.

Even if you don't go for it, still your casualness is turned into serious attention.

The point is, most of the time, it has nothing to do with the quality of product or service, but the entire process is made so intense that it becomes *Now or Never* situation for people. They start considering a normal ordinary thing a ***prized trophy***.

SCARCITY

There is a rule in selling: no urgency, no sale.

The reason is people do not know how much they want a product or service until you suggest that they may not be able to get it.

Generally, people procrastinate their buying decisions. They don't want to lose their hard-earned money. It is only when you threaten to take it away that they step up and make a buying decision.

Human behaviour is such that we are likelier to purchase something if we're informed that it's the last one available in-store or that a special deal will soon expire.

This phenomenon is called Scarcity, where our desire to possess something increases when we find that it is limited in availability.

The scarcity principle is based on some theories of human behaviour, like...

- When opportunities become less available, we lose the freedom of choice. And in order to retain our freedom, we want the item even more than before.

- We consider things that are difficult to possess better than those that are easy to possess. Difficulty to possess the item increases the desire for that item in our mind. So we begin to assign it positive qualities to justify the desire because we don't want others to consider us stupid. And we start looking for logical reasons that if we feel drawn to something, it is because of the merit of the thing.

- We perceive that the products which are in short supply are more desirable, more attractive, and more costly than identical products in abundant supply.

- We find products that have RECENTLY become scarce, more desirable than products that are always scarce.

- We find products that have become scarce due to HUGE demand, more desirable than those which have become scarce due to some mistake.

Capitalizing on our weakness, marketers use the scarcity principle to create the value of their products in our minds. By applying various techniques, they want us to decide **quickly** what to buy.

Marketers know that for us, the joy is not in experiencing a scarce commodity but in possessing it.

Products and Services Which Have Natural Scarcity

Some items in the world are extremely valuable because they are naturally very limited. Either they cannot be produced more, or it's difficult to find them, available only in limited areas.

For example:

- Metals like Platinum, Gold, Silver

- Gemstones like Diamond, Ruby, Emerald, Sapphire

- Fuels like Coal, Oil, Natural Gas, Petroleum

- Land and Freshwater (only 2.5% of the Earth's water supply is fresh water and 70% of that freshwater is frozen)

- Some species of animals

- Trees (paper)

- Rare collectibles, art, and memorabilia

Products and Services with Artificial Scarcity

However, there are many products in which marketers create Artificial Scarcity to increase their value in customers' minds.

For example:

- Shortage of food

- Shortage of vaccination and medicines

- Shortage of vehicles

- Shortage of jobs and high-level skilled workers

- Shortage of schools & colleges, teachers, admission seats

- Patents and Copyrights

In the next volume, I'll talk about different techniques of the Scarcity principle that could be used both offline and online.

Sadly, some unethical marketers use these techniques to create fake scarcity.

My suggestion is: Never fall into this trap. Although it could help these marketers in getting short-term results, in the long-term, it will destroy their reputation in the market.

VOLUME - VI

As you remember in the last volume, I talked about the Scarcity principle of Persuasion, where our desire to possess something increases when we find that it is limited in availability.

Using Scarcity techniques, we can create the value of our products and services in the minds of our prospects and as well urgency to buy now or else ready to lose the deal forever.

However, I warned you of not using Fake Scarcity in your marketing communications... otherwise your customers will stop taking your words seriously.

Also, if you use too much scarcity by bringing the same offers, again and again, it could backfire your marketing strategy.

For example, I have seen some companies which bring discount offers almost every month without any genuine reason.

They try to create scarcity by saying their offer is valid for a limited period. Although it could bring results for some time, in the long-term, it could spoil their reputation.

The problem is not about giving a discount. And the problem is not about applying Scarcity. The problem is about the overuse of discounts and scarcity without providing any genuine reason.

Let me share one of the best examples of how to use genuine reason in providing discounts and building scarcity. I took this example from one of the classic books of all time - *The Robert Collier Letter Book* (If you want to

learn how to write persuasive sales letters, you must read
this book).

Here it is...

(Headline)**: Before the Price Goes Up!**

Dear Sir:

A short time ago one of the old, reliable mills that makes
the finer qualities of woven Madras for shirts began
sending out S.O.S. calls.

They had kept their plant going steadily for months,
thinking that the usual demand would easily take care of
their excess output.

But, with the weather so generally unseasonable, the usual
demand didn't materialize. And there they were heavily
overstocked — and needing money.

If we would take *all* their surplus stock of the finer grades
of woven Madras, amounting to a *quarter of a million
yards,* they offered to let us have them at way below any
price we had ever paid for shirtings in all our years in
business—at *far* less than they could make the materials
and sell them for today.

We took them—the whole quarter-million yards—at a
tremendous savings in cost...

A Bargain You May Never Get Again.

So, you can see in this example that the reason behind the price-cut and scarcity is not only genuine, but it's also believable and dramatic.

The smart customers know that such situations could happen once or twice but not again and again.

So, if the companies are giving heavy discounts again and again without any genuine reasons, first, it could raise doubts in the minds of customers.

Second, after some time, people will start taking their offers lightly. They will stop responding to the scarcity applied in promotions.

Therefore, it's very important to keep in mind that the overuse of any persuasion technique could backfire your efforts resulting in loss of sale and credibility.

Scarcity is one of the most powerful principles of Influence and Persuasion and can bring you tremendous results if you know how and when to apply it in your communications.

There are many ways to use Scarcity techniques, which I'm going to cover in this volume, but first, the question comes why we need to use Scarcity? If our product is so good, then why we need to rely on such persuasion principles?

The answer is: **One of the reasons many people don't buy is they're just not in a hurry**.

It doesn't matter to them whether they buy today or tomorrow or next week or next month or even next year.

It's human nature to procrastinate decisions and actions unless there is some strong reason to act.

"Yes, we like your products, but why we should buy today?" - This is one of the toughest objections every salesperson has to deal with.

When you try to pitch them to buy your product, they will give an excuse that they have already spent half of their life without this product. So it doesn't make a big difference if they buy your product today or tomorrow.

That's why we need to create super attractive offers and provide a solid reason to buy NOW.

In this and next volume, you'll find a lot of ideas and techniques on the Scarcity principle to increase your value and create a sense of urgency in the minds of your customers.

Some people ask me, 'Okay, we understand we need to use Scarcity to create urgency, but why we need to emphasize increasing value if we already know that we have the best products?'

My answer is: **In the world of Persuasion, everything is the perception of the mind**.

It doesn't matter how good your company is… how good your product is… What matters the most is how your customer perceives you, your company, and your products and services.

I want you to remember this point because I have seen many struggling entrepreneurs who have excellent products, but they failed to create the same perception in their customers' minds.

The question is: Why are they not able to create the same value in their customers' minds?

The first reason is their salespeople don't believe in their own products.

The famous sales trainer Zig Ziglar used to say, "Selling is nothing but the transference of feeling from one person to another."

In short, your customer needs to feel the same way that you feel about your product.

So, if you and your salespeople don't believe in your products, then how it's possible to convince your customers that you have the best products available in the market?

This is one of the main reasons many salespeople struggle in their profession, and companies die who rely on such salespeople.

Many salespeople don't agree with me when I make such a remark in my in-house sales training. They counter by saying they fully believe in their products and have no doubts about them.

And then, to prove my point, I take a small test to check how much they believe in their products.

I ask a very simple question, **"How many of you are using the SAME product that you're selling to your customers?"**

Most of the time, only a few hands go up.

Then I ask them, "If you are not using your own product, then how is it possible to ask your customer to use the product that you sell?"

Let me explain with one scenario how important this point is.

Suppose you're selling X brand bike, but you have Y brand bike at your home. The reason could be anything, like:

Earlier, you were in a different company selling Y brand bike.

Or it's not your bike. You're using your brother's bike.

Now one day, while you are riding Y brand bike to buy some groceries from the market, you meet one of your potential customers whom you pitched X brand bike a few days back. Now, what question will come into your prospect's mind?

Gotcha!

Through this example, I want to teach you an important lesson…

It doesn't matter how good you're in prospecting, presenting, and closing… if you fail in expressing your conviction, you will lose the sale.

You see, there are three categories of belief:

1) **Opinion**: Opinion is the weakest form of belief because its intensity is very low.

2) **Faith**: Faith is stronger than Opinion because of higher intensity.

3) **Conviction**: Conviction is the strongest form of belief because of the highest intensity. Here what you SAY and what you DO completely match each other.

So, after conducting this test, the first thing I suggest all salespeople of the company is to discard their competitor's products and start using their company's products even if it's out of their budget.

And not just salespeople, in fact, the entire staff of the company should buy and use the company's products.

If their products are high-ticket items, then the company should make some arrangements on how to finance it for their employees.

The point is, your customer will never buy your product if he doesn't see conviction at your end.

He might think you just want to sell your product to make some commission. After some time, you'll switch to some other job and forget about him.

And the second reason why entrepreneurs are not able to create the same value in their customers' minds is the *Communication Gap* between them and their customers.

I mean, entrepreneurs need to understand and speak the same way their customers processes information inside their brain; otherwise, these entrepreneurs may not be able to create the same value in their customers' minds.

Imagine you have a great product, but you speak in French, and your customer understands only Chinese, so unless you learn and speak Chinese, you'll never be able to persuade him effectively to buy your products. (If you think it's your customer's job to understand and speak French, then please leave marketing)

So, you should understand the subconscious language of your customer and speak the same language while dealing with him if you want to reduce the *Communication Gap.*

I've already covered how your customer thinks and process the information. I've also covered the personality traits of your customer in detail.

 Knowing your customer's personality traits and dealing accordingly helps in reducing the *Communication Gap* between you and your customer.

Another important part of subconscious communication is *Value Gap*, which I'm going to discuss now.

Value Gap

Social Values play a crucial role in our lives. They provide general guidelines on how to behave in society.

Social Values help us to know how others perceive us in society.

Values are the criteria people use in assessing their daily lives, arrange their priorities, and choosing between the alternative course of action.

In short, we all are social animals.

There are various factors which affect our social values like:

- Success in profession

- Wealth and valuable possessions

- High Education

- Association with influential and developed country or state

- Association with prominent and advanced culture... society... family...

- Association with a big company

- Association with famous brands and celebrities

- Physical attractiveness

- Mastery in an important skill-set

- Contribution to society

- And many more...

Based on these factors, we can divide people majorly into two types:

1) High-Value person

2) Low-Value person

High-Value people consider themselves important... whereas Low-Value people consider others important.

So, when a High-Value person, who considers himself superior, meets a Low-Value person... there is a gap in their understanding of each other, which needs to be reduced as much as possible.

I call this difference **Value Gap**.

The bigger the gap, the higher the chances that others misunderstand us... not listen to us... not agree to our thoughts... and not ready to take action on our requests and instructions.

For example, in business, to achieve their targets, sometimes salespeople become desperate to get orders.

Such kind of activities reduces the salesperson's value in the customer's eyes. And simultaneously, it increases the customer's value.

This is not good because the salesperson's desperateness is increasing Value Gap.

And since such things are happening for a long-long time everywhere in the world… so the customer has automatically assumed himself a High-Value breed and salesperson a Low-Value breed.

The bad news is it's out of our control to change customer's perceptions worldwide.

And the good news is we can change customer's perceptions in our case if we know how to increase our value in the mind of the customer.

This is one of the major benefits when we apply scarcity techniques in our sales & marketing.

And it's not just about increasing value. Sometimes we have to decrease our value if we want to sell our services in the market.

Shocking?

Yes, but it's true.

For example, have you ever noticed why in some industries where **audience liking** plays a huge role, for example, entertainment, politics, sports… children of famous celebrities do not get the same success just as their parents?

Of course, I'm not talking about exceptionally competent children.

The reason is unlike their parents, who started their journey as a struggler from a poor background and became enormously successful and popular later, these children are born with a silver spoon.

They already have wealth, possessions, and an advantage over new strugglers to get big breaks inside the industry without proving their competence.

So there is a huge Value Gap between children of famous and rich movie stars...politicians... sportspeople...business owners... and the rest of the public, including their own employees.

That's why they don't get similar kind of love and acceptance that their parents enjoyed, which ultimately leads to failure in the long-term.

In order to avoid such situations, nowadays, celebrities' kids hire smart PR agencies whose job is to influence people through articles, interviews, personal stories that could emotionally connect these kids with the general public.

This strategy used by High-Value people to lower their value in front of Low-Value people to win their hearts is known as **Grounding**.

For example,

- They tell their childhood stories about how their parents were so strict and gave them the same culture and values that they got from their poor parents.

- Or once upon a time, they were having some major illness and how they overcame their problems and bounced back.

- Or in spite of belonging to a wealthy family, they are very humble and never took advantage of their money, power, and position.

- Or how they work so hard day and night to prove they are also equally capable just like their famous parents.

- Or they do lots of social activities, spend time with the poor and helpless people, and do a lot of charity work for some special cause.

The point is whether you're a High-Value or Low-Value person, being a Master Persuader, it should be your major task to reduce the Value Gap as much as possible if you want others to buy your products and services. In short, you need to change the perception of your market about you.

One of the ways to do this is by using scarcity in your marketing communication.

Scarcity can be applied in various ways. It has tremendous power in creating value and urgency and getting immediate action.

Here are some Scarcity techniques that you can use in your work:

Limited Quantity

It's very commonly used by marketers around the world. They love to inform customers that a particular product is in short supply that cannot be guaranteed to last long.

Here are some examples of how to use the *Limited Quantity* technique:

- On product category pages in websites, listing items that are low in stock.

- In an e-commerce website, you can employ scarcity by telling which sizes and styles are out of stock. It's a smart way to show that the product is in high demand and low supply.

- You can also alert your website visitors when a popular item is back in stock. By applying the 'Back in Stock' technique, you can tell them that the item had been sold out due to massive popularity. If they want that item, they should jump on it before it happens again.

- You can also show your website visitors which product is now fully out-of-stock. So, in this way, you can tell them you don't want that it should happen to a product your website visitors are looking at. That's why it's better to buy now.

- Only a few items left.

- Limited edition.

- Not available in any store.

- Two seats left at this price.

- Only 6 rooms left on our site.

- See our last available models.

- Only 3 gold coins per order.

- Only 2 left in the stock (more on the way).

- Only a limited number of items are produced. No more will be made. The moulds will be destroyed.

- Get them while supplies last.

- There are only 10 experts in the world who know this ancient art.

- We are the sole distributor of this imported software in our country.

Limited Time

Marketers love to push deadlines on customers to get a fast response to their offers.

They love to tell customers that unless they make an immediate decision to buy, they will have to purchase the item at a higher price, or they will be unable to purchase it at all.

Here are some examples of how to use the *Limited Time* technique:

- "Sold" signs on the products like furniture, cars, electronics, musical instruments, etc. while walking through stores. These signs create the urgency because somebody else has found a deal, so we should not delay in buying the next hot item.

- In home-shopping TV channels, the little clock running at the corner of the screen. It lets you know how less time you have left to buy.

- The counter on the screen. The counter runs down with every order.

- Available for a limited time only.

- Last day to buy.

- Up to 50% off until Sunday!

- Final Hours.

- The Sale is valid up to 15th January.

- Only a few hours left.

- Don't miss out: Our holiday sale ends tonight.

- QUICK! 50% off ends soon!

- A countdown timer on the website.

- Many people don't pay their bills until the last date.

Limited Quantity + Limited Time

You can use both Limited Time and Quantity in a single offer to make it more compelling to act now.

Here are some examples of how to use this technique:

- Registration is open for two days for new members. Membership will be given only to 100 people on a first come - first serve basis.

- My offer expires on 21st August and is limited to the first 1,000 people who respond. I hope you take advantage of it.

- Admission seats are available for only 150 students who can apply by 30th April Noon. If seats are filled before 30th April, then the application process will be stopped immediately without any intimation.

- To book a table for dinner, please call before 4 pm to check if it's available or not.

Introductory Offer

You can provide an Introductory Offer whenever you're launching a new product or service. Since it can be done only once for every new product so you should try to take maximum advantage of this opportunity.

Here are some ideas on how to use introductory offers:

- You can use both Limited Quantity and Time in Introductory Offer.

- You can give a special discounted price, not available later.

- You can provide some special features or accessories free of cost.

- You can give some special privileges to the first few customers for a long period.

- You can organize launch events where you can give gifts to early customers.

- You can provide celebrity signed models to the first few customers.

Early Bird Offer

Early Bird Offer is quite similar to an Introductory Offer. The only difference, is unlike the Introductory Offer, which can be used only once for each product, the Early Bird Offer can be used again and again whenever you're launching a new event.

Early Bird Offer is used to get fast bookings or enrolments instead of waiting for the last date. Since many people procrastinate their buying decision till the end date so this technique is used to motivate them to act fast.

Offer can be in the form of:

- Discount
- Additional features
- Combo package
- Bonus
- Payment in instalments
- Free after-sales-service
- Additional guarantee/warranty
- Free membership in some private group
- Special financing scheme
- Recognition and awards in the company's events

Special "By Invitation Only" Offer

As the name suggests, here you invite your prospective customers and make this offer exclusive by putting a condition that only those who receive your invitation can buy your products and take benefits of your services.

Examples:

- Sending invites for membership in an exclusive club/social media group/secret society/website.

- Sending invites for attending a high profile conference.

- Sending invites for an interview on TV/Radio/Podcast.

- Sending invites for a new product demonstration.

- Sending invites for lunch with celebrity/business leaders.

- Sending invites for connecting on social media.

- Sending invites for webinars.

- Sending invites for Questions & Answers session.

- Sending invites for parties at homes, offices, schools, community groups, and workplaces. For example, famous Tupperware parties, where products are still sold through a party plan with rewards for hosts and hostesses.

Bonuses/Freebies Available
in
Limited Quantity

During the buying process, the prospect starts feeling anxious at the time of making a buying decision. To get him relieved from anxiety, sometimes we use the **Secondary Close technique**.

Using this closing technique, we try to turn the prospect's focus from indecision to a minor point so that it becomes easier for him to make a buying decision.

If the prospect agrees to the minor point of the deal, he has somehow decided to buy the entire offer.

The minor point can be colour, size, type of model, or any bonus item that he gets along with the main product.

However, in order to build a second layer of scarcity in the prospect's mind, we can limit the quantity of these bonuses.

Here are some examples of how to use this technique:

- This exclusive report is given absolutely free to the first 100 subscribers.

- The company is providing free seat-covers to the first 500 customers.

·	Free car parking for the first 50 bookings due to limited space.

·	Free leather belt with each pair of shoes. Hurry! Only a few belts left.

Bonuses/Freebies Available for Limited Time

Another way to build a second layer of scarcity in the prospect's mind is by putting a limit on time to provide these bonuses, after which one cannot get them free.

Here are some examples of how to use this technique:

- On some rare occasions, a company or an e-commerce website releases a 'gift' every hour with every purchase. This gift is for a limited time—available only on that day, at that specific hour.

- Buy any 5 holiday-items and get a free bottle of red wine. But hurry! This bottle of red wine is available till midnight tonight!

- The offer of a 1-year free additional warranty will expire at 5 pm tomorrow.

Next Day Delivery

Nowadays, people are impatient about delivery and want the items fast.

Since the customer has multiple choices available in the market to buy products, so you can take advantage of their impatience by providing the facility of Next Day Delivery if they accept your condition.

The Next Day Delivery option could also help you in beating competition who can't afford extra resources.

Here are some ideas on how to use the Next Day Delivery option:

- You can use the Next Day Delivery offer to lure people becoming your founding members.

- You can use the Next Day Delivery offer to lure people becoming your lifetime customers.

- You can use the Next Day Delivery offer to sell high-ticket items.

- In an e-commerce website, you can use the Next Day Delivery offer if the cart value is more than X amount.

- You can use Next Day Delivery offer to persuade people to order fast. For example:

- Want it tomorrow? Order within 22 minutes and choose One-Day Shipping at checkout.

- Last Chance: Order by 5 pm today for next day delivery.

Limited Edition

You can come up with limited edition items so that people recognize their value even in the future.

In this way, you differentiate a particular item from all of your other range of products.

Limited edition can be done in various ways, like:

- Producing an item with only a small number of copies.

- Seasonal product.

- A special in-built feature that is not available anywhere else in the market.

- Coming up with a future product with advanced/disruptive technology and distributed to premium customers only for testing purposes.

- Celebrity Signature product.

- New design/taste/colour/fragrance which may not be available later.

- Re-launch of an original or a vintage product, which was extremely popular long time back. But only available in limited quantity or for a short period.

Special Occasion Offers

This is a very common strategy used by marketers all over the world.

In fact, mediocre marketers are so much dependent on it that they come with such offers frequently.

They try to take advantage of local/national/international occasions by giving heavy discounts on their products.

For example:

- This festive season offer of 2-for-1 tea sets is nearly wiped out. If you'd like to get your hands on one of the last tea set, now's the time to do it.

- Buy any LED on or before New Year Eve and get 3-months cable connection free.

You can also take advantage of special occasion offers, but you need to create your own occasions in order to be different from your competitors.

In this case, my only concern is don't get too much dependent on it. It can bring you short-term results, but in the long-term, it could damage your reputation and profits as people will start responding only to your offers.

Here are some ways on how marketers take advantage of special occasions:

- Festival time offers

- National holidays offers

- International Day offers

- Weekend offers

- Birthdays, Anniversary, Foundation day offers

- Historical event offers

Restricted Information

The Scarcity principle is not just limited to commodities. It works equally well with the information.

People are attracted to the information which is not allowed to share with them.

When something is banned, people have a greater desire to receive that thing. Even their attitude turns more favourable toward the banned items than before the ban.

There are many ways in which any information can be made more valuable by making it scarce. Like:

- We find a piece of information more persuasive if we think we can't get it elsewhere.

- We give more value to the information which was available earlier but now is restricted.

- If the news carrying the scarcity of information is made scarce, then it becomes double persuasive.

- Some videos/interviews become viral after getting censored officially.

Moreover, it has been found that **censoring information not only makes it more valuable, but it also becomes more believable.** Because people think there is definitely some truth in that information, that's why it is not shared with them.

Here are some common examples of how some restricted information/news/videos are created:

- Demography/Geography restricted content.

- Censored movies.

- Banned interviews which have exposed someone.

- Officially censored views.

- Lost tapes found recently, which carry very crucial information.

- Classified files.

- The information that is available only to rich, famous, powerful people but not to the general public.

- Revealing secret in the end.

- Suddenly stopping in the middle of the story. Will reveal later what happened next.

Restricted Area

Restricted areas become the talk of the town. The more you stop people from going inside the restricted place, the more they think about it.

Here are some common examples:

- No trespassers are allowed in this area.

- This is a private beach/island/hill.

- This club/restaurant is only for members. Outsiders are not allowed.

- Permission from members of the royal family is required to visit this palace.

- Permission from the forest officer is required to visit this wildlife century.

Recently Become Scarce

If any particular thing becomes less available recently than being scarce all along, then it becomes more desirable.

Here are some examples:

- Due to recent fire at our factory, we are stopping production for the next two months. So, this is the only stock left with us.

- Due to the change in season, our company has decided to stop the production of these items. So, this is the only stock left with us.

- One of our major suppliers is facing some labour issues. That's why we're not getting sufficient raw material to produce more. This is the only stock left with us, and we can't guarantee when our next stock will come.

The products which have become less available recently through social demand are found most desirable of all.

Here are some examples:

- There is a 3-months booking for this model. If you want this model, you need to book today, and there is no chance of getting a single penny discount.

- All other colours are available except for the red colour, which is in huge demand. To get a red colour, you need to book now.

- These islands are one of the most popular destinations in the winter holidays. People from all over the country come to these islands. So, you need to book your flights and hotel as soon as possible. Otherwise, be ready to pay double.

Abandon Emails

If a prospect abandons their cart, send an email letting them know how important your product is for them. And if it's a bestseller item, then tell them that the item is selling fast. If they want the item, they need to buy now before it's too late. Such emails are known as Abandon emails.

Here are some headlines that can pull their attention back to you:

- Oops! How could you miss this _______ (product/opportunity)?

- Are you sure you don't want to look beautiful?

- Are you sure you don't want to become rich?

- Today is your last chance to get this _______(product).

- That's it! We're closing NOW!

- Only a few hours left!

- After 5 hours, this special offer will vanish FOREVER.

Exclusive Offers

There is no limit in applying scarcity wherever you get the opportunity. What you need is a creative mind to come up with new ideas.

For example, you can apply scarcity even to offer itself by making it exclusive.

You can make the offer available for only one time. We call these 'Once-in-a-lifetime Offer.'

You can make the offer available at limited places.

You can limit the ways to grab that offer.

Like these, you should try to make your offers exclusive so that people don't take your offers for granted.

Here are some ideas to use scarcity in offers:

- This offer is not available in stores/online.

- This offer is applicable only if you buy from our website.

- As soon as you close this webpage, this offer will vanish forever.

- This offer is available only for our existing members.

- This offer is available only in limited places (countries/states/stores).

- This offer is valid only if you buy items worth X amount in a particular store in a single day.

- These accessories are given free with only our top model.

- Special discount offer just to clear the inventory.

- Special discount offer only on a particular model.

- Once-in-a-lifetime offer as we are closing this business.

- Special discount offer just to cover our losses due to the recent fire at our warehouse.

The 'Now or Never' Close

While closing deals, you should definitely apply scarcity, especially when you find that the prospect is not in a hurry to buy your product.

The objective of the 'Now or Never' closing technique is to create a feeling of loss in the minds of customers.

If your reputation is strong, the reason is genuine and solid, and your products are valuable in your customers' eyes, you will never wonder why your customers believe your words that the sale would expire this weekend and prices would never be this low again.

Here are some examples of how to use the *'Now or Never' Close*:

- "This car is the last one in stock that is both automatic and red in colour. If it goes later today, we won't get another like it in stock for the next two weeks." Two weeks seems like forever to get the car.

- "Shall we go to the finance manager before she leaves for the day? If you want it today at this special price, you should see her now."

- "I just want to say that it's a superior product which is available at a good price right now. But I'm not sure about the future. Why don't you just take it?"

Closing Questions Using the Scarcity Principle

As you know, in the sales profession, there comes a time where the sales need to be closed. Unfortunately, our customers won't always easily decide to buy.

Sometimes customers are confused.

Sometimes customers are feeling anxiety.

Sometimes customers want to procrastinate buying decisions.

At those times, we need to keep asking Closing Questions using different ideas so that customers don't lose their focus from the deal.

Second, Closing Questions help us in qualifying serious customers.

Third, Closing Questions help us in checking whether we are moving in the right direction to close the deal or not.

Asking Closing Questions at the right time, at the right place, using the right tone and body language is great art, that once you master, could bring you tremendous results.

Moreover, if you start incorporating Persuasion principles and techniques in your Closing Questions, you could outsmart every other competitor in your industry.

Here are some examples of how to use Closing Questions using the Scarcity principle:

- "Do you really want to lose this lucrative deal?"

- "Since the item is not available in our warehouse, would you be willing to book it today and wait for 2 weeks for direct delivery to your home?"

- "Shall we go to the finance department before the manager leaves for the day? If you want it today, you should see him now."

- "If you can't afford to repair your car, what about the ever-increasing fuel price?"

- "As I know that you work full-time, and still if you cannot pay your insurance premium, then how will your family pay the house rent, grocery bills, and kids' school fees if you are not there to work at all?"

- "If you can't afford 2,000 bucks to repair your TV, then how will you be able to afford the greater expense of the new TV you're going to need much sooner?"

- "Since you can acquire this product for just X amount today, to cover all production and shipping costs, don't you think it's more than fair?"

- "If you can't afford to protect your house from rain, won't it be even more difficult to afford the new furniture, TV, refrigerator, washing machine, and house paint after a few more rainstorms?"

- "Should I mark this one SOLD while we discuss how to finance it as per terms suitable to you?"

- "If these are only two models available in the market, which one are you going to choose?"

- "We're almost sold out of this model. Let me check if we can get this model in the size you want. Could you wait here for two minutes?"

- "Let me check with my manager and see if we can arrange immediate delivery? Could you wait at reception for a few minutes?"

- "If you just go ahead and sign this agreement, we can get the process started immediately so that your project doesn't get halted anymore. That's what your major concern is, isn't it?"

In the next volume, I'll talk about some more Scarcity techniques and another powerful principle of persuasion.

VOLUME - VII

In the last volume, I shared a few ideas and techniques on how to use the Scarcity principle in your offerings.

The Scarcity principle is used to create your value as well as urgency in the minds of your customers.

Otherwise, customers will not give you the respect that you deserve.

They will not pay attention to your offerings.

And they will keep procrastinating their buying decisions.

Also, the Scarcity principle helps marketers to capitalize on the human nature of proving ourselves that we are different from others... that we are a unique breed...

And what do we generally do to feel unique and special? How we show others that we are different from them?

By owning or possessing unique and expensive things.

By mastering any rare or crucial skill.

By doing some extraordinary activities that are not expected from normal people.

By achieving some special position in society.

By creating or inventing something new which nobody has ever thought before.

We do such things because this is how we think:

"I am unique and special because I own something that no one else (or very few) has been able to obtain."

Therefore being a Master Persuader, it's our job to make people feel unique and special...

How?

- By building an irresistible desire in customer's minds for our products.

- By creating a Unique Selling Proposition (USP) in our products and services.

- By bringing scarcity in our offers.

- By customizing our solutions.

- By developing personality in our products.

- By giving them information that nobody else possesses in their surroundings.

- By helping them become a hero in their family, work, and society.

I've already talked about how USP and customizing solutions can hit the five senses of our customers.

And now I'm covering the Scarcity part.

Here are some more Scarcity techniques:

Push-Pull

One of the most important points to remember in the Persuasion process is who controls the communication while dealing with customers.

As I always say... either you influence your customer to buy from you OR your customer influences you that he can't buy from you right now.

In any case, one person is always influencing the other person.

To persuade others, it's very important to keep control of communication right from the beginning. It will give you the power of being non-negotiable... means not compromising with your terms.

This is called the **Influence effect**, which is the ultimate form of communication.

Influence is a type of communication with the prospect where the prospect is buying on salesperson's terms without raising any objections. It's a dream sale for every salesperson.

This happens when you master the principles and techniques of Influence and Persuasion.

Your prospect moves to the position held by you.

This is an ideal close for every salesperson because your prospect is buying on your terms and conditions.

Here, the prospect finds so much value in you that he doesn't want to lose the deal.

This is the kind of communication you should aim while closing every deal. And for this, you need to have control over the communication right from the beginning.

However, if the other person tries to control the communication, then you need to apply some techniques to gain back your control.

One such technique is called **Push-Pull**.

It is also known as "Chase Me, and I'll Run."

Push-Pull is a mind game that we play with our customers, colleagues, friends, relatives when we find that others take us too much for granted.

It's human psychology that people want those things that they can't have. And when things are readily available to them, they start taking them for granted.

For example, if you eat your favourite food every single day, then after some time, you start feeling bored and want some change in diet.

Similarly, in our personal and professional relationships, we start getting bored and desperately want some change.

And in this process, we lower the importance of our loved ones, friends, colleagues, associates, partners, vendors because they have become part of our daily life.

As a result, we want to keep control of communication when we deal with them.

Because of this reason, you need to be careful when you're in a relationship with people who are very demanding... who want to have control over communication... who love to dominate others.

If you give others what they want all the time, they will start taking you for granted.

They never worry about getting things from you because they know that you are there to keep fulfilling their requirements and readily available whenever they call. Due to this, they start taking advantage of you.

In such situations, Master Persuaders use the *Push-Pull* technique to win back control of communication.

In the Push-Pull process, you give a little bit what others want and then move away, leaving them wanting more.

So, you whet their appetite by first getting closer to them and then making them want more by not being readily available to them.

You keep repeating this process until you regain control of the state of affairs.

Once you start using the Push-Pull technique, the power in your relationship and communications will shift over to you.

Others will become dependent on your validation and appreciation of their nice behaviour towards you.

Push means pushing others away by saying or doing things that imply you're not interested in them.

It is used when your customer is taking you for granted or not giving you preference or even not giving the respect that you deserve.

Just because to get the deal you've given him too much importance... you're very nice to him and agreeing on all his requests. So, he is enjoying the control of powers.

Such things happen in marriage also, where you provide your unconditional caring, loyalty, and devotion to your spouse to prove your love, but your spouse doesn't value it.

Such things happen in friendships also where the person whom you consider your best friend is not too much inclined towards you. Instead, he likes to hang out with others.

Such things happen in offices also where your colleagues keep assigning you more and more work without any appreciation and rewards.

Instead of begging for their attention, appreciation, respect... you need to make them realize that they might have lost you by disappearing and acting distant.

Here are some ideas on how to show your Push behaviour...

·   Do things that show you're not needy.

·   Don't be readily available all the time. The more available you are to your prospective customers, the more at ease they're going to be with the way things are right now. They don't feel any pain and pressure to immediately buy from you.

·   Use dissociation techniques to show that you have no interest in what's going on in other's life.

·   Hang out with the people whom your best friend doesn't like.

·   Tease the person about something he doesn't like to talk about. For example, any funny incident, remembering which, still embarrasses him... or any of his old bad habits, for which he used to get punishments... or his native town or school that has earned a bad reputation these days.

·   Show your selfishness. A dark side of yours.

·   Give a strong message in your office that you have no feelings for incompetent employees.

·   If your customer is rude to your colleague and bothers him too much, then tell your customer politely that your colleague is upset with their behaviour. That's why you're assigning someone else for customer service.

- In your office, if your senior is assigning too much work to you without any appreciation, then stop responding to his every request. Don't need to answer his phone calls all the time or reply very briefly.

- Reduce your habit of calling people back when you see their missed calls.

- Skip or leave social events where you don't get attention and respect.

- Skip useless meetings that you have to attend just for the sake of attendance, as directed by your superiors. You need to tell them directly or indirectly that your time is valuable and not meant for listening to others on matters which are not relevant or important.

- Postpone or cancel meetings where your customer calls you just to waste your time instead of giving any business or talking something important.

Whereas **Pull** means you're saying or doing things that imply you're very much interested in them.

You need to show your Pull behaviour when the other person is confused about why you're acting so strange and cold, and because of this, he starts approaching you again.

In your personal and professional relationships, due to your Push behaviour, the other person subconsciously starts thinking that maybe he plays an important role in your life. And he doesn't want to lose this importance.

He tries his best to make sure you don't push him again. To avoid that pain, he invests more and more time with you. He agrees with your thoughts and points. Ultimately he gives you control of the communication.

This is the right time to apply for the PULL technique.

The more he behaves nicely with you, the more you reward him with your Pull behaviour, which he subconsciously enjoys a lot.

Here are some ideas on how to show your Pull behaviour...

- You're happy with their behaviour and reward them through your friendly attitude.

- Invite them out for lunch and have a long chat. Tell them how much you appreciate their support. But don't tell why you were so cold and distant.

- Do things to take their attention towards you.

- You say something positive and upbeat.

- Do things to seduce them.

- Do things to impress them.

- Give sincere compliments to the other person's achievements.

During the Pull process, you need to be careful of not disclosing your reasons for Push behaviour. Let them guess what they have done wrong.

If they feel responsible for your cold behaviour, they will begin to invest more and more time, money, energy with you to avoid such pain again.

When you achieve mastery in the Push-Pull technique, you can use it several times whenever you see a change in people's behaviour.

You can use it fast... like both Push and Pull in a single sentence.

Here's one of the ways how to do it:

You can use the Push-Pull technique by giving complement but not making any commitment. For example:

"Wow! Your product is amazing. You'll definitely find an investor who is interested in such products."

You can even increase the effectiveness of the Push-Pull process by quickly doing Push-Pull-Push-Pull-Push-Pull-Push-Pull--- in a single paragraph...

For example:

"Due to huge demand, we are glad to announce that we are opening membership of our club (Pull) for a limited period

(Push). There is an Early Bird Offer of 20% discount (Pull) for only the first 50 new members (Push). Any resident of this city can apply for membership (Pull) but only 1 person from 1 family (Push)."

Using Push and Pull together makes your offer incredibly attractive. It increases the desire to buy as well as the fear to lose the opportunity.

The Push-Pull technique can also be carried out using body language without uttering a single word. Make it dramatic and keep the other person confused about your behaviour.

When you use the Push-Pull technique, you need to be careful about how the other person is responding to it. Here are some points you need to remember:

- You have to be cautious that you don't over-push the other person away.

- Don't over-dramatize the situation.

- When you apply this technique, it should look natural and not deliberate and manipulative.

- When you tease during the Push process, be careful of not hurting others.

- Don't try too hard to impress the other person during the Pull process.

In business, you can use the Push-Pull technique when you find that:

1) The customer considers himself a High-Value person and you a Low-Value person.

This is one of the most common problems salespeople face while dealing with customers. Here are some reasons why it happens:

- You look too much needy and desperate to get the deal.

- You're forcefully trying to tell your story.

- Your communication and presentation skills are extremely weak.

- Your body language is poor.

- You've low self-esteem.

- You give too much importance to the customer.

- You're intentionally trying to impress the customer.

- Whenever you make a joke, you're looking at others for their approval.

Activities like these will confirm your customer that you're a Low-Value person and therefore **widen the Value Gap** between you and him.

In such situations, you need to think creatively, how to use the Push-Pull technique to increase your value in the customer's eyes.

2) The customer is still unsure about you

Suppose you're talking to a customer, and you notice that he is still unsure, confused, and trying to distance himself from you for whatever reason.

In this case, instead of showing your desperation, you should apply the Push-Pull technique.

For example, when you find that he is looking confused, stop your presentation... stop convincing him... and start asking some hard-hitting questions to check whether he really needs your product or not. Like:

· "I'm sensing that there is an issue somewhere. Where did I go off track?"

· "There seems to be some confusion in your mind that's causing you to hesitate to move further. Do you mind if I ask what it is?"

· "Has anything changed since our last meeting?"

· "Is this product/service what you are exactly looking for?"

· "How far apart still are we?"

· "Did I do something wrong in the last meeting that I'm not aware of?"

·	"What do we have to do to make a deal today?"

·	"What do you think we should do next?"

·	"Have you convinced yourself, or should I tell you more?"

·	"How will the final decision be made after the committee meets tomorrow?"

·	"Why don't I do an online presentation for your top management if they still have queries?"

·	"Did you get a chance to talk to your boss about what we discussed last time?"

·	"Have I covered everything? If yes, then let me know how soon would you need this?"

·	"Let me know who is going to finalize this deal? You or your boss?"

·	"I find you a bit distracted today. Let me know, will you be available tomorrow to discuss this or shall I continue?"

·	"Just between you and me, what do you think is going to happen after this presentation?"

·	"Is the price of this product out of your financial range?"

·	"I feel as if I'm missing something in this meeting. What do you think I'm missing here?"

·   "Given all the details of this investment, would you be in a position to make a quick decision?"

·   "Are we thinking along the same lines in terms of features and price?"

·   "What do you think will it work for you?"

·   "I get the feeling that you are not too happy with what I've proposed here. Am I right?"

·   "Does this make sense to you so far?"

·   "What do you think your boss will think about what we've put together?"

·   "Do you need this right away?"

·   "Did I do something wrong in the presentation?"

·   "Does our idea appeal to you?"

3) The customer is taking you for granted

This generally happens when you're already in some relationship with the other person.

For example:

- Employer-Employee relationship

- Pre-Sales and Post-Sales relationship

- Business partnership

- Shareholders, stakeholders, investors relationship

One of the reasons why some business partnerships and marriages are not successful is one partner starts taking the other for granted, which hurts the other person's feelings, self-respect, and expectations.

Similarly, in business development, if your prospects and customers take you too much for granted, it could hurt your relationship and potential sales.

Here's one scenario:

Suppose you're fulfilling every demand of your prospect.

Whenever he asks for you and your team, you immediately come to his place, leaving all your other work.

Even you and your prospect have become good friends.

However, in spite of all these efforts, your prospect has still not given you any business.

The reason is he has started taking you for granted.

Such professional friendship is one-sided. If your prospect really considers you a good friend and keeps taking your advice and help... then he must have given you a nice chunk of business. Otherwise, he is just taking advantage of you.

It's a Lose/Win situation.

Let's consider the opposite scenario...

Suppose your prospect gives you order considering you as a good friend, but after getting the deal, you stop talking to him, thinking he might be no more useful to you. In this case, you've taken advantage of your friendship with him.

It's a Win/Lose situation.

Such kind of experiences results in bitterness.

To create a Win/Win situation, both you and your prospect should continuously gain from the relationship.

Coming back to the point of what to do when your prospect is taking you for granted?

In this case, you should apply the Push-Pull technique to increase your value in your prospect's mind.

How?

Here's one tactic called **1-2 step**...

Next time whenever you go for lunch with your prospect, take one of your existing satisfied customers along with you.

Now you've to apply a 1-2 step technique while having lunch with them.

In this technique, whatever attention you're giving to your prospect, you need to give double of it to your existing customer. And it's not just limited to talking... It includes looking, listening, even laughing at jokes.

In this way, you're indirectly sending a message to your prospect that you consider your existing customer a Higher-Value person as compared to him.

Now it's a human nature that we can't tolerate our close friend, associate, partner, lover, or even spouse finds someone else more desirable... more interesting... more respectable than us.

So, in order to win your attention, he will try to prove to you that he is also a High-Value person. And one of the easiest ways to do this is by giving you some favour, which you consider highly valuable, for example, business.

Some people may not feel comfortable using the Push-Pull technique because they are worried they may lose customers while pushing them away. They don't want customers to think that they are uninterested or unavailable. They are afraid that if they act distant, their customers may forget about them.

The question I want to ask these people how they feel when their customers don't pay respect to them despite their years of experience?

How do these businesspeople feel when their customers give business to their competitors despite their good behaviour and customer service?

What's the use of being a nice person if your customers take you for granted? What's the use of fulfilling all their demands if they don't appreciate you for bringing happiness and comfort in their life?

The point is how your customers are going to realize how much they need you if you don't give them the chance to need you desperately?

Sometimes, people need a rude awakening to understand the importance of others. It is your job to realize your customers how big a loss they have to face if they lose you.

Your customer will want you back if you use this technique properly. It's better to start using this technique slowly until you master it.

While using this tactic, you need to be careful about two things...

First, this should look unintentional from your side.

Second, your prospect should not get hurt because of your behaviour. Otherwise, this technique could be backfired if not performed properly. Instead of rewarding you, the prospect may punish you without dirtying his hands.

Now I'm sharing a Scarcity technique that is used when we approach customers for the first time. It is used to disarm strangers in rejecting us.

When we approach strangers, their defences are naturally up. The reason could be anything. They may find us unpleasant, uninteresting, irritating, too much pushy...

So, their automatic reaction is rejection. For example:

"I'm busy right now."

"Not interested."

"Let me think about it."

"Please don't call again."

Slowly, salespeople start facing the fear of rejection while approaching new prospects.

It is called **Approach Anxiety**.

Many salespeople leave their profession just because of this fear. And just because of this fear, many people don't want to join the sales profession or start a new business and even ready to live a mediocre life.

The below Scarcity technique can be quite handy while dealing with new prospects.

False Time Constraint

A False Time Constraint technique is used to convey to others that you're a High-Value person who has huge respect for his time.

Since you've limited time so you're reassuring your prospective customers that you'll not take too much of their time.

It allows them to relax because even if it turns out that they don't like you, they know you'll be gone soon.

By using the False Time Constraint technique, you want to show your customers that...

- You're coming from a place of abundance.

- You're coming from a high-value place.

- You're an authority of some kind.

- You're a social or busy person.

- Your time is scarce.

- You can't waste your time on unnecessary things. If you find something interesting in what people say, you continue the conversation. Else, you simply eject.

- You are always in a hurry.

In sales, when you are approaching customers, their natural inclination is to guard their time. They don't want to be solicited.

When you approach your customers, they start wondering...

- "How long is this person going to stay here wasting my time?"

- "How long is this meeting going to last?"

- "How can I get rid of him?"

It's because, in their mind, they consider themselves of High-Value and you as Low-Value. (Remember, I told you in one of the earlier volumes that Sales is generally not considered high profile profession. I also told you reasons.)

And it's quite obvious that since now we are living in a hyper-competitive environment, where the customer has many choices and is regarded as a king; the need for survival is becoming a big concern in salespeople... to the point that, because of many desperate salespeople, the Value Gap between customers and salespeople keeps increasing day by day...

The situation has become so bad that even highly qualified self-employed professionals like doctors, lawyers, chartered accountants, engineers, stock analysts are using desperate tactics to get new clients.

If they are so desperate to get business, imagine what the situation is for average salespeople working in small private companies.

No, it's not at all wrong in being competitive to bring new business for survival. After all, everyone wants to make money to live a better life.

The problem is in their approach to get business. The problem is in their cheap tactics. The problem is in their clearly visible desperation to get new clients. Ultimately, all these things are increasing the Value Gap between them and their customers.

That's why one of your primary jobs as a Master Persuader is to reduce the Value Gap between you and the other person.

The second reason is if you are a stranger to your customers, they start feeling uncomfortable because they don't know about your intentions.

In such situations, customers automatically reject you when you approach them. That's why it's very common to find salespeople having "approach anxiety" in meeting new customers.

So, apart from reducing the Value Gap, we also need to make them comfortable.

When you use the False Time Constraint technique...

It makes you look like you are an important person whose time is scarce and valuable.

It lowers the defences of the other High-Value person.

It makes them feel assured that nothing weird is going to happen.

It confirms that you're not going to cause any inconvenience to them.

False Time Constraints can be very useful when you're introducing yourself... when you're meeting your prospects for the first time in their office or a public place like exhibition, seminar, airport, club, etc.

Here are some examples of how to use this technique:

- "Hello Mr. Prospect, I just saw your stall in the hall no. 5. From there, I got your reference. I think my products could be quite useful for your company so wanted to discuss the same. But right now, I can only stay for a minute as nobody is there in my stall. So, let's have a quick chat now, and then we can discuss in detail at your office sometime later."

- "I have to leave after this session. My friends are waiting for me. Call me and give your feedback if you want to continue these sessions."

- "I can't stay for more than an hour as I have one more appointment this afternoon."

- "I have to meet my friends in a few minutes, and I've got to go, but let me ask you one thing real quick..."

·   "I have to leave for my office immediately, but before I leave, let me check the status of the Purchase Order with you..."

·   "Oh... it's already late. I should leave now. But let me share one more important feature which is in huge demand these days..."

·   "I have to get back to the meeting... it's going to start in 15 minutes. I just want to know your opinion on our new product..."

·   You can also use this technique on groups of people. For example, you can arrange a small party where you invite some existing as well as prospective customers. And you can tell them, "There's a bunch of interesting people to meet here, including our satisfied customers. If time permits, I want to talk to everyone at least for two minutes and see how I can help them."

Here's one scenario where a prospect uses False Time Constraint to show his high-value to a salesperson:

Salesperson: "Hello, Mr. Prospect, are you free right now? I want to show you something."

Prospect: "Show me fast. I'm leaving in 10 minutes for urgent work."

Salesperson: "Yeah, I've also to leave in 5 minutes as my boss is coming from head office for an urgent meeting. But while I was passing through your office, I thought to show you the data that you were asking in the last meeting. Let's see over here for a minute..."

So, in this case, to counter the prospect's False Time Constraint, the salesperson also used the same technique, in fact, two times.

"Just a Second" Approach

Sometimes, when you approach a customer in some public place, he holds his hand up to reject you immediately, before you utter a single word.

At that time, you can use the **"Just a Second" approach** to reduce the chances of automatic rejection.

Generally, we use "just a second" phrase when somebody is occupied in a crowded place, and we want to tell them that he forgot his credit card on the table or she left her purse in the shop, or we want his signature on some document.

Whenever we encounter such a situation, this phrase is registered in our mind as something important or urgent. And because of these multiple registered experiences in our mind, the "Just a Second approach" is now programmed to trigger an autopilot reaction to pay immediate attention to the person who is using this phrase.

"Just a Second" approach is again a form of False Time Constraint technique. Say something to capture the target person's attention like:

- "Just a second…"

- "This will take just a second…"

- "I need to steal you for just a second…"

- "Before I meet my boss, I want to talk to you for a second…"

- "Hold up a second; I just had a question."

- "Hey! Wait for a second! I just wanted to tell you something important. I saw you standing over here, and…"

- "Before I send my final proposal, I want to talk to you for a second…"

- "Let me sneak in here for a moment please…"

Using such phrases will get an autopilot reaction from the customer that it's something important to tell. So don't runoff.

Moreover, during the conversation, most people don't even remember that you started your conversation with just a second approach, but it lasted for a few minutes until your purpose of the conversation is achieved.

Body Rocking

Body Rocking is a non-verbal form of False Time Constraint technique where you're expressing through your body language to High-Value customers that you're not needy and may leave them at any time. This creates a feeling of loss in your customers, and they want you to stay there.

This happens when the High-Value person stops showing interest in you or still having some resistance towards you, especially if you're a salesperson.

Here's how to use the Body Rocking technique:

- You slightly turn away or move back one step but then come back again and continue your discussion.

- Waving your hands to someone else and then continue the discussion.

- Taking a one-minute break to answer an important call and then continue your presentation.

- While talking to a person during a morning walk, instead of stopping, keep on walking.

However, too much physical movement without any reason shows your nervousness, lack of confidence, and poor body language (Low-Value).

Your objective is to move in a manner that will perceive you as a person with high social status (High-Value).

Please note that you are using False Time Constraint and Body Rocking techniques against High-Value people who are showing some kind of resistance. If you apply these techniques against a Low-Value person, it could backfire the whole process.

Since a Low-Value person has low self-esteem, he might think you are trying to prove him inferior. This will increase Value Gap, ultimately leading to dislike and even hate towards you. (Remember, I talked about the Grounding technique in the last volume)

Now I'll move to the next principle of Persuasion:

Law of Contrast

When we talk about Influence and Persuasion, we need to remember that in the world of Persuasion, everything is a perception of the mind.

It means whatever value we are assigning to some product or service is based on how we perceive that thing in our mind.

If we find something important, urgent, or useful than other items in the same category, we assign it a higher value.

On the contrary, if we do not detect any change after using a product, then we consider it similar to others.

In short, Contrast is the root of all perception. Contrast is the difference between two things when placed in time or across space.

One of the easiest ways to understand how Contrast works is by watching a Bollywood movie song where the hero is dancing along with 20+ background dancers. If they all wear the same colour dress, then it's become difficult for the audience to find where the hero is. That's why the colour of his dress is kept different from others to make a sharp contrast. This is an example of visual contrast.

Similarly, on the front cover of the magazine, you'll see that the colour of the dress of a model and product is in sharp contrast with the surroundings so that the reader's eyes go straight to the product.

Recently I watched the movie *Parasite*, where the director has beautifully used the contrast principle to show the lifestyle of a rich vs. poor family.

Higher the contrast between two items, the easier for us to separate them in our minds. On the contrary, if the contrast is very low, between two or more items, it's become difficult for us to identify which is better or mediocre... which is beneficial or dangerous... which is economical or expensive in the long run.

If the contrast is very low, it makes us confused and even paralyzed to make a decision.

For example, when the frog is dropped in hot water, it will immediately leap out.

But when the same frog is placed in a pan of warm water, then it eventually gets boiled alive if the temperature of the pan is increased gradually. Simply because frog cannot contrast temperature increments.

And it's not just animals; even humans' minds can be easily deceived using contrast.

For example, when you put your right hand in hot water and left hand in cold water for at least 30 seconds and then put both hands in normal water, to hot hand, it feels cold, and to the cold hand, it feels hot.

Likewise, when you pick up a heavy box and then a lighter one, you will feel the second box much lighter than it actually is.

Another example is how we feel when we experience the same thing but in different scenarios.

Suppose you lose a major deal, and while coming out of a prospective client's office, you see a big dent in your car. The way you behave would be totally different from how you behave if you get the deal before you saw that dent.

Although the dent is the same in both cases, your reaction would be different depending on how emotional your experience is immediately prior to that incident.

The point is we tend to evaluate things by comparison to accessible referencing rather than in absolute terms.

Every day we apply the principle of contrast in all senses to make judgements.

For example:

We use contrast in the visual sense, like comparing bright and dark colours.

We use contrast in the auditory sense, like comparing loud and quiet sounds.

We use contrast in the kinesthetic sense, like comparing hot and cold temperatures.

We use contrast in the gustatory sense, like comparing bitter and sweet tastes.

We use contrast in the olfactory sense, like comparing stinking smell and strong perfume.

The Principle of Contrast is based on human behaviour fact that how our minds get affected and make decisions when we are shown two different alternatives of the same product or an idea in succession or simultaneously or close together.

In business Principle of Contrast helps in finding a better deal between two or more options when we use our emotional and logical reasoning.

When we see an advertisement or walk into a store, we compare items in our minds to check how product X is better than product Y.

That's why smart marketers use the Principle of Contrast to influence customers' perceptions of their products.

Here are some techniques based on the Principle of Contrast:

Before and After

This is one of the most common ways to demonstrate the benefits after using the product.

If you run advertisements, you can clearly show the sharp contrast by a LIVE demonstration, which is extremely believable.

You can show how painful and difficult it was to carry out the work before buying your product. And now, after buying your product, the same work has become pleasant and hassle-free.

You can also show the data in the form of test reports, results, statistics, report cards, graphs, charts, photos, etc. to convince your market how effective your product is.

You can also take testimonials of your satisfied customers in the 'Before and After' format.

Here are some industries which extensively use 'Before and After' technique in their marketing:

- Fitness and Weight Loss
- Software
- Manufacturing
- Training and Development
- Home Care products
- Beauty and Health Care

Direct Comparison with Competitors' Products

Another way to use the Principle of Contrast is directly comparing your product with your competitors' products. It can be done in various ways, like:

- Simultaneous demonstration of yours and competitors' products

- Comparing statistics

- Check-listing of features and benefits on a website, newspaper, brochure

- Bad-Good-Bad-Good-Bad-Good... format

- Providing Samples

- Using Decoy

- Using a website that gives side-by-side comparisons of different products along with their website links

- Showing complaints of competitor's product along with your customers' testimonials

- Test drive

Here's an old American advertisement that talks about how a customer can run his car without spark plugs and can get more gas mileage and more power if he puts "fire injectors" in his car instead of the old-fashioned plugs.

The advertiser uses the technique of 'Direct Contrast with Competitor's Product' to convince the reader.

Notice the structure of the ad. It's Bad-Good-Bad-Good-Bad-Good....

MECHANICS AND ENGINEERS READ THIS CAREFULLY

And for you mechanics and engineers let me tell you why fire injection must give you these results.

A spark plug jumps a spark of electricity across an air gap. This is the most wasteful and power consuming way to get electricity from one place to another and it limits the size of the spark.

A fire injector fires on the surface of an electrical conductor. This is the most efficient way to get a big powerful spark into your cylinder.

On ordinary spark plugs the air gap between the electrode and the firing point is always getting bigger because the electrode is always burning away. This means you have misfiring which means loss of power plus wasted gas plus raw gas to damage the cylinders and piston rings.

On fire injectors there is no air gap and no electrode to burn away. That means maximum gas explosion which means full power, full economy and no raw gas to wash away the oil protection from cylinder walls and pistons.

A spark plug accumulates filth and carbon because of inefficient firing. This means you need regular cleaning, setting and expensive replacement!

A fire injector never needs cleaning or setting. It actually "breaks in" and becomes more efficient with use. It will actually outlast your car, delivering maximum efficiency without servicing or replacement.

A spark plug gives you a thin skimpy spark that actually blows out under pressure of less than 120 pounds.

A fire injector gives you a heavy powerful flame that will not blow out at pressures far heavier than those created by even the highest compression engine.

With ordinary spark plugs you are using, or should be using premium gas which costs from 4 to 8 cents more than ordinary gas, and despite this you're getting inefficient, wasteful gas consumption.

With fire injectors regular gas will give you up to 8 more gas miles per gallon, up to 31 more horsepower, plus easier starting in all weather. Add these savings together and see for yourself why I say that fire injectors will pay for themselves every single month that you drive your car.

Ordinary spark plugs have to be replaced regularly. In some of the new high-compression cars, a set of plugs will burn up in a couple of months.

A fire injector installation is guaranteed for the life of your car without cleaning, servicing, or replacing.

These are some of the reasons that the U.S. Air Force pays premium prices for surface supported injectors for their aircraft and why you will ultimately find fire injectors in all automobiles.

VOLUME - VIII

In the last volume, I talked about the Principle of Contrast and some of its techniques.

Contrast is one of my favourite Persuasion principles because it is super-effective in beating competition if one knows how to use it properly in communication.

The Contrast makes your customers perceive that you are better than your competitor.

In the world of business, everything is the perception of the mind.

No matter how good you are in your craft, it has no value if your customer doesn't think so.

No matter how innovative your ideas are, it has no value if your customer doesn't think so.

No matter how revolutionary your products are, it has no value if your customer doesn't think so.

No matter how knowledgeable you are in your field, it has no value if your customer doesn't think so.

No matter how user-friendly your services are, it has no value if your customer doesn't think so.

The point is: If you want to survive and thrive in a hyper-competitive market, then you need to make your customers perceive that you are better than others.

Here are some more techniques based on the Contrast principle:

Markdown Price

This is a common technique used by marketers to highlight the new discounted price.

First, you show the original price and then strikethrough it and put the new discounted price.

Like this:

$~~100~~ 75

If you show only the discounted price, people will not recognize the value of discount because they are not able to compare the original and discounted prices in their minds.

But when you put together both the old and new prices, people can see the difference in front of them, which increases the chances of buying your product.

Limited Choice Close

Humans are naturally indecisive in nature.

When you present too many varieties of your product the customer's mind is paralyzed in deciding what to buy.

That's why give only 2 to 5 choices if possible.

By giving your customers a few limited choices, you relieve them from the anxiety of decision making.

Choices can be in the form of size, colour, taste, duration, price, quality, etc.

You might be wondering if choices create anxiety in customers, then what's the need of giving choices? Why not just focus on selling one product?

The reason is: **If you give no choice, it creates psychological reactance in customers.**

What is Psychological Reactance?

It's an unpleasant feeling, resistance, protest against people, offers, rules, and regulations that are threatening to one's freedom.

It's a feeling generated in people when someone is taking away their freedom, or limiting their range of choices, or forcing them to do only what they say.

For example: If a salesperson desperately keeps insisting you buy his product today, then what will you do?

Even if you were interested in the salesperson's product... even if you found his product best and cheapest... then also you will decline his offer. In fact, you may do the opposite of what he says.

Simply because nobody can force you when and what you should buy or not. Nobody has the right to take away your freedom of choice.

Psychological Reactance plays a very important role in our personal and professional life.

Master Persuaders love to play with Psychological Reactance. I'll cover this topic in-depth later.

Now coming back to the Limited Choice Close, if you don't give any choice to the customer, they will show resistance.

It's human nature to compare a product with another. It gives them the satisfaction that they have taken the right decision.

But if you give too many choices, the customer will get confused about what to buy or not.

That's why keep the focus on offering limited choices if you want to sell more.

Consultant Close

Suppose you want to buy a new LED TV. You go to a nearby electronics retail store to casually see what's available in the market.

When you enter the store, a salesperson approaches you to know what you're looking for.

But you politely send him back saying, "We'll see ourselves. No need for your assistance." You're uncomfortable that the salesperson will keep trying to sell you even if you're not prepared to buy it today.

You move towards the section where all LED TVs are displayed. For 15-20 minutes, you keep standing there looking at TVs.

While going through these LED TVs, you find that although they are of different brands, they are quite similar to each other in appearance, price, features, and warranty period.

Also, you find that in the same price range, the top branded models have slightly fewer features than less popular brands.

So, you are confused about what is right for you.

If you buy a top brand, you will miss one or two important features.

And if you buy an unpopular brand, then you may always doubt its quality. Also, you have to keep justifying your family and friends why you chose a less popular brand.

The reason for your confusion is that you have been presented with so many TVs but with very low contrast because of which you're not able to decide which TV is right for you.

It's human nature that you hate putting too much stress in your mind, especially in the cases of making buying decisions. To remove this stress, you keep looking for shortcuts.

The busier you are, the more you search for shortcuts, particularly in making those decisions that have low significance in your life.

When you face this situation in purchasing online, one of the most frequent shortcuts you choose is to buy the best-selling product or the product with maximum top reviews.

But when you face the same situation in a retail store, the shortcut you choose is to ask the salesperson to guide you what is right for you.

Now the same salesperson whom you've ignored earlier is no more a salesperson for you. He has now taken the role of a consultant whose job is to understand your requirements and then suggest the best options.

Contrast Stories & Case Studies

You can use the principle of contrast in case studies, stories, examples to tell the difference what happens to people who use your products & services against those who don't use them.

Here is an example of a famous Wall Street Journal sales letter, considered as the most successful letter of all time.

Written by freelance copywriter Martin Conroy the letter was first sent out in 1974 and mailed continuously for over 25 years.

This letter is known as the "Billion Dollar Letter" because it brought over a billion dollars in selling newspaper subscriptions.

This letter is also famous by the name "Two Young Men..." because of the **contrast story** between two young men who graduated together, but 25 years, later they are positioned at a very different place.

Here is the opening of this sales letter:

....

Dear Reader,

On a beautiful late spring afternoon, twenty-five years ago, two young men graduated from the same college. They are very much alike, these two young men. Both had been better than average students, both were personable and both – as young college graduates are – were filled with ambitious dreams for the future.

Recently, these men returned to their college for their 25th reunion.

They were still very much alike. Both were happily married. Both had three children. And both, it turned out, had gone to work for the same Midwestern manufacturing company after graduation, and were still there.

But there was a difference. One of the men was manager of a small department of that company. The other was its president.

What Made The Difference

Have you ever wondered, as I have, what makes this kind of difference in people's lives?

It isn't a native intelligence or talent or dedication. It isn't that one person wants success and the other doesn't.

The difference lies in what each person knows and how he or she makes use of that knowledge.

And that is why I am writing to you and to people like you about The Wall Street Journal.

For that is the whole purpose of The Journal: To give its readers knowledge – knowledge that they can use in business.

....

So, you can see that this letter starts with a short story of contrast between two young men.

Although it's a short story, it has a strong connection with what we all face in our lives.

Right from our childhood, we are directly or indirectly competing with our siblings, cousins, classmates, friends, and neighbours. We don't show on the face, but somewhere inside, we hate to lose to them.

By making comparisons with these people, we decide how successful we are.

Competition with near and dear ones is a very strong emotion that marketers can use in their promotions, stories, case studies.

Here are some ideas that you can use in contrast stories and case-studies:

- Successful vs. Unsuccessful (used in the Two Young Men sales letter)

- Rich vs. Poor

- Powerful vs. Weak

- Modern vs. Traditional

- Good vs. Evil

- Employer vs. Employee

- Small vs. Big

- Spiritualistic vs. Materialistic (For example, a famous book title: *The Monk Who Sold His Ferrari*)

- New vs. Old

- Beautiful vs. Ugly

- Saving vs. Investing

- Smart vs. Dumb

- Good vs. Great (For example, a famous book title: *Good to Great*)

- Skilled vs. Unskilled

- Healthy vs. Sick

- Digital vs. Physical (gained huge popularity during Coronavirus Pandemic)

- Dreamer vs. Practical

- Boss vs. Subordinate

- Forgiveness vs. Punishment

- Social vs. Lonely

- Winner vs. Loser

- Luxury vs. Ordinary

- Fast vs. Slow

Here are two emails that I wrote using the Contrast principle:

1)   Good vs. Great

....
....

Subject: **Good is the enemy of Great**

Do you feel satisfied when someone says you did a good job?

If yes, then you need to go through the story of the rabbit and turtle that you read during your childhood.

In that story, the rabbit went to sleep in the mid of the race as he was overconfident that the turtle was far behind him. He kept on sleeping while turtle won the race.

The same thing happens with people who think they are doing a good job.

They are satisfied with their work because they find themselves better than their peers, neighbours, and competitors in their local area or community.

But actually, they have fallen into "Good Trap."

They don't realise they are living in a kind of aquarium, where they might be considered as a decent performer, or even a hero, or a celebrity.

But when these same good performers compete with people of other cities, states, or countries, they lose.

Why?

It's because they were satisfied with their good performance in their small world and never thought about exploring and challenging other strong players of their game.

Next time whenever you feel satisfied with your good performance, ask this question to yourself:

"Compared to what?"

Remember, "Good is the enemy of Great."

If you feel satisfied with your good performance, you will never push yourself for bigger goals... bigger challenges... bigger rewards...

Moving from Good to Great requires a lot of hard work and sacrifices. That's why very few people get the title of Great.

There have been many good leaders, but very few great like Lincoln and Gandhi.

There have been many good inventors, but very few great like Edison and Tesla.

There have been many good manufacturers, but very few great like Ford and Honda.

There have been many good sportspeople, but very few great like Pele and Bradman.

There have been many good marketers, but very few great like Hopkins and Ogilvy.

There have been many good entrepreneurs, but very few great like Gates and Jobs.

There have been many good actors, but very few great like Pacino and De Niro.

Some of these great guys had very little formal education. But it didn't stop them from learning and growing. Their SELF-EDUCATION kept them moving forward while dealing with obstacles.

Moving from Good to Great is difficult but not impossible.

What is required the most is just your devotion.

....

2)   Smart vs. Dumb

Subject: **"The customer is not a moron. She's your wife."**

"The customer is not a moron. She's your wife" is a famous quotation attributed to legendary ad executive, David Ogilvy.

Sadly many marketers don't take his advice seriously.

They keep making big claims in their advertisements.

They are more interested in people liking their ads instead of ACTING on their ads.

They keep coming with new products without studying their market.

They keep coming with huge discount offers without making profits.

They keep expanding their team with executives who have never sold a product in this ruthless world.

They don't listen to their customers' feedback.

And the worst part is they overestimate their own intelligence and underestimate their market's intelligence.

They forget the lifecycle of a product starts with a hungry market and ends with a saturated market.

However, there are some intelligent marketers who keep studying their market day and night and keep updating their products, services, and communications accordingly to get customer's attention.

Do you want to know what they study about their market?

....

Contrast Headlines

Using the principle of Contrast in headlines is a very effective strategy in taking the attention of busy people because it creates conflict in the mind of people.

It happens because we are a slave to our daily habits and scheduled activities. We act like robots doing the same thing every day and all day. Most of our tasks are generally planned without doing anything completely different.

Moreover, our mind is always engaged in multiple thoughts.

That's why our attention goes to things which are unusual, unexpected, out of the league, and contrary to the general pattern.

Here are some famous book titles and advertising headlines which have successfully incorporated the Contrast principle:

- Rich Dad Poor Dad

- The deaf now hear whispers

- The lazy man's way to riches

- At 60 miles an hour the loudest noise in the new Rolls-Royce comes from the electric clock

- Good to Great

- When doctors feel "rotten" this is what they do

- Often a bridesmaid never a bride

- How I made a fortune with a "fool idea"

- Pride and Prejudice

- Why models stay young till sixty

- How I raised myself from a failure at 29 to become a $250 per day success

- Think small

- Angels & Demons

- For the woman who is older than she looks

- Beat the races by picking losers

- This pen "burps" before it drinks - but never afterwards

- The God of small things

- First he whispers, then he shouts...

- How a bald-headed barber helped save my hair

- The university of the night

- The monk who sold his Ferrari

- Why you should open the window before you close the door of a Volkswagen

- At 4 1/2 she's reading 3rd-grade books

- Starting next Tuesday, the Atlantic Ocean becomes only one-fifth as long

- War and Peace

- Feeds waste gas fumes back into your engine

- To men and women who want to work less and earn more

- Get rich slowly

- How a fool stunt made me a star salesman

- Life after Life

- How to retire at 40 instead of 60

- How to have a cool, quiet bedroom – even on hot nights

- Who else wants a whiter wash – with no hard work

- Thinking, fast and slow

The Contrast Close

The Contrast technique is very useful when you want your prospect to compare your product and service with others. It can be price, quality, offer validity, guarantee, warranty, etc.

Examples:

- If your prospect says, "Your price is quite high." You should immediately ask, "Compared to what?"

- If your prospect says, "You've only two years warranty." You should immediately ask, "Compared to what?"

- If your prospect says, "Sometimes, we want different features in your product." You immediately ask, "How does your current vendor handle that?"

- If your prospect says, "Let me check with the purchasing department if we can buy today or at least within this week." You immediately reply, "I am so glad you are purchasing now because the price will go up in 30 days."

- When you say to a prospect, "This is very competitively priced", she might not take your words seriously. But when you present a price comparison from a magazine, website, or a price list from your major competitor, there is a higher chance she will believe you.

- "Our products belong to the highest price category in this market. Still, we are selling more than ever before. Would you like to know why so many people from all over the country are buying our products even though we charge more?"

- "There are many customers like you who have thoroughly examined our product, compared it with our competitors, and decided to pay more for it, even when they could get something cheap somewhere else. Would you like to know why these customers chose us against our competitors?"

Anchor

Suppose you are coming with a new product in the FMCG market. Since it's completely different from what already available in the market, so you are having an advantage of no competition.

But there is one problem also. You have no reference to consider what should be the price of 500ml of your product.

After long discussions with your product development, sales & marketing teams, finally, you decided on the price of your product. And within a short period, the product is a huge success in the market.

However, as expected, your new product started facing competition not just in similar kinds of brand name, ingredients, packaging, and quality but also in price.

Okay, we know that many competitors shamelessly copy the products which are successful in the market.

But the question is: why your competitors chose the same price? They could have gone for a much higher or lower price if they want.

It's because the price of the original product has set an anchor not only in the mind of your competitors but also in your customers.

Even if your competitors come with a better version, then also they will face difficulty selling at a higher price. The reason is it's very difficult to replace the set anchor with a new anchor.

This happens not only in the FMCG industry. The same pattern you'll find in other industries too. Like Software, Real Estate, Automobile, Electronics, etc.

So, what is an Anchor exactly?

An Anchor is the initial piece of information based on which all negotiations, arguments, estimates, decisions are made.

Setting up an Anchor in a customer's mind creates a frame of reference for valuing your product.

For example, in the case of Markdown price, where you cut the original price and show the new discounted price like this ~~$999~~ $499, $999 is the price anchor for the final $499 sales price.

By setting up the anchor of $999, you instantly raise the value of your product in the mind of the customer. And then, quoting the discounted price of $499 immediately after the anchor price, you raise the value of the discount in the mind of your customer.

An Anchor can be a piece of information.

An Anchor can be a number, a unit of measurement.

An Anchor can be a price.

An Anchor can be a standard of quality.

An Anchor can be a standard of reputation.

The Anchor holds a great deal of influence over future evaluations. It becomes standard for the rest of the negotiations.

The Anchor can influence the estimated value of an object.

The entire process of setting an Anchor and making subsequent biased judgements is known as **Anchoring Effect**.

Here's how it works...

As we rely too heavily on the first piece of information, and similarly, give too much weight on the first number put forth in a discussion for further adjustments, so **start with a reference point and then keep making incremental or decremental adjustments to it.**

Before we set an Anchor, we need to do our homework properly. We should have studied our market and competition and be aware of our strengths and weaknesses.

If we have done our preparation well, we can make an aggressive first offer expecting that our offer will anchor the entire discussion to our advantage.

Here are some scenarios of how people play with an Anchor smartly:

- Manufacturers, product developers, marketers keep increasing the price of their bestselling products at regular intervals if their competition is extremely weak. This helps them make more money, which they invest in R&D.

- During negotiations, once one of the parties states their first price offer, the anchor is set. And once the anchor is set, it becomes the starting point for all subsequent negotiations. This deliberate starting point can strongly affect the range of possible counteroffers.

The counterbid to the first quoted price is the second anchor. It is also called the **counter anchor**. If the first party has set an anchor of a very high price, by using a counter anchor of the low price, the other party can try to defuse the primary anchor.

If the other party wants to defuse the primary anchor, they have to make it clear to the first party that the quoted price is simply not acceptable. They are miles apart on price.

Finally, this whole process of offer and counteroffers results in a mutually beneficial agreement.

The advantage of using a high price anchor is that whatever lower price is quoted in later discussions, it sounds reasonable even if that lower price is still higher than market value.

- If you're going to deliver a speech in a conference or debate, try to take the first slot.

After you deliver a solid presentation, it sets an anchor in the mind of the audience.

The audience will expect a similar presentation from your competitors and colleagues, if not better, at least equal to yours.

- Suppose you're desperately looking for a new job. Based on industry standards and your past experience, you're expecting a salary of $100,000.

But before you tell your expectations, the interviewer offers you a salary of $65,000.

Now in order to get some sort of agreement, you make a counteroffer of $75,000, which is far less than what you think you're worth.

- Suppose you're living in a 10-storey building where one of your neighbours recently sold her flat at a much lower price than prevailing market rates.

Once this news is spread, it sets an anchor for negotiations in the minds of other people who are interested in buying a flat in your building.

The problem could become more serious for residents if a few more flats are also sold at a lower price in yours and adjacent buildings in a relatively short period. It could influence people that there is some problem in the entire locality, thereby lowering the market value for a long time.

The point is high anchor price draws our attention to positive qualities, whereas low anchor price draws our attention to flaws, especially in cases of uncertainty. As I told you earlier, when we are busy and uncertain, we look for shortcuts.

- The initial price in your quotation should be precise and specific instead of making it general.

It reduces the chances of large adjustment while making counteroffers.

The more specific the initial price, the better chance to close the deal at a lower adjustment to the initial price after negotiations.

For example, if you quote $100,000, you may get a counteroffer of $95,000 ($5,000 adjustment to the initial price). But if you quote $99,750, you may get a counteroffer of $98,250 ($1,500 adjustment to the initial price).

Primacy and Recency Effect

Suppose you want to shift to a new house on rent. The real estate agent takes you on a tour to show you five houses according to your requirements.

Out of these five houses, four are quite similar in structure and slightly above average. But the fifth house is out of the league. It is the nicest and the most expensive location out of the five.

Since it's the last stop, your family decides to spend more time checking each room of the house even though the rent of this house is above your budget.

After spending almost a half-day with that real estate agent, when you reach back home, you can't stop thinking about the fifth house, consider it the best option because of contrast with other houses, and make your mind to take it.

The question is why the real estate agent didn't show the nicest house before other properties? He could have started your property tour by showing this house to set an anchor in your mind.

First, he knew by experience that people like to see a few more options before making a final decision. It rarely happens that people close the deal the moment they see the first item.

Second, being a salesperson, he wanted to spend more time with you to build rapport. So, he planned to show you the best house later.

Now the question is: why didn't he show the nicest house in the 3rd or 4th position?

It's because of the Recency Effect.

According to the Recency Effect, the most recently presented item is most likely to be remembered best.

It means:

People remember the LAST thing much longer than what they have seen earlier.

People remember the last advertisement much longer than other ads.

People remember the climax of movies and novels much longer than the mid-part.

People tend to buy a similar item again what they have recently bought. That's why E-commerce companies keep suggesting items that are similar to your last purchase.

The opposite of the Recency Effect is the Primacy Effect, according to which people remember the FIRST thing much longer than what they have seen later.

Both Primacy and Recency Effects are the parts of the **Serial-Position Effect,** which predicts how items from a list are remembered based on their **position** in that list.

Humans tend to recall the first and last items in a series best and middle items worst.

Now the question is: If people can also remember the first items, then why that real estate agent didn't show the nicest house first in case he ignored the first two reasons?

The answer lies in the length of the list of events and time taken from the first to the final event.

If the number of events between first and last is high and there are some interruptions between the sequences of events, then people generally remember the last event. This means the Recency Effect is stronger when the time taken from the first to the final event and length of the list increases.

And if the number of events between first and last is low and there is no or less interruption between the series of events, then people generally remember the first event. This means the Primacy Effect is stronger when the time taken from the first to the final event and length of the list decreases.

Since you spent a good amount of time seeing a total of 5 houses, so, your chances of remembering the first house are quite low. Therefore, the real estate agent used the Recency Effect contrast technique on you.

On the contrary, if you saw only 3 houses fast without any interruptions, chances of remembering the first house are quite high.

This technique is not limited to real estate. You will find the same technique used in shops selling dresses, furniture, lifestyle products, household items, etc.

Here are some ideas on how to use Primacy and Recency Effect in your communications like daily conversations, sales presentations, infomercials, job interviews, love/marriage proposals, political speeches:

- If you want whatever you say to be stand out in someone's mind, then say it at the beginning or wait for the end of the event.

- If you want to reveal a secret, make sure you disclose the most important information right at the end.

- In your business proposal or sales presentation, don't forget to summarize all the key points in the end.

- If you're going to deliver a long session, it's better to break up the session into shorter presentations.

- If you're running a restaurant, instruct your waiters to either start or end talking with the most special (and expensive) items on the menu.

- While giving a sales presentation, start and end with the biggest benefits. If there are any flaws in your product, tell about them in the middle of the presentation.

Rejection-then-Retreat

This technique is famous by various names, like:

- Door-In-The-Face

- Concession technique

- Larger-than-Smaller request

- Expensive-then-Economical request (A modified form of Rejection-then-Retreat technique)

- Rejection-then-Retreat

This technique is very often used in negotiations.

Here's how it works:

First, you make a very high and unreasonable request, which is rejected by the other party.

And then you make a smaller and more reasonable request which is readily accepted by the other party.

This happens because the other party clearly sees the contrast between the first and second requests.

Secondly, when you provide concession to the first rejected request, the other party feels obligated to agree with your smaller request.

The other party feels that since you've made a fair compromise, now it's their turn to pay back the favour.

In this process, the other party fails to recognize that it was actually the smaller request that you wanted the other party to agree right from the beginning.

Let me explain the process arithmetically...

You were interested in the X request.

But instead of making an X request, you made an X+Y request. The other party declined your request.

So, you made a concession of Y and reduced your request to the only X. The other party agreed to your X request.

So, you got exactly what you wanted in the first place, that is, X.

The point is: if you directly make a smaller request first, then neither there is any reference against which contrast can be seen, nor there is any obligation against your favour of concession.

It's human nature that if someone gives us concession, we feel obligated to return that favour with concession.

In the above case, your concession was moving from Larger to a Smaller request.

And the other party's concession was moving from No to Yes.

Expensive-then-Economical Request

A product is never cheap or expensive in absolute terms. It's all relative. People want to compare your product with others in order to determine the value of your product.

It's a human tendency to get the best reward for the least money and effort.

That's why people always look for a bargain.

They keep looking for offers here and there until they find the best deal.

And they want to keep with the crowd instead of moving to extremes.

For example, when you present the three models of the same product with a difference in features and price, most of the time, the customer chooses the middle model.

Like in the case of buying coffee in a café, most people choose a medium coffee as opposed to a small or a large **because it's more than the least and less than the biggest.**

Of course, it's easy to decide (the middle one) when you have only 3 options on the table.

But what to do when you have many options?

What should you pitch first? I mean, should you pitch the top OR bottom range of products first?

The answer to this question lies in how people behave while shopping.

It's human nature that we make compromises while shopping. We always look for a bargain. Instead of going to the extreme option, we choose the second-best option.

That's why you should always present the top-end, the most expensive item first to your customer. If he doesn't buy the most expensive item, the chances are much higher that he goes for 2nd or 3rd most expensive item.

Now suppose you present the least priced item first. Then chances are higher the customer selects 2nd or 3rd least priced item as a compromise.

This is because by presenting the costliest or cheapest product, you have set the anchor in the mind of the customer. Now that price has become a reference point for him to make a decision.

Therefore you need to use the **expensive-then-economical strategy** in your advertisements, proposals, presentations, offerings, menus, display items in the shop if you want to make more money in sales.

Likewise, when you are personally showing items to the customer in a retail store, show the highest priced item first, second highest next, and so on. Chances are higher that customer buys 2nd or 3rd highest priced item as a compromise.

Let me explain with an example:

Suppose you're a computer dealer having models ranging from $500 to $3,000.

Since you want sales desperately, the chances are higher that you will pitch the lower-range items first, hoping to immediately trade the customer up when he comes to your shop.

Now I want you to run a test for one month and see the results yourself.

In the first 15 days, start showing visitors **the low end of the line**, i.e., $500 onwards, and then encourage them to consider more expensive models. This is basically a traditional trading approach followed by most of the stores.

After 15 days, calculate the average sale price of computers sold in that period.

In the next 15 days, start showing visitors **the high end of the line**, i.e., $3,000, regardless of what they want to see, and then show the rest of the line, in declining order of price and quality.

After 15 days, again calculate the average sale price of computers sold in that period.

The objective of conducting this test is to check and verify yourself the effectiveness of the Expensive-then-Economical technique.

If you show the customer the most expensive item first, then the customer will spend much more money than if you show the most economical item first.

You can run the same test online also by listing the price of all your products on your website in ascending and descending order for 15 days each respectively.

You can do testing simultaneously also by taking half of the traffic to a webpage where prices are mentioned in ascending order and the other half traffic to a webpage where prices are mentioned in descending order.

If you're in Direct Selling, you can use the same technique to check what the average order value is when you pitch high-range products first against low range products.

One of the biggest lessons I have learned in Marketing is to keep testing techniques even if you're satisfied with your performance.

Test... Test... Test... is the secret of great marketers.

Here are some areas where you can use the Expensive-then-Economical technique effectively:

- If you're an automobile salesperson, use the top-end model of car for test-drives.

- If you run a restaurant, put prices on the menu card in descending order.

- If you run an infomercial on TV, demonstrate the top model, which has all the features.

- If you own a general store, put bigger bottles and packets in front at the display counter.

- If you're asking for donations, start with a big amount.

- If you're selling tickets for match, seminar, or conference on websites, stores, and counters, display the price in descending order.

- If your friend wants to give you a gift and asks your interest, demand an expensive item.

- If you're appearing for a job interview, demand a high salary.

- If you have a sales page on your website where you bring online visitors to buy your product, you can add an **Exit Popup** to pitch cheaper versions of the same product, if in case a visitor is leaving the sales page without buying.

A simple question: What's the advantage of selling higher-priced items against lower-priced items?

The answer is: It increases order value. As a result, you can make more money in commission.

For example:

Suppose your commission is 5% on whatever product you sell in your store.

Now, if you sell a $100 item, you earn $5 as a commission.

If you sell a $1,000 item, you earn $50 as a commission.

And if you sell a $10,000 item, you earn $500 as a commission.

So, it's always better to sell a higher-priced item.

Comparative Hypnotic Words

Comparative words are used in sales pitches, presentations, demonstrations to show how effective, efficient, cheap, superior your product is as compared to competitors.

Here are a few Comparative words:

- Faster
- Slower
- Fancier
- Lighter
- Stronger
- More
- Better
- Nicer
- Quicker
- Easier
- Cheaper
- Bigger

- Smarter

- Brighter

We are using such words right from our childhood days whenever we compare two things. That's why these words have developed an in-built believing power that hypnotizes our mind in agreeing with Persuader.

By subtly using these words, you can increase the effectiveness of your communication.

Remember, everything in this world is the Perception of Mind.

No matter how passionate you are... how much money, time, and energy you invest in yourself and your business... how many sacrifices you make... it has no value if your customers don't perceive the same.

VOLUME - IX

Let me start this volume with a quote of a master public speaker Reid Buckley:

"If you are not continually learning and upgrading your skills, somewhere, someone else is. And when you meet that person, you will lose."

So, next time whenever you feel satisfied with your performance, and start considering yourself a good marketer or salesperson, ask yourself:

"Compared to what?"

I'm sure you'll definitely find someone better than you. It means you need to keep challenging yourself.

Now let's talk about some more techniques based on the principle of Contrast.

Good Cop/Bad Cop

It is one of the oldest and most popular psychological tactics used in negotiation and interrogation.

Although it was originally designed for interrogation, it became the part of business negotiations due to its hard-bargaining nature.

Good Cop Bad Cop tactic is also called:

- Mutt and Jeff
- Friend and Foe
- Joint Questioning
- Working together but in opposition
- Fear and Relief

As the name suggests, Good Cop/Bad Cop involves two police interrogators who take the opposite approach while interviewing the suspect.

The opposite approach means one interrogator behaves nicely with the suspect and the other interrogator behaves harshly.

However, they both are working together towards a single objective – to get a confession or crucial information about the crime from the suspect.

Both interrogators may confront the suspect at the same time or one by one.

The aim is to make the suspect feel the sharp contrast between the personalities of two interrogators.

Interrogators use Good Cop/Bad Cop technique when they see the unwillingness of suspects to cooperate with them and provide the information they are seeking.

The suspect's non-cooperation makes one of the interrogators furious. He takes the role of "Bad Cop" and starts showing his negative stance towards the suspect by becoming aggressive... making derogatory comments... using abusive language... accusing and threatening the suspect of serious consequences... even to the extent of applying his muscle power.

In this way, the "Bad Cop" builds fear, disliking, antipathy in the mind of the suspect for him.

As per the plan, this is the perfect time to introduce the other interrogator who is going to play the role of "Good Cop".

The Good Cop can be introduced in multiple ways:

- Sometimes Bad Cop leaves the room saying that he is going outside for a few minutes due to some urgent work but coming back with more punishments if the suspect still refuses to cooperate.

- Sometimes Bad Cop stays there and asks Good Cop to talk to the suspect and tell him about his bad temperament and reputation in dealing with people who refuse to cooperate with him.

- Sometimes Bad Cop turns himself into Good Cop. He takes the suspect to another room and treats oppositely to how he behaved earlier.

- Sometimes, right from the beginning, Good Cop shows his positive stance towards the suspect by continuously defending him from the Bad Cop.

Unlike Bad Cop, Good Cop is polite and sympathetic in general. He appears supportive and understanding towards the suspect.

He offers the suspect some food and drinks.

He asks the suspect about his family, education, home town, hobbies, etc. to let his guard down and make him comfortable.

The Good Cop even plays down the moral consequences of the crime by using phrases like:

- "Such things happen at this age."

- "Even me and my wife have lots of fights. And sometimes I don't know what to do."

- "My father was also accused of cheating his business partner. But my father was not a bad man. It was our poor financial conditions that compelled him to do so."

- "My experience is also bad in maintaining personal relationships. So, I can totally understand what has gone with you in all these years."

By playing down the moral consequences of the crime, the Good Cop lowers the barriers so that the suspect admits what he did and saves a bit of face and dignity.

The Good Cop even confesses that he also doesn't like the Bad Cop but has no powers to stop him.

And then he suggests to the suspect that it's better to cooperate and tell them whatever he knows otherwise, he is afraid that Bad Cop can go to any extent to extract the information from the suspect.

Good Cop also promises that if the suspect is ready to cooperate, he will try his best to save the suspect from any further punishments.

Due to the sharp contrast between Bad Cop's rough behaviour and Good Cop's friendly attitude and sweet treatment, the adamant suspect starts listening and trusting Good Cop's words.

He requests the Good Cop for his support and protection from the Bad Cop. And in return, he will provide all information.

The question generally asked: "Why is there any need to use "Bad Cop"? Even Good Cop is sufficient to use his friendly attitude and soft approach to take out information from the subject."

The answer is: **The sharp contrast between two cops' interrogation styles makes the carrots offered by Good Cop sweeter and sticks offered by Bad Cop harsher.**

Many times people don't value good things until they see how bad the world is.

Similarly, many customers don't value good companies, products, offers, services, employees... until they see what terrible things are available in the market.

So, the suspect may not value the nice behaviour of Good Cop until he sees the offensive behaviour of Bad Cop.

Secondly, when people experience fear and then relief, one after another... the contrast between two emotions (Fear and Relief) is so extreme that they start losing their sense. They become disoriented. Their ability to think critically is switched off. They become compliant... ready to go along with suggestions without thinking.

Here are some common characteristics of Bad Cop:

- Unreasonable

- Doesn't listen to others

- Aggressive, impatient

- Rude, mean, temperamental

- Abusive, violent, physically threatening

- Uncompromising, not willing to negotiate

- Adamant; keeps objecting on a particular point.

Here are some common characteristics of Good Cop:

- Reasonable

- Cordial, empathetic, kind

- Nice behaviour, speaks softly.

- Friendly, understanding, caring attitude

- Opened to listen to other's points

- A dependable, trusted person who wants to build a long term relationship

- Reassures positive consequences if the subject agrees to comply

Good Cop/Bad Cop in Business

Because of its effectiveness, the Good Cop/Bad Cop technique is used heavily in business negotiations.

The reason is that the Bad Cop sets up the Good Cop easy to deal with during and after closing the deal.

Capitalizing on this advantage, the Good Cop encourages the other party to accept their recommendations to make concessions and even to give in.

Here's an example of how this technique is used in sales negotiations...

Suppose you're a startup company developing softwares and mobile apps.

After a long cycle of multiple meetings with a big prospective client, you have reached at the closing stage where you have to meet their two key executives. One of them is a tech manager, and the other one is the head of purchase.

When you are discussing with the tech manager how you're going to train their staff on your advanced software, suddenly, the other manager interrupts you and starts talking about commercials.

She expresses her worries about how you're going to meet their demands on time.

She starts digging about your previous business dealings.

She asks in detail about your background... why you left the job and started your own venture... how you're hiring people... how you're able to manage day-to-day operations and expenses...

She tries to downgrade you by saying:

"You're a very small company."

"You have limited resources."

"You're new to this industry."

And when you try to answer her queries... she becomes more dominating... takes a tough stand... acts aggressively... and starts making unreasonable demands...

She realizes that you're getting defensive and desperate to get the deal, which makes her more aggressive on her demands.

And now the moment comes when you start thinking that you're going to lose the deal and all your previous efforts will go in vain.

But wait...

Before you could think about what to do next... the tech manager jumps into conversation to save your poor soul.

The tech manager tells the purchase head that she doesn't agree with her.

She objects her rude colleague by saying:

"Despite being a small company, you're brilliant in your work."

"Your software has some advanced features which could be useful to us."

"Though we have never worked with such a small company, we are satisfied with your technical expertise."

You find the tech manager quite polite... reasonable... pleasant... and easy to deal with...

However, the purchase head gets furious and becomes more aggressive.

She starts arguing with the tech manager and points out more faults in your company.

She even refers to the company's policies and talks about previous bad experiences.

Finally, the purchase head threatens to discontinue the conversation if you don't go according to their terms and conditions.

And then, as per plan, the purchase head goes outside for 10 minutes due to some urgent work.

Due to purchase head's rude behaviour... your fear, desperation, worries can be clearly seen through your body language.

Taking advantage of the situation, the tech manager suggests to you, "Listen carefully! I really want to work with you. But your price is quite high, which our company will never accept. Our purchase manager is working in this company for a long time. So, our top management will go according to what she says. It's better to think about price and other terms... and come with a better offer. I can just recommend you above other competitors, but you need to support me with a better deal."

It's not just sales negotiation where Good Cop/Bad Cop is extensively used. Even in new recruitments, this technique is used regularly these days, where candidates need to go through multiple interviews before the final selection.

Here the role of Bad Cop is played by the owner, senior boss, HR manager, consultant, psychologist to find out candidates' weaknesses so that they don't demand a high salary.

If it's a single interview where both Good and Bad Cops are sitting together... in such cases, Good Cops are speaking most of the time. And when they find things are not going in their way, Bad Cops start talking with the candidate.

Who Should Play The Role of Bad Cop and Good Cop?

When using this technique, it's very critical to decide who should play the role of Bad Cop and Good Cop?

Bad Cop should be played by a person who is an outsider... temporarily available... not going to play any significant role once the deal is done.

Whereas Good Cop should be played by a person who has to build a long-term relationship with the other party... who has to communicate regularly with them...

By adding Bad Cop to the team helps Good Cop in saving face and maintaining relations. If Good Cop wants to say "no"... or wants to delay the decision... he blames Bad Cop so that he can keep negotiation positive.

Adding Bad Cop also helps in buying more time to do proper research and homework instead of rushing to close the deal or to say "no" to it.

Ultimately, Bad Cop takes all the blame so that Good Cop can remain in a trusted relationship between two parties with less risk of being the target of any retained hostility.

Here are some professionals who are generally kept as Bad Cop in negotiations:

· Purchase Manager

- Attorney

- Accountant

- HR Manager

- Super Boss

- Business Partner

- Outside Committee

- Investors and Bankers

- Auditor

- Government Regulators

- Business Advisors

- Board of Directors

- Professional Negotiator

- Office colleagues

- Media

And even spouse.

It's quite common to see politicians and bureaucrats playing Good Cop/Bad Cop in politics as it helps in their daily negotiations.

Suppose the minister plays the role of Bad Cop.

Because of his blunt comments in press conferences, tweets, meetings, he has earned a reputation of a tough, aggressive leader who is straight forward... not easy to deal with... wants others to work according to his terms... doesn't use diplomatic language... can't tolerate mistakes of others...

Whereas, his team of bureaucrats plays the role of Good Cop. They work opposite of his style... behave nicely with others... answer all tough questions... maintain relations with media... arrange parties and functions and invite key people... involve in social activities...

The minister's team tries to show his soft side. They talk about how hardworking he is... how honest he is... how much he hates corruption... how he wants everyone to work together on social issues... how he wants to build this world a better place for a living...

However, it is not at all necessary that the leader always plays Bad Cop, and subordinates play Good Cop. It can be vice-versa, depending upon what suits their personality.

For example, if the leader is conscious about image and acts diplomatic, then it's better to become Good Cop.

And if the leader is blunt and politically incorrect, then it's better to become Bad Cop.

Disadvantages of Good Cop/Bad Cop

Although Good Cop/Bad Cop is one of the most common techniques used by interrogators and negotiators, it has some disadvantages, like:

- Because of its overuse, this technique can be easily identified by the other party.

- There is a fear that because of his outrageous behaviour, the Bad Cop may push away the other party from closing the deal.

- In interrogation, Bad Cop's behaviour could make suspects and witnesses more adamant in not providing any information.

- Since negotiation tactics are considered as manipulation by some people, so it can destroy relationships and trust between the two parties.

- By frequent use of the Good Cop/Bad Cop technique could hurt one's reputation and image in the industry.

- Without planning and practice, this tactic could backfire.

- Sometimes negotiators get too much involved in game playing that they lose focus on achieving the outcome.

How to Counter Good Cop/Bad Cop Situation?

Top negotiators play this tactic so subtly that you may not even realize that you're in a Good Cop/Bad Cop situation.

It is not necessary that always two people are required to execute this technique.

Sometimes only one person plays both roles.

Sometimes Bad Cop prefers playing behind the scenes.

Sometimes, only the reference of Bad Cop is given to convey who is the real authority. For example, the husband (Good Cop) says, "Last time when I went for such a deal, my wife (Bad Cop) threatened me to leave me forever."

Sometimes the department plays the role of Bad Cop. For example, Good Cop may say:

"I don't think I could get it approved by Accounts/Legal/Auditors/Editors."

Sometimes a big team plays this tactic where half of the team acts as Bad Cop, and the other half acts as Good Cop.

Sometimes no human is involved in playing the role of Bad Cop. Instead, company policies, rule books, procedures, credit policies, computer software play the role of Bad Cop.

Whenever you find yourself in a Good Cop/Bad Cop situation, the first thing you need to keep in mind is that both Good and Bad Cops are on the same side. Both of them want to close the deal.

Here are some ways to counter this lethal technique:

- If you're feeling the pressure of Bad Cop, take a break and go outside for a few minutes to change the mood. Or, if possible, terminate the session. When you come back, they have to start again to build pressure.

- Tell them politely that you're aware of the Good Cop/Bad Cop negotiation tactic. So it's better not to use it.

- Shift your entire focus on Good Cop and ignore Bad Cop.

- You can counter the Good Cop/Bad Cop tactic with the same tactic. But it requires preparation.

- If the Bad Cop acts too much aggressively, simply walk out of the room.

- Confuse them. Act opposite to what they expect from you.

- Put all blame on Bad Cop for not having the deal.

- If they keep playing this tactic, tell them, "Let me bring my Bad Cop before we move further."

- You can create your own set of rules and regulations which act as Bad Cop to justify your position on the issue.

- Put a condition that you want to negotiate only with the decision-maker.

- Politely accuse the Bad Cop of their rude behaviour. Raise doubts on their intention. Ask questions like:

"Don't you like me, sir?"

"Why are you so rude to me?"

"Have I done something wrong to you?"

"Don't you want to get this deal?"

"Are you interested in some other party?"

"May I know what your real problem/objection is?"

Just Noticeable Difference

In the last volume, I discussed the Anchor.

The Anchor is the initial piece of information based on which all negotiations, arguments, estimates, decisions are made.

Setting up an Anchor in a customer's mind creates a frame of reference for valuing your product.

Now, what happens when the price of your product is anchored in the minds of your customers, but after some time, the cost of manufacturing increases? The reasons could be various like:

- Increase in price of raw materials.

- Shortage of raw material or labour.

- Increase in transportation costs.

- Cutthroat competition.

Some companies tackle the Anchor problem by coming up with a different low-grade brand in the same product category where they have the liberty to reduce the quality as well as the price to kill competition. However, they don't make any changes to the original brand. In this way, they maintain the reputation of their original brand.

Another way to deal with such situations, some companies either increase the price OR reduce the quality, size, and quantity below a value called **Just Noticeable Difference**.

What is Just Noticeable Difference (JND)?

Just Noticeable Difference is the scientific term that describes the minimal amount of change between two stimuli that a person can detect.

JND is also called **Differential Threshold** or **Weber's Law** as this concept was discovered by a nineteenth-century German scientist named *Ernst Heinrich Weber*.

It's is a specific amount that must be changed for a difference to be noticeable. It can be measured in physical units and is a constant proportion/percentage of the reference level.

JND can be applied to all senses. For example, how much difference in brightness, darkness, colour, design, volume, tone, pitch, pressure, weight, sweetness, sourness, fragrance should be made to be noticed by you.

According to Weber's law, a significant difference in the level will depend on the intensity of the initial stimulus. This means the difference is not an absolute amount but relative to the intensity of the first stimulus. Let me explain with some examples:

Example 1: If you increase the brightness of the light bulb inside a room, where light is very dim, the change in brightness is easily noticed by people. But if you increase the same level of brightness of a light bulb outside the room in the sun, it's very difficult to notice the change.

Example 2: If the price of a $20,000 car is increased by $500, it may go unnoticed by people because, in contrast to $20,000, $500 is a tiny amount, i.e., 2.5% change in the original price. But if the price of the same car is increased by $5,000, it may get immediately noticed by people.

Now suppose in the above car example, instead of increasing the price, the company offers a discount of $500. Again it may go unnoticed by people because $500 is a tiny amount as compared to $20,000. But if the company offers a discount of $5,000, it may take everyone's attention.

However, this tiny $500 becomes a considerable amount for you when you're buying a $1,500 laptop.

The question is: how this JND theory plays an important role in business?

It has been seen in the business world that whenever companies want to share the good news to the consumers, they project it big and most important thing the consumers will ever get. And if these same companies wish to reduce size, weight, quality, or increase the price of the product, they ensure they don't make it visible to the consumers.

Now here comes the role of JND.

Often companies want to make changes in products and services to reduce the cost of manufacturing, packaging, shipping, maintenance, etc.

To reduce this cost, one of their most common strategies is applying JND in their business so that people don't notice what negative changes they have done. Otherwise, customers may think the product is not worth the price. **To**

avoid this, they either increase the price or reduce the quality and quantity just below the JND.

Since the rise in cost is inevitable, therefore manufacturers and marketers are always trying to determine the relevant JND for their products.

However, the role of JND is not only limited to make negative changes. It is equally used in creating positive changes.

Companies make positive changes to improve their image, update themselves with the latest trends, develop a stronger position within the market, and also to protect themselves against the competition.

But they want to do it in a way that customers notice these positive changes without any shocks and frustrations.

If customers don't accept these changes, companies could lose their market share, loyalty, and profits. **To avoid this, they make these positive changes at or just above JND.**

But how do marketers determine the limits of what consumers will accept?

It depends on **consumer thresholds**. When the change between two stimuli reaches the threshold, the change becomes recognized. And when the change is below the threshold, it is not being recognized by others.

When this change crosses the threshold, it could affect the value of the product perceived by the customer.

For example, if the quality and quantity remain the same, but the increase in price crosses the threshold limit, the value of a product, as perceived by the customer, decreases.

Similarly, if the price remains the same but the decrease in quality or quantity crosses the threshold limit, the value of a product, as perceived by the customer, decreases.

The threshold for each product is different. That's why it is not easy to find out JND. It requires conducting multiple trials and then finding the smallest difference participants could detect at least 50 percent of the time.

Let's say a company finds out that the JND for their product is 5%.

Now, if a company makes some positive changes in their product like improving quality, updating packaging, increasing size, lowering prices then in order to make this improvement noticeable to customers so that they get the confidence they are getting a good deal, the quantity of improvement will be above 5%.

Whereas if a company quietly wants to reduce its costs and losses or increase profit margins, it will either increase the price OR reduce the quality and quantity below 5%, so that it is not noticed by customers.

And if someone notices this difference, they might not find it so much significant.

But for these companies, it could make a huge difference when they multiply this hardly noticed difference (for example, 5%) with thousands or even millions of items.

And it doesn't stop here.

These companies keep on increasing price or reducing quantity and quality below JND from time to time. And people hardly noticed that. These unnoticeable differences eventually add up to big changes but prevent their market from being taken by surprise.

Similarly, companies keep improving their products at or above JND from time to time. This becomes much more important if the company and its competitors have similar kind of features, design, colour, taste, odour, etc.

But brands are afraid of making big changes as their loyal customers may not like it. For example:

- Brands don't change their packaging too much. Otherwise, it could increase the risk of rebranding.

- If a food & beverage brand changes the ingredients of their popular product to make it healthier, there are chances that customers could taste the difference and may not like it.

- If a brand makes major changes in its logo, customers may get confused and consider it some other brand.

In short, to get someone's attention hit them with more than a feather but a lot less than a baseball bat.

If companies keep improvement below JND, then all their efforts will be waste because this improvement is unlikely to be noticed by people.

And if companies keep improvement significantly larger than JND, then again all their efforts are waste because:

- Companies end up spending more than what is required to elicit the necessary response (for example, taking customer's attention).

- The customers may not like the new changes.

- The companies may irritate the customers through their repeated boastful messages about their new improvements.

- Since customers are getting more for less, new big positive changes may reduce the level of repeat sales.

Here are some points about the Just Noticeable Difference that you need to remember:

- If you're shopping for items in discount Sale, you need to check carefully if the store has reduced the size/quantity/quality of the discounted products in comparison to non-discounted products.

- Even a small price change in lower-priced items looks much bigger than the same price change in higher-priced items.

- Sometimes companies reduce the weight of the product but keep the packaging size and price the same as before.

- A famous branded product requires a smaller discount to be perceived as a bargain as compared to a local product.

- Big brands keep making positive changes in their logo... design... packaging... slogan... advertising... in almost every aspect of the product... to improve their image. But they are afraid that customers may reject these sudden changes. Therefore, these companies make changes gradually and keep it just above JND so that customers don't get sensitive about it.

- The difference between two odd-number prices is perceived bigger than two even-number prices.

- If you're offering products on Sale, you need to provide discounts at or just above JND if you want to attract customers' attention immediately. Suppose the JND of discount is 20%. So, if you give a discount of less than 20%, then your campaign may fail if customers do not notice your offer. And if you give a discount of more than 30%, then you're losing money from your pocket to take the attention of your customers.

- Even a small increase in the price of cheap items could decrease their sales. But the same small change in the price of expensive items may not affect at all.

The 'Add-on Accessories' Close

Suppose you go to a reputed mobile store to buy an expensive mobile handset.

Once you finalize the model and move towards the billing counter, the salesperson or her colleagues want to show you something else that you may like.

For example:

- High quality mobile cover

- Bluetooth headphone

- Scratch-resistant screen protector

- Wireless earphone

- Antivirus software

- Extended warranty

Of course, these are all mobile accessories that you may require as you have purchased a new handset.

But the question is why they have not pitched you the entire package at a time?

Why are they bringing these items separately? In a big store, each of these items may be pitched by a different salesperson.

Why are they not focusing only on selling mobile handsets?

Let me answer the last question first.

One of the rules in Selling is to increase the order value (also called cart value in online shopping) as much as possible because we don't know when this new customer will come back again to our store (or website) to buy something else.

As you already know…

It's very difficult to attract new people.

It's very difficult to convert strangers into customers.

It's very difficult to sell our other products to new customers.

And it's very difficult to bring the existing customers back to our website or shop.

That's why when you get a new sale; always try to increase the order value to make more money.

This is one of the fastest ways to cover your marketing and advertising costs and even reduce the break-even time.

Referring back to the above example… Since you've already bought a mobile phone and are not interested in buying more handsets, so the best way to increase the order value is by selling you mobile accessories.

Now coming to the first and second questions, the answer is… if the salesperson tries to sell you all accessories along with a mobile phone as a comprehensive solution, it naturally increases the total cost in your mind, which could increase your anxiety and delay your buying decision.

But the salesperson knows you're a superhot qualified case since you've just bought an expensive mobile phone and still you're inside the store.

So, she uses the **Add-on Accessories technique** to sell other items. This closing technique is used just after the main product is sold.

The objective is to bring up the extras INDEPENDENTLY of one another so that each small price seems INSIGNIFICANT when compared to the already bought larger one.

Here are some examples where you can use this closing technique to increase your order value:

Example #1: **Retail Clothing Store**

Suppose a man enters a fashionable men's clothing store and says that he wants to buy a three-piece suit and a pair of shirts. If you are the owner of that store, what would you show him first to make him likely to spend the most money?

The trick is to instruct your sales team to sell the costly item first.

Sell the suit first, because when the time comes to look at shirts, even expensive ones, their prices will not seem as high in comparison to the price of a three-piece suit.

The price of a three-piece suit sets an Anchor in the mind of the customer.

If you pitch him an expensive shirt first, he might shy away from spending so much money on a shirt… but if he has just bought a three-piece suit which is obviously much more expensive than a shirt, the price of the shirt does not seem excessive.

The same principle applies in buying other accessories like tie, belt, socks, etc. to go along with his new suit.

Example #2: **Restaurants**

Restaurant waiters normally take your entire meal order first, and once you're done, add on dessert requests.

If the price of dessert is a bit costly as compared to other nearby restaurants, still you'll find it cheap if you compare it with the expensive meal you just had.

Example #3: **Automobile Dealerships**

If you're a salesperson in an automobile dealership, what to do once the new car is sold?

Start adding accessories options like a car cover, seat cover, FM Stereo, GPS navigator, sunshades, tire inflator and pressure gauge, extended warranty, vacuum cleaner, car freshener, Bluetooth, air purifier, glass cleaner, car shampoo, etc.

The trick is to sell these accessories independently to each other.

For example, once your customer has purchased the $20,000 car, she may find it worth spending a few hundred more for deluxe rust proofing.

These are a few common examples to show you how to increase order value once your main product is sold.

In your case, you need to brainstorm with your team what accessories you can add in your business to maximize cart value.

This technique works equally well in the service industry.

Comparison-Affordable technique

It is also called the *Reduction to the Ridiculous technique.*

It involves making your deal sweeter by breaking down the price into monthly, weekly, daily, or hourly prices so that customers can easily digest the price.

Salesmanship is all about how you change the perception of your product, price, company, services, people, competition, etc. in people's minds. *Reduction to the Ridiculous* is one of the Contrast techniques in how you present the offer in the minds of the customers.

Actually, the price is the same, but in order to avoid automatic rejection by the customer once he knows the full price, we contrast the breakup price with his daily expenses.

For example, comparing the breakup price of your product with the cost of tea, coffee, cold drink, groceries, petrol, movie ticket, newspaper subscription, club membership fee, snacks, utility bills, rent, medicines, clothes, etc. on which customer spends money regularly.

The objective is to break the price down into small amounts so your customers can afford it. In this way, you're making it easy for them to buy.

Here's one example to show you how this technique works:

Suppose you're a salesperson in a car dealership. A prospect comes to your showroom and wants to buy a $17,000 car. She has already arranged for money. It's a cool deal where you just have to complete formalities and deliver a car to her as soon as possible.

You request her to sit in the waiting area while you do all the paperwork.

But she prefers to see other cars in your showroom to kill time.

Within a few minutes, you notice that she is staring at a recently launched $22,000 model. She is paying attention to every detail. She is checking interiors, engine, front and backlights, and even shows interest in taking a test drive.

You suggest to her to buy this model if she is so interested.

After thinking for a while, she says no as the price of this model is $22,000, whereas she is having a budget of $17,000. Although she is going to use a new car for at least 5 years, an extra $5,000 is too much for her.

Now here's a small test for you to check your salesmanship.

If you think yourself as a customer-oriented salesperson who always thinks about the best interest of your customer, then what will you do? Convince her to buy a $22,000 car or sell a car in a $17,000 budget?

Where is the salesmanship? In selling $22,000 car or selling $17,000 car?

You see, most salespeople would like to sell the customer a $17,000 car.

Why?

First, she is financially qualified for $17,000. And she already made her mind to buy that car. So, why to confuse her?

Second, salespeople are afraid that if they try to change customer's focus from the $17,000 model to some other model, they might lose the sale.

Well, my views are different.

Suppose the customer buys a $17,000 car from you. Now for the next few days, she enjoys driving her new car. And she has almost forgotten a $22,000 model.

But one day, she sees that $22,000 model parked outside her office. She comes to know that her colleague has bought it. She congratulates her colleague and reveals she also wanted to buy the same car, but due to financial constraints, she couldn't buy it.

Her colleague says she was also planning to buy a cheaper car. But then she thought she is going to drive a new car for the next 3 to 5 years, and if she doesn't buy her favourite car, then every day she will blame herself for making the wrong decision.

After listening to her colleague, your customer starts regretting not buying a $22,000 car.

And somewhere in her mind, she blames you for not convincing her to buy this new model.

Now my some tough questions to you…

First, don't you think for just getting the sale, you turn your new customer into an unhappy customer who will never buy from you again?

Second, if your customer had a budget of $17,000 to buy a new car, then she could have purchased from anywhere… from any other dealership… heck, even online. Then what's the use of you? What's your role in selling? Why does your dealership need to hire and retain people like you? You're just working as a clerk to complete the formalities… NOT as a salesperson.

Third, ask yourself: where is the real salesmanship? If you think you did right in selling a $17,000 car, then I don't agree with you. Because from my point of view, you did NOTHING. Your customer was already sold on a $17,000 car. The real salesmanship was selling in a $22,000 car, which your customer fantasized about owning and driving.

Fourth, if you remember, I talked about **Need vs. Want** in one of my previous volumes. In this case, your customer's **need** was $17,000 car. But her **want** was a $22,000 model. If you focus on selling needs, then sorry to say, pal, you'll never become rich; if you're in the profession of Sales. Top salespeople are always interested in selling wants. **The real skill is converting Want into Need.**

Fourth, suppose you get a chance to correct your mistake. Instead of selling a $17,000 model, you convince her to buy a $22,000 model. My question is: What's the actual sale done by you if she agrees to buy a $22,000 model?

Think about it.

Think…

Think…

It's $5,000.

Yes, the actual sales done by you is only $5,000.

The reason is: Your customer was already sold on $17,000 before entering your showroom.

It was that extra $5,000 where she needed your help to convince her. Of course, you can't expect from your customers that they will ask you to convince them. It's your job to read their mind, particularly their unconscious signals.

In this case, your only job was to make your customer accept that $5,000 figure in her mind.

How?

By using the Comparison-Affordable technique, reduce that monster figure into a ridiculous amount.

Here's how it works:

Suppose your customer is going to use this new car for at least 5 years.

Step 1: Now divide this extra $5,000 price by 5 years, i.e. $5,000/5 = $1,000 per year.

Step 2: Divide $1,000 by 12 months, i.e. $1,000/12 = $84 per month (in round figures).

Step 3: Divide $84 by 30 days, i.e. $84/30 = $2.80 per day.

Closing Question: "Ms. Prospect, can't you spend $2.80 per day for your desired car? It's even less than what you pay for a cup of coffee."

Just see the comparison of $5,000 against $2.80, which is quite affordable for your customer.

So, by using the Comparison-Affordable technique, you're reducing price resistance by breaking the price down to its lowest common denominator. (For example, instead of saying to your customer that one-year membership will cost you $600 plus tax plus shipping, you can say that price is even less than $70 a month.)

And then, simply compare the price of your product and service with a daily cup of coffee OR bottle of beer per week OR dinner out one night per month.

Compare your price to something that your customer consumes on a regular basis.

The Secondary Close

It's a smart way to turn your prospect's focus from indecision to a minor point. You make it easier for him to make a buying decision. If the prospect agrees to the minor point of the deal, he has somehow decided to buy the entire offer.

The Secondary Close helps the customer to get relieved from the anxiety that always accompanies a buying decision.

Examples:

- "Do you want this with the factory tires, or do you prefer some other company's tires?"

- If a person is considering buying a bike, washing machine, mobile, bag, etc. use a secondary close by asking, "Would you prefer this in red or silver?"

You have changed the prospect's focus from purchasing (major issue) to the colour (secondary issue). By confirming the colour, he has decided to buy the entire product.

- "Would you like this delivered, or would you rather take it with you today?"

You have changed the prospect's focus from uncertainty to delivery (secondary issue).

1965 Letter Selling The Mercedes-Benz 190 Diesel

It's one of the most famous sales letters of all time.

This letter was responsible for selling one of the first diesel cars of Mercedes in the USA. At that time, Mercedes decided to junk the production of diesel cars because of some disadvantages associated with it. Like:

- At that time, Diesel fuel was not available everywhere.

- Gasoline was relatively cheap in those days.

- Diesel engines were very noisy as compared to standard gasoline engines.

As a last resort, they turned the project over to Ed McLean, a direct marketing expert in the USA. He wrote this sales letter targeting wealthy individuals who could be persuaded to buy a diesel car.

Just see yourself how beautifully McLean has compared the benefits of a diesel engine with a gasoline engine.

Also, I have bold some sentences where the principle of Contrast is used smartly and effectively.

....

Dear Sir:

"Forget it, Heinz," the experts told me. "It just won't sell here."

They were talking about the Mercedes-Benz 190 Diesel -- **a car that is owned and driven daily by over 500,000 people overseas.**

"Americans won't buy it," said the experts. **"Why pay $4,068 for a German car with a noisy engine when for $891.37 more they can get a Cadillac?"**

I had reason to believe the experts were wrong. Some Americans have paid $4,068 for this German car with the "noisy engine."

As a matter of fact, if it wasn't for the "noisy engine" many of these Americans wouldn't have found out about the car. While in Europe, they saw Mercedes-Benz Diesel cars and noticed the noise made by the engine. Fascinated, they asked questions.

And what they learned from European drivers up and down the high-speed Autobahns convinced them the Mercedes-Benz Diesel is a great car.

As for the noise, they found it does sound different from a gasoline engine. In fact, a few people may give the car a second look as you idle at a traffic light. But you won't be bothered by the sound above 25 miles per hour. Some 190D drivers report they actually enjoy the unique sound of the Diesel. Many owners tell me, "If it didn't make a little noise, people wouldn't know it's a Diesel!"

Mr. John J. Gray of Albany, Oregon is one of these owners.

He travels all over the western U.S. for his firm, Kashfinder, Inc. In the past 7 years, he has driven his Mercedes-Benz Diesel car 652,000 miles.

"652,000 miles is a long way to drive one car," writes Mr. Gray. **"It has taken me 7 years -- during which my faithful Mercedes-Benz Diesel has run more efficiently and far more cheaply than any car I have ever owned. And the car still doesn't rattle..."**

Recently, we asked other Mercedes-Benz Diesel car owners in America:

"If you had it to do all over again, would you buy another of these automobiles?"

Before I tell you their answers, I'd like to reveal what I learned from the U.S. Automobile Manufacturers Association. **I asked them how many Americans buy the same make and model of car they owned previously. They told me that fewer than four out of ten do.**

Yet, when we asked our Mercedes-Benz Diesel car owners in America if they would buy another Mercedes-Benz Diesel, better than nine out of ten said YES.

The experts were wrong about these Americans. But one question remains unanswered for me.

How many other Americans want a great motorcar?

I'll soon know the answer.

You -- and a small number of others -- have been selected
to receive the most unusual offer ever made by a car
manufacturer.

I will pay for all fuel, all motor oil, all oil filters, and all
lubrications on the new Mercedes-Benz 190 Diesel for the
first 15,000 miles you drive it.

**This offer is from Mercedes-Benz of North America. It
is not from your Mercedes-Benz dealer.** It will not affect
your trade-in or terms in any way. I feel certain you will
like this car and will help me spread the word about it.

That's why I can offer you all fuel free. All motor oil free.
All oil filters free. All lubrications free. All are yours free
for the first 15,000 miles you own and drive your new
Mercedes-Benz 190 Diesel.

**No other manufacturer of a full-size 4-door sedan in the
entire world could afford to make this offer.**

I can make it because the Mercedes-Benz 190 Diesel
averages over 30 miles per gallon of diesel fuel -- **and
diesel fuel costs 1/3 less than gasoline in many states.**

In fact, the 190 Diesel regularly saves its owners more than
50 percent on fuel costs alone.

And, like all Mercedes-Benz cars, the 190 Diesel is so
finely machined it uses scarcely any motor oil.

That's not all.

The 190 Diesel never needs a tune-up. It has no carburetor to adjust or replace. No spark plugs, no points, no condensers, no distributor.

Mechanics will tell you that many cars need a new set of rings after 75,000 miles.

John Gray -- the Diesel owner in Oregon -- reports his car didn't need a ring Job until after it had gone 275,000 miles!

Even crack mechanics are surprised by that. We build the Mercedes-Benz 190 Diesel so that, with normal care, it will last for hundreds of thousands of all oil filters, and all lubrications for the first 15,000 miles you drive your new Mercedes-Benz 190 Diesel.

So please accept my invitation to drive a 190D and reach your own personal, private judgment.

Simply return the enclosed card in the postage-free envelope. I will also send you a special brochure called "The Amazing 190D."

My offer expires Monday, August 16, 1965, and is limited to the first 1,000 people who respond. I hope you take advantage of it. Thank you.

Yours truly,

____

....

This is one of the examples of how to incorporate principles and techniques of Persuasion in your sales pitches, presentations, advertisements.

It's not only the contrast principle that is used in this sales letter. There are other Persuasion techniques, as well.

Imagine how effective we become in sales when we start applying Persuasion in our daily communication.

I'm not talking about one or two tactics.

I'm talking about using five, ten, or even more techniques **simultaneously** with so precision and well-timed that people consider you a **natural** persuader.

VOLUME - X

I want to start this issue with the topic of the Coronavirus Pandemic that has turned the world upside down.

Coronavirus has severely impacted our lives and economy.

The question is: why is Coronavirus so dangerous? What are the factors which make it extremely lethal?

Is it because of the high infection rate?

Is it because of the high mortality rate?

Is it because of its invisibility?

Is it because of no vaccine available to protect ourselves?

Of course, all these factors make it difficult for us to fight and defeat Coronavirus.

However, I want to add one more reason linked to a lethal Persuasion technique that has made us highly vulnerable to covert attacks from people who know how to use this technique.

This technique is based on the Principle of Contrast.

Before I discuss this Persuasion technique and how some advertisers, marketers, and salespeople are using it subtly... let me show you how Coronavirus has used the same 'technique' to capture our body.

You see, the reason Coronavirus was able to spread so quickly is LOW CONTRAST in symptoms between people who are Normal and who are Infected by this deadly virus.

We have heard many stories in the past few months that an infected person without showing any symptoms met many people outside the home.

And when the person came to know about his or her infection, the virus was already spread to people whom the infected person met recently, especially near and dear ones.

Even there were cases where general doctors became victims of Coronavirus while treating patients who didn't show any 'major' symptoms.

Still, many people who test positive are either asymptomatic or show mild symptoms.

I think it's a big concern and should not be handle lightly.

Why?

The reason lies in human's perception of how they identify good and evil.

As you know, in the last 2-3 issues, I'm talking about the Principle of Contrast. I told you that the higher the contrast between two items, the easier for us to separate them in our minds.

On the contrary, if the contrast is too low, between two or more items, it's become difficult for us to identify which is better or mediocre... which is beneficial or dangerous... which is economical or expensive in the long run.

So, higher contrast between people tells us who is Good or Evil to us...

But what will we do if the contrast between good and evil is so low to the level that a Wicked person is behaving exactly like a Good person?

As I mentioned earlier, **if the contrast is too low, it makes us confused and even paralyzed to make a decision.**

Just like in the case of the Coronavirus pandemic... where unless the test is done, we are not sure who are the infected people, if they're behaving quite normal.

I'm talking about asymptomatic COVID-19 patients who do not display any symptoms at all while incubating the virus in their bodies. They are **silent spreaders** who are transmitting the virus to a lot of people since they go on with daily lives just like they normally do, meeting friends, family members, colleagues, and even strangers.

Okay, we understand that these silent spreaders are not aware that they are infected with this deadly virus.

But what about others? I'm talking about people who are meeting asymptomatic patients. Why are they not cautious of silent spreaders? Why do they easily become victims of the virus carried by their near and dear ones?

It's because it's human nature that we generally don't doubt people who are not strangers to us. In fact, it has become our old habit, which is not easy to leave even in crazy times like the Pandemic period.

Here's how people think in normal circumstances...

We are not suspicious of those who are nice and close to us.

We don't protect ourselves from those whom we think are harmless.

We don't surround ourselves with a protective shield to save ourselves from known ones.

We don't show resistance to people whom we are comfortable meeting and talking to.

In short, we are not conscious of our family members, friends, relatives, and colleagues as we don't perceive any threat from them.

On the contrary, we are highly suspicious of strangers as we don't know who they are... What is their background? What is their hidden intention?

We teach children not to mingle with strangers.

We don't allow strangers to our home.

Even in business, we don't want to hire and work with strangers because we are afraid that tomorrow these people could turn into unethical business partners, conmen, competitors, or may get involved in some scandal which could spoil the reputation of our business.

But we can't always keep ourselves surrounded by near and dear ones. We have to go out and meet new people.

That's why we learn to identify differences between right and wrong people.

How?

By observing the behaviour of strangers, learning from our past experiences, and using mental shortcuts, we try to find out who genuinely wants to help us and who wants to hurt us.

One of the mental shortcuts is finding a sharp contrast between the behaviour of bad and good people.

For example:

We consider those people Good who are work very hard. And consider those people Bad who take unethical shortcuts to achieve their purpose.

We consider those people Good who are kind to others... who help others... And consider those people Bad who make fun of others... who play politics and conspiracies...

But what will you do when the contrast between bad and good, unethical and ethical, stranger and known is very less?

Just like what we witnessed during the Coronavirus Pandemic, in some cases, there was low contrast in symptoms of an infected and normal person.

I know it's not good news, but the point is low contrast could lower our defences if we rely on our shortcuts. Our casual attitude towards harmless situations and people makes us extremely vulnerable to those who know how to take advantage of low contrast. This phenomenon is known as...

The Illusion of Invulnerability

If you remember, I shared an example in one of my previous issues that when the frog is dropped in hot water, it will immediately leap out.

But when the same frog is placed in a pan of warm water, then it eventually gets boiled alive if the temperature of the pan is increased gradually. Simply because frog cannot contrast temperature increments.

Similarly, human minds can be easily deceived using contrast.

The Illusion of Invulnerability means we're most vulnerable at those very moments when we feel that we're in the least danger.

As you know, we're always suspicious of crooks, thieves, fraudsters, selfish, and pushy people... and somehow we're prepared to deal with them if in case we face any threat from them.

But we forget that the greatest threat is from people we're unprepared for.

Of course, all of us should be optimistic about our present and future. We should believe in our abilities. We should remain positive and calm to handle tough situations.

In fact, many of us have already tasted some kind of success. Whether it's bringing good marks in the exam... bringing tons of sales... running a successful business empire... or enjoying a great relationship with family and friends...

But it doesn't mean we are invulnerable.

It doesn't mean we are unbeatable.

It doesn't mean we are unconquerable.

It doesn't mean we are immortal.

It's good to be optimistic, but over-optimism leaves us psychologically disarmed.

The Illusion of Invulnerability stops us from thinking about problems.

The Illusion of Invulnerability could lead us to be unprepared for dangers lying ahead. Ignoring weaknesses and difficulties doesn't help us in becoming positive. It makes us arrogant and dumb.

Many traditional business empires vanished from the earth just because they ignored upcoming problems. They were living in the Illusion of Invulnerability. Whereas some small businesses survived and thrived just because they acknowledged they are small and weak and need to protect themselves from big sharks.

That's why stop thinking that you are invulnerable. And start loving problems. In fact, the world's greatest entrepreneurs are those who find opportunities in problems.

Who Are The Victims of The Illusion of Invulnerability?

Whoever lives in an illusion that they are naturally immune to danger, and therefore no preparation is required from their end are automatically ready to become the first victims when the problem arrives.

Here are some characteristics of people - who live in the Illusion of Invulnerability, which increases their chances of getting attacked by others.

- People who have overconfidence.

- People who unrealistically believe in a bright future.

- People who believe bad things are not going to happen to them.

- People who have inflated images of themselves.

- People who think they are different.

- People who think they are better than average people.

- People who think nobody can take advantage of them.

- People who think nobody can manipulate them.

- People who refuse to acknowledge their weaknesses.

- People who are not prepared for the worst.

- People who don't learn lessons from the past and never bothered about the future. They just live in the present.

- People who believe they are immune to diseases, natural disasters, death, unemployment, losses, and even divorce.

- People who ignore problems assuming sooner or later will be automatically get resolved. So, what's the use of thinking about problems because it causes stress?

- People who expect miracles in their lives.

- People who are too much dependent on administration, parents, boss, company, economy, gurus, friends and relatives, and even God.

- People who tend to focus only on strengths and deny their shortcomings.

- People who blame others on parameters like intelligence, personality, competence, behaviour, etc. for problems in their lives. But when they face similar problems in their own lives, they blame circumstances.

- People who think nobody can influence, persuade, or sell them.

- People who think Advertising doesn't work.

Now, the point we need to discuss is what the role of the Illusion of Invulnerability in Sales & Marketing is.

For this, we need to understand what these people who are suffering from the Illusion of Invulnerability think about Advertising, Sales, and Marketing guys?

What is the General Perception of Salespeople?

As I told you earlier, the Sales profession has earned a terrible reputation all over the world.

The word "Sales" has now become a Bad anchor in the minds of people.

I still remember the facial expression of my intellectual family members and relatives when I told them the first time that I've moved into the Sales profession. For them, moving from the respectable Profession of Engineering to a low-grade Profession of Sales was like that I've moved to 'Underworld'!

Here is the general perception of salespeople in our society:

- Salespeople are desperate.

- Salespeople are aggressive.

- Salespeople are greedy.

- Salespeople are fast-talking.

- Salespeople are not intellectuals.

- Salespeople are not sophisticated.

- Salespeople are shameless.

- Salespeople are always pitching their products and services.

- Salespeople make big promises.

- Salespeople are pushy.

- Salespeople are scam-artist.

- Since salespeople love making money, they can go to any limits for getting sales.

- Salespeople are experts in taking out hard-earned money from people's pockets.

- Salespeople are experts in selling overpriced and useless items. And once they sell the product, they will never come back.

- Salespeople have no interest in the well-being of customers. They are selfish and just want to achieve their targets.

- Salespeople are too direct.

- Salespeople have no self-respect.

- Salespeople love to criticize their competitors.

- Salespeople's pet words are: "We're the best"... "We're No.1"...

- Salespeople wear expensive, stylish clothes and accessories to look attractive just like a con artist.

- Salespeople are smart but not knowledgeable.

- Salespeople are unethical.

The same perception is for marketers and advertising guys.

No, this general perception is not automatically created in the minds of people.

Many of these points are true. The credit goes to desperate sales guys, manipulative marketers, and unethical advertisers due to which the entire industry has earned a poor reputation.

Unfortunately, because of this general perception, many good people suffer. Even if they work hard, then also it's not easy to change this general perception.

That's why to counter this general perception, some smart marketers and salespeople use a cunning technique based on the Principle of Contrast so that people don't easily recognize them. It's called...

Psychological Disarmament

It basically means to do the exact opposite of general perception so that people remain in the Illusion of Invulnerability that they are not dealing with people whom they're feared the most.

In this way, these salespeople remain under the radar and sell their products without facing any skepticism, resistance, and rejection.

Psychological Disarmament has made us highly vulnerable to covert attacks from people who know how to use this technique.

The deadly Coronavirus has used the same technique to capture our bodies.

Here are some examples to show how some marketers, salespeople, advertisers, and fundraisers are using Psychological Disarmament subtly, especially on those who think they can't be easily influenced and persuaded to buy products and services...

Example #1

As we know, many customers dislike dealing with aggressive, pushy salespeople. However, the same customers react differently; when they deal with those marketers and salespeople who already know about it and use the Psychological Disarmament technique to counter people's dislike.

These lethal marketers and salespeople do the exact opposite of what people generally perceive about them so that they don't face skepticism, resistance, and rejection from customers.

Just like what we see in movies, how undercover agents work to gather information about an enemy.

Here are some seducing characteristics of lethal marketers and salespeople who use Psychological Disarmament as their main weapon:

- They are family men/women.

- They are non-threatening.

- They don't like talking too much. They prefer listening. In fact, some of them are introvert.

- They are trustworthy.

- They are reasonable.

- They are sweet, soft-spoken, and polite in nature.

- They are not self-centred.

- They have a good sense of humour.

- They are indirect. For example, they use stories, metaphors, and analogies to influence customer's minds.

- Instead of pushing hard to sell their products, they love to seduce their customers.

- They sell through references.

- They are master in building an instant rapport with customers.

- They are masters of disguise.

- They first become friends, then consultant, and then salespeople.

- If they are selling to Low-Value people, they behave like an Average Joe who is also part of the same society where the customer lives. (Remember the *Grounding* technique that I discussed in one of the previous volumes?)

- They are good at Account Mapping. They keep trying to find out a common link between them and target customers.

- They don't use the "Sales" word in their job title. Instead, they call themselves:

    - Consultant

- Coordinator

- Advisor

- Specialist/Expert

- Application Executive

- Business Development Associate

- Sales Engineer

- Customer Support Representative

- Business Manager

- Key Account Manager

- Regional/Country Head/National Manager

- Guru/ Public Speaker

- Relationship Manager

- Team Leader

- Copywriter

Example #2

Another example I want to discuss is from the advertising industry.

Many people consider advertisements only what they see or listen to on TV, magazines, the internet, social media, billboards, and radio.

But smart advertisers know that people skip, resist, and reject messages which clearly look like an advertisement. That's why these advertisers use different ways to disarm people psychologically about their real intentions, that is, to promote their products and services.

Let's take the example of **Format**:

Advertisers use different formats of communication and promotion, which are still not accepted as hard-core advertising by people.

They keep the Format of advertising in such a way that people don't recognize that it's actually an advertisement. It helps advertisers in avoiding skepticism, resistance, and rejection from the market.

Here are some formats which go under the radar of the market:

- Interview

- News

- Seminar

- Jingle, Rhyme, and Song

- Documentary

- Blogs and Articles

- Social media post

- Editorial (In newspaper and magazine, advertisements in the editorial format are called Advertorial)

- Video Sales Letter

- Webinar

- Q & A session

- Product launch event

- Book

- Contest

- Frequent Asked Questions

- Podcast

- Sponsorship of sports and fundraising events

- Free health check-up camp

- Parties and meetups

- Public Relations (PR) stories

- Corporate Social Responsibility (CSR) activities

- Press Release

- Subtly showing brand name or logo in movies and video games

Example #3

Another example is the *Hare Krishna movement* that was struggling financially in North America in the late 1960s.

At that time, the members of this society showed up in their orange robes and mostly-shaven heads, dancing and chanting on the streets while begging for funds.

However, Americans didn't like their looks and outfits... found their acts quite weird. They were reluctant to provide the members with any money and support.

Since it became hard for members to raise money so they thought about changing their image and decided to overcome this negative bias among Americans.

How?

By transforming themselves.

First, the members abandoned street chanting in robes.

Second, they are solicited in airports, train stations, and other public places where there is a lot of pedestrian traffic.

Third, they dressed and groomed in a modern style to avoid immediate recognition.

Fourth, in public places, the members gave the people passing a gift, for example, a flower, a book, a magazine. And once the person had the gift in his or her hand, they asked for a small donation.

Fifth, today, many members are from the mainstream, for example, corporate executives, professionals, students, etc.

Triple The Value

Suppose you're a dealer of a B2B or B2C product that is easily available in the market.

Assuming you don't have any exclusive agreement with the manufacturer, customers have a choice to buy from you or your competitors.

Also, the product manufacturer has given strict instructions that no dealer can reduce the end-customer price to win the sale even at the cost of their own margins.

Now, it all depends on the customer from where he or she wants to buy the product.

The question arises: how the customer will decide from where to buy... from you or your competitors?

Well, it depends on who provides the most value to the selfish customer.

That's why the customer is called "King" these days.

If you are selling a product, people are more likely to buy it when they see an extra value.

Giving value to your target customer is what going to win you that customer, not just for today's sale, but for the entire life.

Your job is to make Value/Price seem bigger than it is. You have to make them feel that there is so much value in doing business with you that they would never even think about going elsewhere. This becomes much more important if you're running a small business.

Remember always, try to provide at least triple value to your customers so that they never think about going to your competitors.

Whatever you are selling, try adding a discount, bonus products, a warranty, or anything else that will give the impression of a good deal.

Here are some ideas on what value you can add to make your offer more lucrative. As a marketer, you need to make a killer combination of values which suit best to your business.

1. Coupon and Discount Codes

2. Warranty/Guarantee

3. E-book

4. Audiobook (in multiple languages)

5. Free trial

6. Daily/weekly/monthly analysis report

7. Personal advice

8. Customization

9. Free sample/ test drive/ beta program

10. Early Bird Special Discount Offers(for a limited period)

11. Free/paid upgrades

12. Podcast

13. White Paper

14. Webinar

15. Bundling of products & services (for example, a combination of most popular services with the ones that barely gets noticed but remember that it should be a logical package which makes sense to the customer)

16. Online classes

17. Videos (in multiple languages)

18. Easy to buy from anywhere

19. Easy to deliver to anywhere

20. Multiple ways of accepting payment

21. Fast delivery of products

22. Adding different levels of service based on customer's size, frequency, or amount of purchase (for example: silver, gold, and platinum levels of service)

23. Better design with safety features

24. Free shipping

25. Add-on: Small day-to-day useful items related to business service

26. How-to guides

27. Articles/Blogs/Daily Tips

28. Deep knowledge of products and services

29. Free demonstration at client's place

30. Round-the-clock 24/7 customer support (phone/online/physical/live chat)

31. Easy to use even for a layman

32. Multiple ways to contact the company

33. Fast action on complaints (a standard timeframe to reply and act on complaints could become the company's USP)

34. Free installation and service

35. No-Haggle - No-Hassle pre and post sales process

36. Do-It-Yourself tutorials and kits for product repairs

37. Easily available cheap spare parts

38. Service centers located near to customer's place

39. Recognizing and rewarding outstanding customers when they buy certain levels from you (for example:

Platinum customers, Hall of Fame customers, Premium customers, etc.)

40. Beautiful, easy to handle, and protective packaging

41. Money-back guarantee

42. Any time unsubscribe option

43. Any time change of subscription plan

44. Instruction manual (in multiple languages) on how to use the product

45. Membership to a closed group on social media

46. Mobile App

47. Free games, toys

48. Analysis/Statistical tools like graphs, charts, diagrams, calculator on a website

49. Access to previous projects, research data, case studies, customers' feedback

50. Attention to detail

51. Special arrangements to meet, interact, and share experiences with other customers

52. Opportunities to work with other customers

53. Special training to customers from time to time

54. A personal touch in business communication and customer support service

55. Assigning a personal assistant, an account manager, a dedicated phone line, a dedicated customer care representative to every big client

56. Special features and discount coupons to loyal customers

57. Free Wi-Fi access

58. Knowledgebase & Resource library

59. Industry/Insider/Technical Reports

60. Very active on social media

61. Add-on plug-ins

62. In-built templates

63. Personalized customer experience

64. Comfortable seating, free entertainment, beverages and snacks, and public restrooms

65. Daycare center for employees' kids

66. Free meal for kids on weekends in a family restaurant

67. More quantity at the same price instead of giving a discount

68. Newsletter (Free/Paid)

69. Infographics

70. Sharing personal recipes to loyal customers

71. Free evaluation & quote in case of selling highly specialized or customized service

72. Interviews with industry experts

73. Transcripts of videos

74. Sharing a list of favourite resources to gather information

75. Sharing swipe file

76. Partnership with others that complement the company's products

77. Coaching/Consulting sessions (One-to-one/Face-to-face/Phone/Online)

78. Cheatsheets

79. Survey/Quiz/Test/Inspection along with suggestions for improvement

80. Checklist

81. Advanced technology and automation

82. Online tracking of vehicle/shipment/kids going to school

83. Pilot project/Proof of Concept/Prototype

84. Environment-friendly product material/infrastructure

85. Build an online customer community where customers from worldwide interact with each other and share ideas and information.

86. Maintain every customer's record.

87. Share progress reports of customers with them periodically.

If you're providing these values, you need to remember that customers may not value your free items since nothing is invested from their side. So, they have nothing to lose if they don't buy your product and services after using your freebies.

Providing Freebies could lead small businesses to bankruptcy.

That's why Freebies should play the role of **Incentives** instead of just giveaways.

The point is to let your customers work hard to get your Freebies. It's better to take something immediately from customers in exchange for your Freebies.

For example,

- Give a one-month free trial for software/subscription service if the customer gives credit card information and agrees to monthly billings once the trial period is over.

- Give a free online gift/sample in exchange for an email sign up OR online survey OR refer a friend.

- Give unexpected extra incentives to customers who spend a minimum purchase amount on their orders.

- Give discounts in exchange for commitment (for example, Letter of Intent).

- Ask your customers to participate in the quiz, interview, podcast, debate, contest, get together, conference, product launch, or an important event in exchange for Freebies.

- Ask for customer feedback/view/comment in exchange for Freebies. However, one should remember that Freebies should not influence the customer to say positive things. It should be unbiased views.

Feature Comparison Checklist

When you're selling a competitive product, you need to remember that your customers are always wandering in the market because they are selfish in nature.

They want to know:

- Which product is the best fit for them?

- Who provides maximum features?

- Who provides the highest discount?

In short, they want to know who can provide them the **best deal**.

If they're looking for a product that you have and when they come to your place, there is a chance that they don't buy immediately because they are still looking for better offers.

In such cases, one of the best ways to hold them and buy from you is by providing a **Feature Comparison Checklist**.

You can say to your prospective customers that why to waste time and energy in going to other places when they can compare all features of your products with your competitors' products by just sitting at your office.

If you're running an online business adding Features Comparison Checklist becomes much more important to stop your visitors from leaving your website.

A Checklist involves making a list of all features and benefits of yours and all your competitors in such a way that your customers can easily pick out the best points of yours and weak points of your competitors.

Product Features	Company A	Company B	Company C
Feature #1	✓	✓	✓
Feature #2	✓	X	✓
Feature #3	✓	X	✓
Feature #4	✓	X	X

A Checklist is one of the smart ways to answer your customer's objections. It's one of the best ways to show your superiority against your competitors. And very important if you're in an extremely competitive business and want to kill your competition mercilessly.

Now the question arises what different kind of features you can use for comparing your strengths with competitor's weaknesses?

Here are some ideas for you that you can use for comparison:

- How long are you in business as compared to your competitors?

- What is the size of the plant, office, employees?

- What is the length, weight, height of your product?

- How many resources do you have?

- Do you have a world-class laboratory?

- What is your annual turnover?

- How many years of experience do you have?

- What are the raw ingredients used in your product?

- What is the latest technology used in your product?

- What are the advanced processes that you have used in manufacturing?

- What is the maximum speed of your product and service?

- What is the cost of using your product per hour/kilometre/kilogram?

- What is the Maintenance Cost?

- What is the average life of your product and service?

- How long your product and service can perform without any break?

- What geographical advantage do you have? For example, where is your Research & Development/manufacturing unit/service centres located? Similarly, from where do you buy your raw ingredients?

- How fast can you deliver the product?

- How many followers do you have on social media?

- How many customers (local/national/international) do you have?

- How many awards have you won?

- What is the guarantee/warranty period?

- How good is the quality of your product in terms of percentage? For example: purity, freshness, natural, strength, anti-corrosion, waterproof, etc.

- How much power/fuel does your product consume? Is it environment friendly?

The 'Why Buy/Why Not Buy' Close

Take a sheet of paper and draw a line down the center.

On the left-hand side, write 'Why Buy' and on the right-hand side, write 'Why Not Buy'.

Why Buy	Why Not Buy

In the left column, you give all the reasons why the prospect should buy your product today.

Now you go to the right column.

You start this list by saying, "One of the problems you mentioned is…" Here you mention the 'major' objection (only one) that prospect raised during the presentation.

Then you remain quiet and let your prospect list the other reasons why he should not buy your product.

Now you add the totals on both sides.

If you've played smartly, you will have far more 'Why Buy' reasons than 'Why Not Buy' reasons.

And then you can say to your prospective customer, "Reasons for buying my product are much more than not buying. So, why not close the deal today as I've presented all my points very logically and absolutely fairly?"

The Alternative-Choice Closing Questions

This technique is used when the prospect is bit confused or making a delay in giving the order.

It's our job to assist our customers in buying our products. We have to find out all their objections, prepare answers to these objections, and even then also if customers are trying to procrastinate, we have to move them towards closing the deal very smoothly.

Sometimes, a Closing Question is enough to change customer's focus towards Closing. Like, in the case of asking **Alternative-Choice Closing Questions,** which is based on the Principle of Contrast. The prospect is asked to choose between two options in the confirming process.

Just, for example, I'm sharing three ways to use Alternative-Choice Closing Questions. There could be many ways to ask such questions, depending on how creative you are.

1) Closing Questions to Divert Prospect's Focus on the Type of Model

- "Would you rather take the large or medium size?"

- "Would you like the advanced version or the regular?"

- "Would you prefer the blue one or the purple one?"

2) Closing Questions to Divert Prospect's Focus on the Mode of Delivery

- "Would you like to take it with you, or should we send it out?"

- "Shall I ask the company to ship it as soon as possible, or would two weeks be better?"

- "Are you in a rush, or would Wednesday be all right?"

3) Closing Questions to Divert Prospect's Focus on the Billing Process

- "Do you want it billed in your name or your wife's name?"

- "Would you like to have your own bank finance this, or would you like to go with us?"

- "Would you want to make a large deposit initially so that monthly deposits are smaller, or would you go with a small deposit and larger monthly deposits?"

- "Do you want us to use your credit card, or are you going to pay by cash?"

- "Would you prefer that we send the billing to your office or your factory address?"

In the last 2-3 volumes, I've shared many techniques based on the Principle of Contrast. It is one of my favourite principles of Persuasion because if applied correctly, timely, and precisely it could help you in showing your superiority against your competition.

Many times people don't value good things until they see how bad the world is.

Likewise, many customers don't value good companies, products, offers, services, employees... until they see what terrible things are available in the market.

Now the question comes should we keep waiting... hoping that one day customers will find out themselves how good our products are and how bad our competitors' products are.

Well, I don't think so.

Being a Master Persuader, it's my job to reach out to my prospective customers.

Being a Master Persuader, it's my job to communicate with my prospective customers.

Being a Master Persuader, it's my job to listen to the problems of my prospective customers.

Being a Master Persuader, it's my job to tell how my products and services are going to change the lives of my prospective customers.

And being a Master Persuader, it's my job to kick out my competitors from the minds of my prospective customers.

Sometimes I use a direct approach. And sometimes, I use indirect, subliminal, covert approach.

But I can't wait, hoping that one day my prospective customers will surely find out what is right and wrong for them.

I can't leave my customers to procrastinate.

If I believe in the quality of my products and services... if I believe my products and services are going to change the lives of my customers forever... if I believe I'm much better than my competition... then it's my duty to use all sorts of ethical Persuasion techniques to convert my prospects into lifelong happy customers.

VOLUME - XI

Let me start this volume by taking a short test on your shopping IQ.

Suppose you go to a famous designer store to buy a new dress for your birthday party. After exploring 20-25 dresses, you finally choose two dresses from which you have to buy one.

But there is one problem.

Dress A is perfectly fit in size... price is according to your budget... but not so stylish.

Whereas Dress B is very stylish... price is according to your budget... available in your favourite colour... but it's slightly tight in fit.

Now you're confused. You've already spent two hours in the store. You like both these dresses and want to buy one of them. But both have one major drawback, which is making it difficult for you to make a decision.

Since the positives and negatives balanced each other, both options are looking equally good to you.

Sometimes you decide to go with Dress A. Other times you decide to go with Dress B.

Your mind is completely paralyzed.

The salesperson, who is showing you all these dresses for the last two hours, also wants to close the deal.

To close it fast, he decides to apply a technique on you, which could help you in making a buying decision.

He suggests one more dress for you which he forgets to show you earlier as it has newly arrived in the store. This Dress C is very stylish... size is okay... available in your favourite colour... but the price is almost double of Dress A and B.

Now, what will you do?

Here's one possible scenario.

Before Dress C, you were comparing Dress A with Dress B. There is a significant difference between these two in terms of style, size, and colour.

But when the salesperson showed you Dress C, you started comparing Dress C with B because both of them are quite similar in terms of style and colour. However, Dress B is slightly tight in size, and Dress C is out of your budget.

Due to the high price of Dress C, you now find Dress B (which is quite similar to Dress C) a great deal if you compromise with the size.

And since nobody wants to miss a great deal, you finally buy Dress B.

After buying this dress, you praise yourself for making a smart decision but, it's actually the salesperson who should get credit for closing the deal because of his use of a Persuasion technique called...

Decoy Effect

In the above example, the asymmetry of the third dress reframed your choice. It shifts the comparison from the first two dresses to the third dress and the dress from the first two, which is most similar to the third dress.

This process is called the Decoy Effect.

The Decoy Effect is also called the Attraction Effect or Asymmetric Dominance Effect.

The Decoy Effect is a technique of Influence and Persuasion whereby people are influenced to make a specific change in preference between two options when also presented with a third option that is asymmetrically dominated.

When there are only two options, people tend to make decisions according to their personal preferences. But the presence of an asymmetrically dominated option increases the chances of people preferring the dominated option.

This addition of the third option could be unintentional, but in marketing, generally, it is added intentionally to influence customer's decisions.

The third option is asymmetrically dominated when it is inferior in all respects to the first option, but when you compare the third option with the second option, it is inferior in some respects and superior in others. If the third option fulfills this condition, then it's called a **Decoy**.

However, it is not necessary that Decoy can be used only between two options. It can be more than two options. And it can be more than one Decoy.

The Decoy Effect is used by marketers to offer either a low-quality, or low-quantity, or overly-priced product alongside with the target product that they really want you to buy.

In this way, the Decoy is perceived as a similar but less attractive product that ultimately increases the attraction of the target product. That is why the Decoy Effect is also called the Attraction Effect.

The objective of Decoys is to help in increasing the sales of the target product by sacrificing their own worth. Decoys are great team players. They are not intended to sell.

They are used to nudge customers away from the competitors and towards the target product that is usually the more expensive or profitable option.

The irony is, in comparison with Decoy and other competitors, the target product is now presented as the best deal in terms of an increase in perceived value (quality, quantity, extra features, etc.).

Why Marketers Use Decoys?

Because Marketers know that customers are self-centered... always looking for the best for the least.

It's a human tendency to buy cheaper versions so that people can save their hard-earned money as much as possible.

On one side, if customers are given two or more options in terms of price, they generally go for lower price versions, especially in cases where they are trying a new product... or in cases where they are still having some doubt about the product or company capabilities.

On the other side, smart marketers always want to sell their highest-priced products simply because it brings more revenue to the company.

To accomplish this objective, these marketers keep trying new strategies that could influence the customer's mind to go for a higher version without any major push.

The Decoy Effect is one of such techniques based on the Principle of Contrast through which customer is easily persuaded to buy the target product that the company wants to sell the most... even if the customer is presented with multiple choices.

In this way, salespeople easily sell what they want to sell without looking desperate or pushy in the eyes of the customer.

How the *Decoy Effect* Works?

There are a few steps that marketers follow for applying the Decoy Effect technique in their business to sell their most expensive products and services:

1) Choose a target product that you want to sell the most. Generally, the target product is the most expensive or the most profitable.

2) This target product should have more features and benefits than any of your other products. And because of this reason, it should be the highest-priced item on your list.

3) At least two options should be available to customers to buy what suits them most.

4) Measure how many orders you are getting for the target product every day.

5) Now add a Decoy, as another option in your products.

6) While adding the Decoy, you need to remember that the objective is to make this Decoy asymmetrically dominated by your target product in order to make the target product more attractive in the customer's mind.

7) Keep the options limited (not more than 5) to increase the effectiveness of the technique. Greater choice complexity increases anxiety and therefore hinders the decision-making process.

Here's an example of how the Decoy Effect works:

Suppose you're selling a kitchen utensil in two sizes:

Option A: Small size @ $15.

Option B: Large size @ $27.

As we have seen, people generally buy low-cost items unless they see a huge value in buying the expensive version.

So, most of the customers in your shop choose Option A.

But to bring more revenue, you desperately want people to buy the higher-priced item.

In my e-book 'Become A Master of Closing Sales,' I talked about how customers continuously compare the value of your product with their hard-earned money needed to pay to get it.

So, if you want to sell your larger-size product more, **you have to increase its perceived value in the minds of customers.**

Here's how you do it.

At present, the customer has only two options – the smallest-size product (Option A) and the largest-size product (Option B).

But now you deliberately add an Option C – a medium-size product @ $25.

Let's see what happens…

Earlier the customer was comparing Option B with Option A. Both of them are quite different in size.

But now the same customer starts comparing Option B with Option C and finds that for just $2 extra, she is getting the much larger size of your product… which is a great deal.

Option C is nothing but a Decoy employed by you to increase the sales of your target product, that is, Option B.

So, what will happen finally by adding this Decoy?

First, it reduces the sales of Option A.

Second, it increases the sales of Option B.

And what about Option C?

Don't worry! Nobody will buy Option C because people are smart, not stupid.

It is called the Decoy Effect in which the medium-size product (Option C) is asymmetrically dominated by the largest-size product (Option B).

The Decoy Effect encouraged your customers to go for the highest-priced option (Option B). People's cognitive biases skewed its value. Customers see a good increase in value in terms of money between medium and large size.

As I said earlier, Decoys are great team players who sacrifice their own worth to increase the value of the target product that you actually want to sell.

So, next time you go to the market or visit an online store and get excited to see a new option added by a brand… check carefully; whether that new option is added to give you more choices or it is just a **strategically placed Decoy** to influence you to buy a target option which the brand wants to sell the most.

Here are some examples of how marketers use Decoy to sell their target products.

This example is from the subscription business…

Suppose you're running a magazine publishing company selling subscription in two ways:

Option A: Digital subscription @ $130.

Option B: Digital + Print subscription @ $210.

As we've seen, people generally tend to go for lower price options if there is a vast difference in the prices of two options. So you may be also facing the same problem; that is, most people are buying only Digital subscriptions (Option A).

But you want to increase the revenue of the company for which it's important to sell the higher-priced item (Option B).

In order to increase the revenue, you decide to influence your customers towards Option B by increasing its value in the minds of customers.

How?

By bringing Decoy in the form of Option C.

What is Option C?

Option C is the print edition of your magazine @ $195.

Before this Decoy, the customer was comparing your Option B with Option A and buying the latter one because of the huge difference in prices.

But now, after the addition of Decoy (Option C), the customer gets the opportunity to compare the price of Option B with Option C and decides to buy the former one because the customer is getting both print and digital edition by just paying $15 extra.

In this way, you succeed in increasing the sales of Digital + Print subscriptions, your target product.

The reason for adding this Decoy is to shift the customer's focus from comparison between Option A and B to a comparison between Option B and C.

The point is the customer always wants the best deal available in the market, and you are taking advantage of this human nature.

Ironically, the more penny savers are the people… the more smart spenders are the people… the more chances are that they get seduced by the best deals. But actually, they are buying those items that companies want to sell the most to make more money.

Of course, by adding Decoy, there are chances of reducing the sales of Digital edition, but there are equal or more chances of increasing the sales of your highest-priced edition.

Let me explain arithmetically...

Suppose before adding Decoy (Option C), out of every 100 orders, you were getting 60 orders of Option A and 40 orders of Option B.

But after adding the Decoy, the sale of your Digital edition is reduced to 40 orders, and the sale of Digital+Print edition is increased to 60 orders, and there is no order for the Print edition.

So, now check yourself whether your revenue is reduced or increased and by how much.

Before adding Decoy (Option C):

Revenue of Option A: $130 X 60 = $7,800.

Revenue of Option B: $210 X 40 = $8,400.

Total Revenue: $7,800 + $8,400 = $16,200.

After adding Decoy (Option C):

Revenue of Option A: $130 X 40 = $5,200.

Revenue of Option B: $210 X 60 = $12,600.

Total Revenue: $5,200 + $12,600 = $17,800.

Total increase in Revenue after adding Decoy: $17,800 - $16,200 = $1,600 (9.9%).

In this way, you can keep testing different offers and check yourself what is working and what is not working.

In some cases, I have seen that marketers keep the Decoy's price the same as the target product's price. Like in the above example, you keep the price of Option C @ $210 instead of $195.

Of course, it may further increase the sales of the target product (Option B), but it also makes the customer more suspicious that why the company is keeping the same price of Option B and C? Is it a mistake or deliberately done?

Let's take another example. It's in the computer industry.

Suppose you want to buy a pen drive. You go to a nearby shop. Only two brands are available in that shop.

Brand A has four varieties according to storage capacity.

16 GB @ $5

32 GB @ $8

64 GB @ $12

128 GB @ $20

Brand B has only one variety according to storage capacity.

64 GB @ $17

Brand B is expensive because it's an old and famous brand.

Whereas, Brand A is a comparatively newer brand with less advertising. People are not too familiar with this brand.

You think that for just $3 extra (as compared to Brand B), you're getting double storage in Brand A even though you haven't heard about this brand before.

So, the chances are that:

1)   You ignore the popularity of the brand and buy Brand A - 128 GB pen drive.

2)   Or if in case you don't need 128 GB, then also there are higher chances that you again buy 64 GB pen drive of Brand A because it is $5 cheaper than Brand B.

The question is, why only one variety of Brand B was available in the shop despite being so popular?

Here are some reasons:

First, because of only one variety available in Brand B, it becomes easy for you to compare two brands – those varieties which are very similar to each other.

Second, if more varieties are added in Brand B, then you spend more time in product comparison that could delay your buying decision.

Third, generally, retail stores get a low margin on popular brands. The reason is these brands spend heavily on marketing and advertising so that people prefer their products as compared to other local or less advertised products when they go shopping.

That's why, like in the above example, retail stores keep only limited models of the famous brand because they are getting low margins… and more models of less popular brands because they are getting higher margins.

But the question is, why is there any need to keep a famous brand in retail stores if they get lower margins?

Here are some reasons:

1.   People want to have choices before making a buying decision. They want to enjoy their shopping experience. By not providing 'choice' is a direct threat to their freedom.

2.   Big brand names attract customers to retail stores. If you keep only local products, it reduces traffic on your website and physical store.

3.   By keeping a model of a famous brand which has some shortcoming (for example, high price, inferior quality, less features, lower quantity, etc.) automatically increases the value of your local product model, which is very similar to that famous brand model but is a better option in terms of quality, quantity, features, price, etc.

The point is, this model of the famous brand is strategically used to act as a Decoy to sell the target product, in which you're making higher profits.

Let's take one more example, this time from Politics.

Suppose you're contesting an election for the post of President in your industry association.

You're young, post-graduate, popular, and also Ex-Vice President of the Association.

Whereas, your opponent is old, graduate, popular, and two times Ex-Vice President of the Association.

Since both you and your opponent have some strong qualities, it's becoming difficult for members to decide whom they should vote for?

If members want a young leader who is highly qualified, then you're a preferred choice.

And if members want a highly experienced leader, then your opponent is a preferred choice.

While members still thinking about whom they should vote for, one more member applies to contest the election for the same post.

The third candidate is young, post-graduate, but never served earlier as Vice President, and also low in popularity.

Now things changed dramatically. Because of this third candidate, who is also young and highly qualified but lacks two other important attributes, members get attracted to you.

The reason is the same members who were comparing you with the second candidate have now started comparing you with the third candidate because of similarities between you and the third candidate.

The third candidate, who is actually a Decoy, is asymmetrically dominated by you. This Decoy Effect has increased your value in the minds of members.

Here's an example of how Decoys help in selling bundle products.

Suppose the main product is priced @ $500, and the accessory is priced @ $100, but the bundle of main product and accessory is priced @ $525.

In this case, both standalone main product and accessory act as Decoy to drive the sale of bundled products.

Marketers use Decoy quite often in a real estate business.

Before showing you a perfect house according to your needs, a real estate agent shows you:

- An old or abandoned house

- Or an expensive house which is out of your budget

- Or a house which is quite far from your desired location

The objective of showing such houses is to increase the value of the target house that the real estate agent actually wants to rent you. It may have some shortcomings but not as big as what you just saw in a decoy house.

Why Are Decoys So Effective?

Here are some reasons why Decoys are so effective:

- Decoys change how customers value the target product.

- The key function of Decoys is not only to make the target product look good but to draw attention to it.

- Decoys save customers time, make them happy, and help them make safe decisions.

- Decoys reframe the decision around qualities that are easy to compare and away from qualities that are difficult to compare.

- Decoys help in making quick decisions, especially when the customer is confused with multiple choices and not able to decide what to buy. When there are multiple choices, the customer feels anxiety. To reduce this anxiety, the customer tries to simplify the buying process by considering only one or two key attributes to make a fast decision.

- Decoys help in making stress-free decisions. People feel they are making rational, informed decisions.

- Decoys reduce the salesperson's efforts to push customer for the order.

- Having Decoys to make the target product perceived as the smartest option can significantly impact customers' choices even if they have never heard about that brand before.

- Comparison with Decoys offers customers an easy justification for an otherwise random decision. Because of Decoys, now customers have a readymade reason to explain their preferences.

- Without a Decoy, it's difficult to understand the importance of a product's feature in terms of monetary value. Decoy helps customers in realizing the worth of that feature.

- Decoys change the focus of customers from a competitor's product to the target product.

- Decoys influence how customers think about their decisions.

- Generally, Decoys force customers to focus only on ONE attribute instead of multiple aspects. And it's quite obvious that when customer focuses only on one attribute, the chances of getting distracted due to other features get diminished. Ultimately, the customer is most likely to make a buying decision. And this is what every marketer wants.

- Adding a Decoy makes a customer more likely to judge the product not on price but on quality or quantity or performance or whatever she thinks is the most important attribute… or suits her personality the most… or reflects her own identity…

- Decoys appeal to the customer's desire to avoid loss. Loss Aversion is so strong that $100 feels twice as expensive when it's a loss instead of gain.

One question asked in my sales trainings is why marketers use a similar product for Decoy?

It's because people are not too capable of comparing things that are very different from each other and have very distinct applications or advantages.

On the contrary, when people compare things that are quite similar to each other, even a minor difference can be clearly seen that could influence their buying decision.

Generally, a Decoy is a slightly lower priced but with a much lower quality product. Or a Decoy is a much higher priced with a slightly higher quality product.

However, it's not only quality and price; in fact, there are many factors on which Decoys are compared with the target product.

Here are some of those:

- Quantity of items received at the same price

- Quantity and type of items in a combo offer. For example, a restaurant uses a Decoy in menu with three options: a) Burger @ $5 b) Burger + Cold Drink (medium size) @ $8 c) Burger + Cold drink (large size) + French Fries @ $10

- Duration of subscription

- Format of subscription

- Discount

- Quantity of free Bonus/Accessories

- Size (weight, height, length, and breadth) of the product

- Colour, design, style of product

- Speed and Storage capacity (comparing Decoys on this factor is common in computer and electronics store)

- Number of cups served (by a coffee maker machine)

- Power consumption, Battery life

- And many more…

How to Measure the Effectiveness of Decoy?

It's crucial to check the effectiveness of Decoy to know whether it's helping you in selling your target product or not.

Here are some ways to measure the effectiveness of Decoy:

- By comparing the frequency of liking or choosing the target product instead of other products in the presence and absence of Decoy.

- By comparing the readiness of customers to pay for the target product instead of other products in the presence and absence of Decoy.

- By comparing the number of increased sales in the presence and absence of Decoy.

- By comparing the number of missed sales in the presence and absence of Decoy. Missed sales should be counted for all products and not just the target product.

- By noticing how many times customer easily identifies that you have deliberately put Decoy to sell your target product.

Some Important Points Related to the

Decoy Effect

1)　Since some marketers keep the price of Decoy and target product same it's possible that customer gets suspicious of the same price and doesn't buy anything.

To avoid such problems, marketers should put some conditions to get the target product at the same price as Decoy.

For example, if a print newspaper is offering 5 days subscription per week (Decoy) @ $10 and 7 days subscription per week (Target Product) again @ $10, then the customer may get suspicious how two different subscriptions can be offered at the same price when one subscription has a big advantage over the other.

In such cases, companies put the condition, like, to get 7 days subscription per week @ $10, the customer needs to pay by cash only, OR the customer needs to pay one month in advance, OR the customer needs to pay by credit card.

The point is companies have to provide a logical reason if they are offering two options at the same price, even if it's apparent that one option has a big advantage over the other.

2)   Relativity is the key element in the Decoy Effect. Our brains are programmed in such a way that we are not good at judging absolute values. That's why marketers use Decoys to increase the value of the target product in our mind.

For example, if you're selling an expensive item, you need to justify its value to the customer. Moreover, when you're selling standalone products, it's not easy for customers to understand its value.

But when you compare your expensive product's features and benefits with inferior products, services, and offers… customers realize why this product is more expensive than others available in the market.

However, still, they may go for cheaper options for various reasons. Remember, customers don't want the best product with the most features and benefits. They want the best deals available in the market. They are seduced by the great deals.

That's why marketers use Decoys, for example, offering inferior products and services at a slightly lower price, so that customers now get attracted to your expensive product instead of buying cheaper items.

Fear of missing out on great deals is so powerful that customers may ready to spend more money even if they have to borrow from someone.

3) Sometimes big brands are not ready to use inferior products as Decoys because they are afraid it may hurt their reputation in the market.

However, they want to use Decoys to increase the value of their expensive products and to attract new customers who haven't used their products before.

To counter this problem, they set up a new low-value brand with a different name. The objective is to sell cheaper and inferior products that act as Decoys, but without letting customers know that this new brand is actually their sister company.

4) Decoy doesn't need to be always an inferior product whose job is to help to sell the highest-priced or most profitable product. A Decoy can be the highest-priced item because of which a moderately priced item looks like a bargain.

How to Combat the *Decoy Effect?*

The Decoy Effect takes advantage of your subconscious tendencies to act irrationally. Your own greediness makes you fall victim to the Decoy Effect.

Simply because your focus shifts from your basic needs to getting the maximum number of features in the least amount of money.

Ultimately, it results in spending more money from your pocket than you actually planned to spend.

Here are some tips to combat the Decoy Effect:

- Whenever you're shopping, always be conscious of the Decoy Effect.

- Don't make an impulsive decision. Instead, think about the choices you're making.

- Focus on exactly what you want and how much you want.

- Calculate and compare the cost of the product per unit.

- Focus on the initial two items that are quite different from each other in attributes like features, price, quantity, format, etc. For example, Small vs. Large size; Cheap vs. Expensive; Basic vs. Advanced; Online vs. Physical.

- Be aware that if there are three or more options, there are chances that one of the options is used as a Decoy.

Now let's discuss another technique based on the Principle of Contrast.

Reverse Psychology

(Don't read further if you're satisfied with your Sales)

You must have seen a picture having a big red button in the middle and above it is written:

DO NOT PRESS

It is based on the Reverse Psychology technique that in order to persuade highly skeptical people, we need to request them to do the opposite of what we actually desired.

The Reverse Psychology technique, also called 'Anti-Marketing' or 'Don't buy my product,' is based on **Reactance theory,** according to which many people have a negative approach towards direct and forcefully applied instruction, suggestion, command, pitch, and will do the opposite of what you ask them to do.

According to Reactance theory:

People hate being told to follow the rules.

People hate being told to do what they don't want to do.

People hate being controlled or manipulated.

And people hate being sold to products and services.

In short, people have natural resistance whenever they feel their freedom of choice is taken away, or their options are being limited.

Ironically, when the Reverse Psychology technique is applied, people think they are doing the opposite of what you want them to do, and in this way, they are teasing you... rejecting you... insulting you... downgrading you... but in actual they are doing exactly what you wanted them to do.

However, the Reverse Psychology technique is not applied to everyone. Many people are agreeable and compliant by nature.

They welcome new suggestions.

They are inclined to agree to requests.

They accept changes.

They are open-minded.

The Reverse Psychology technique is applied particularly to those who show the following characteristics:

- People who are mostly resistant to sales pitches and promotional offers.

- People who are skeptical or pessimistic by nature

- People who hate bragging

- People who don't believe others and question their sincerity

- People who don't easily mix up with strangers

- People who think their freedom is restricted by others (for example, children think their freedom is restricted by their parents and try to do those things which their parents don't allow them to do)

To deal with such people, many professionals use Reverse Psychology techniques ethically in their respective trade. For example:

Therapists use Reverse Psychology techniques to treat resistant patients.

Prosecutors use Reverse Psychology to pull out confessions from criminals.

Advertisers use Reverse Psychology to take the attention of readers.

Salespeople use Reverse Psychology to close deals faster.

Here are some examples of how people use Reverse Psychology in their daily lives:

How a mother uses Reverse Psychology technique on her child:

"I was going to give you ice cream after homework, but I don't think you're able to finish it fast."

How a tennis coach uses Reverse Psychology on a recently enrolled trainee:

"I think you've some qualities of becoming a great tennis player. But you lack the self-discipline to wake up early in the morning and practice for a few hours every day. So, it's better to leave tennis for some time and just focus on your studies, friends, and parties. You have a whole life to learn tennis."

How a therapist uses Reverse Psychology on her patient:

"Every night before sleeping, you're allowed to have negative thoughts. Just think only negative that time."

Advantages of Reverse Psychology

Reverse Psychology should not be a part of daily communication. It should be used when you find that people are reluctant to follow your requests.

If you start using Reverse Psychology frequently, it starts losing its effectiveness.

Reverse Psychology helps in multiple ways:

- Gets immediate attention

- Lowers resistance

- Increases believability

- Since it's unexpected, so the person is not prepared for how to counter it.

- Encourages others to take your challenge.

- Makes your products and services more desirable.

- Builds your image as non-pushy.

How to Apply Reverse Psychology?

Here are some ideas about how to apply Reverse Psychology:

- Accept your fault.

- Make fun of yourself.

- Say, "This is not for you."

- Instruct not to do what you want them to do.

- Put restrictions on people's freedom of choice.

- Ban crucial information.

- Make your products and services a forbidden fruit that people want to eat but not allowed to eat unless they fulfil certain conditions.

- Challenge others to prove you wrong by performing better.

- Reinforce the customer's autonomy by using phrases like "Whatever you decide is fine with me. After all, it's your choice. You have to use that product. Not me."

Reverse Psychology in Sales, Marketing & Advertising

Reverse Psychology could be very effective in Sales, Marketing, and Advertising if you want to sell to tough customers.

Many skeptical people hate sales guys, advertising, and promotional events... don't agree with big claims... and don't buy the overly pitched product even if it's a perfect fit for them.

To persuade such people, marketers use Reverse Psychology in their promotions smartly, subtly, and sometimes sarcastically.

Here are some headlines that used Reverse Psychology to influence and persuade people.

- Warning! Do Not Read This Unless You Are Already Rich!

- Do Not Call

- Don't Buy This Jacket

- Do Not Lick This Page

- Don't Join The Army. Don't Become A Better You.

- Give Her No Applause. Don't Dance To The Song At All.

- We Could Fill This Page With Interesting Information About Our Research Company, But Research Indicates You Wouldn't Read It.

- We Are No.2. We Are Trying Harder.

- For More Information on Lung Cancer, Keep Smoking

- Smart Critiques. Stupid Creates. Be Stupid.

- Read this, you piece of shit!

- The Dumbest Guy In High School Just Got A Boat

- A Warm Welcome To Death (no smoking campaign)

- We Like Our Clients Because Of Their Money. They Like Us Because Of Our Honesty.

- The Last Thing We Want To Do Is Sell You A Copier

- Don't Buy Our Sugar-Free Cookie Dough. We Wouldn't Want You To Accidentally Low Weight.

- Doughnuts Are Bad For You

- This Advertisement Is Probably Not For You.

- Read Something Else Because Most People Don't Get It.

Here are lines of some famous advertisements which used Reverse Psychology technique to take immediate attention of people:

· **Read this you piece of shit!**

If you're offended by this advertisement you should be.

Nobody should be treated like this.

Yet, unfortunately there are millions of people around the world who
are...
....

There are still over 100 million slaves in the world. Each one probably has a story as pain-filled as these.

Anti Slavery International campaigns for the abolition of slavery. We know that it's only by making the facts of these people's lives known and by bringing slavery out into the open that we'll ever destroy
it..

· "Forget it, Heinz," the experts told me. "It just won't sell here."

They were talking about the Mercedes-Benz 190
Diesel -- a car that is owned and driven daily by
over 500,000 people overseas.

Doughnuts are bad for you.

So are cream cakes, lie-ins and loud rock music.

So is sugar. If you take it in your tea, stop immediately. If
you take two sugars in your tea, obviously you are trying to
commit suicide and it's a cry for help. Don't do it. Your life
is
precious...
....

At Krispy Kreme, we think the key to life, by which we
mean eating doughnuts, is balance. Sure, if you eat them
morning, noon, and night and they are brought directly to
your armchair, then that would be bad. But then if you've
never felt the pleasure of eating a delicious fluffy original
gazed doughnut hot off the line and, heaven forbid, you get
stuck by lightning, well surely that would be really bad.
Really really bad.

Quite frankly, the American Express is not
for everyone. And not everyone who applies
for Card membership is approved.

However, because we believe you will benefit
from Card Membership, I've enclosed a special
invitation for you to apply for the most honoured

and prestigious financial instrument available to people who travel, vacation, and entertain.

·   We would like you to try Fanta's new taste, deliciously orange. Yes, right now!

Just tear off a piece of this page, pop in your mouth & enjoy a Fanta by tasting this Ad!

·   **A Few Encouraging Words For The Totally Incompetent**

It's perfectly alright to be incompetent for hours on end.

I am. And so is everyone I know.

Of course, being of this persuasion, I shall never be able to afford a bottle of Beck's Beer. Which is why the people who sell Beck's Beer got me to write this ad ....There, feel better now, don't you? After all, the price of a bottle of Beck's Beer may well be so high as to be audible only to highly-trained bats, but at least you're not the only one who'll be never able to afford it.

·   Let me explain. I don't care whether your child is six years old or twenty – boy or girl – in grade school, high school, or college. It makes no difference how badly that child is doing in school today – how difficult it is for him to concentrate... how poor his memory maybe... how much a prisoner he is of crippling mental habits... how terrified he may be of mathematics, or grammar, or social studies, or even the hardest science course.

· To The Man Who Will Settle For Nothing Less Than The Presidency of His Firm

And who is willing to make the incredible sacrifices necessary to get there in the shortest possible time.

Here is the most realistic handbook ever written for you – and you alone.

This is a private advertisement.

It is not meant for ninety nine men out of every hundred. These men do not have the drive – the impossible pride – the absolute compulsion to succeed that this advertisement demands...

Here is one example of how I used Reverse Psychology partially in one of my emails.

....

Headline: **How to fire good employees and destroy your business?**

Today I'll talk about the *Lalaism* culture that still prevails in many traditional companies.

Ironically, business owners of many *Lala* companies feel very proud of exploiting their employees, sucking their blood in the name of hard work, not providing a healthy environment, and enough salary (and incentives) just for the sake of saving money to make more profits.

They don't want to recognize the importance of the human resource, the most important asset in any company.

Lalaism culture badly affects the mental health of employees to the level that they quit their job.

No company can survive for long, where hardworking employees are not treated well.

Where there is incompetence at the top level, you will find *Lalaism* culture deeply rooted in their company.

If you like *Lalaism* culture and want to promote it inside your company, then here are a few tips on how to fire good employees and destroy your business without dirtying your hands...

- Try to find out stupid mistakes that could be easily corrected by softwares, but you want your good employees to do it manually in order to keep them engaged in some work no matter how useless it is. For example: calculations in MIS reports, grammar mistakes, keeping records of all physical bills for reimbursement, admin work, etc.

- Insult good employees in front of juniors and interns to show your bossism.

- Make such arrangements where you and your bootlicker colleagues get all the credit instead of deserving people.

- Never organize training and development activities for good employees who can become better in their skills. You need to be insecure and remember that after getting trained, they might leave your company.

- Award and encourage those employees who blindly follow the rules of the company and never question you and other authorities.

- And penalise those employees who apply creative and out-of-box-thinking and in this process make some mistakes... who question you... who argue with you... and who want to change company rules if they find any flaws.

- Whenever there is an increment time... start talking about recession, company losses, losing some big deals, the slow response in the market, etc.

- Assign a lot of powers to your bootlicker employees by creating an impression that they are very loyal to the company or have devoted many years of their life in your company. However, you need to be careful that you don't talk about their incompetence and poor performance.

- Conduct useless meetings daily where you talk about all those things like politics, sports, movies which have nothing to do with your business. Since good employees have productive habits, like completing work on time, they will automatically stay late in the office to finish urgent work.

- Assign your favourite bureaucrats to keep interfering with the good employees' work. Your objective is to make them frustrated without coming into the picture. Your image will always remain clean & clear.

- Organize parties and family events and make it compulsory for everyone to attend. Tell your pet subordinates to make a note who is skipping. Now you get a reason for not paying attention and listening to some people inside your office.

- Create such panic situations where your good employees desperately need your favours. This requires some genius manipulation from your side. And in return for your favours, you can demand their blood, toil, tears, and sweat.

If you're already doing things like these in your business, then Congratulations! You are going to destroy your company very soon.

Keep up the good work!

A Special Note

Just like other Persuasion techniques, Reverse Psychology can be referred to as either ethical or unethical depending on the intention of the persuader.

For example, if marketers are using the Reverse Psychology technique or Decoy Effect just for the sake of selling without understanding the needs, desires, and personalities of their customers... then, of course, it's unethical.

But if marketers really believe that products could change people's lives, then I think these marketers should apply such tactics as we know that:

People procrastinate.

People have different personalities and communication styles.

People are penny-savers... they don't want to lose their hard-earned money, and that's why they compromise with cheap or basic items... and later realize their mistake.

People are easily attracted to discount offers.

People, in general, buy heavily advertised items even if those products are poor in quality.

People don't buy from strangers. Instead, they are looking for references.

Very few people like to try new products and services. And some of those want it for free.

It's not easy for small businesses to beat giant companies.

Because of these reasons (and many more), we have to think out-of-the-box. We need to develop our creative skills. We need to explore unconventional ideas.

When we don't have enough money and resources to fight with old and big players... we need to be much more effective, creative, and competent than our competitors.

VOLUME - XII

I created this course so that small business owners, self-employed professionals, and sales & marketing professionals could learn the principles and techniques of Persuasion that I used to teach in my in-house and public workshops.

This is because many times, I received inquiries from people that they can't afford my expensive in-house trainings at their premises, or they can't leave their work and come to the city where I generally conduct my public workshops.

The second reason was I wanted to reach people globally since my customers are from various industries irrespective of age, gender, geography, and occupation.

In this issue, I would like to answer some common questions that my participants used to ask in my workshops.

Before I talk about this, let me make myself clear. Since you're studying this course, no matter you're a business owner or a self-employed professional or an employee working for someone else, I assume you aspire to become rich.

Q) How can an ordinary person become rich?

Before I answer this question, I recommend you reading three classic books that have influenced millions of people, including me.

The first book is *Think and Grow Rich*, written by Napoleon Hill. Although there are controversies regarding the author of the book, the book is absolutely a goldmine. It was perhaps the first book that told wealth is directly related to how we think.

This single book brought a revolution in America by revealing the secrets of the wealthiest people of the early 20th century. This book changed the whole concept of becoming rich.

Andrew Carnegie, considered as one of the richest men of all time, assigned a project to Napoleon Hill to interview wealthy people in America like Henry Ford, Thomas Edison, Alexander Graham Bell to find out their secrets behind their success.

He wrote *Think and Grow Rich* and *Laws of Success* based on that research.

Earlier, people used to assume that most rich people inherited their money. The rich were rich because of 'old' money.

But this book changed the whole concept of becoming rich.

As the title suggests, becoming rich depends on your MINDSET. Mastering your money has more to do with psychology and mindset than anything else.

Here's a quote from the book which became immensely popular:

"Whatever the mind can conceive and believe, it can achieve."

So, it's what you THINK that matters the most in becoming rich.

First of all, to become rich, you must have a burning desire for what do you want in life.

Second, you must know and follow the method of transforming that desire into its material counterpart.

But it's not as easy as it sounds.

You have to cultivate the power of imagination to make existing things better or to create completely new things.

You have to deal with your basic fears, especially fear of criticism and poverty.

You need to develop an unshakable belief in yourself that you can achieve your burning desire in a specific period.

In short, this book suggests anyone can become RICH if he or she knows how to control the process of their thinking.

Now, I come to the second book that has again influenced millions of people worldwide.

It's *Rich Dad Poor Dad*, written by Robert Kiyosaki.

This book is considered as one of the best personal finance books in the world.

I recommend reading all three books of the Rich Dad Poor Dad series, especially the second, *Cashflow Quadrant*, which explained the difference between four classes based on how they make their livelihood.

These four classes are:

1. Employee

2. Self-employed (and small business owner)

3. Business owner (big)

4. Investor

An Employee works for the system. A Self-employed is the system. A Business owner creates, owns, and controls the system. An Investor invests money into the system.

Again *Rich Dad Poor Dad* book tells us that anybody can become rich if they learn and follow how Rich people work every day.

The book talks about the author's educated dad, whom he considers POOR, and his friend's businessman dad, whom he considers RICH.

The book explains the difference between rich and poor, based on their daily habits, work, and values. For example:

- Rich people know how to make money from money. Whereas poor people's lives revolve around expenses and savings.

- The rich buy assets, the poor only have expenses, and the middle class buys liabilities they think are assets.

- Rich people don't work for fixed income. Instead, they like to take a share from sales or profits. Whereas poor people work to pay bills on time. Their focus is to get a raise in salary.

- Rich people want to build a business that pays all their expenses. Whereas, poor people are looking for a secured job and benefits.

- Rich people use other people's time, energy, knowledge, and money to grow their business and wealth. Whereas, poor people use their own time and energy to make income.

- The only difference between a rich person and a poor person is what they do in their spare time.

- The Poor and Middle class have been programmed from an early age to mind everyone else's business and ignore their own business.

- Rich people focus on increasing their passive income either through building a system-based business or by acquiring assets that provide long-term residual income.

Here are some key points discussed in the Rich Dad Poor Dad series:

- Financial struggle is often directly the result of people working all their lives for someone else.

- Pay yourself first.

- If people who own system-based business leave their business for a year and return, chances are they find their business growing better than what they left. Whereas if self-employed professionals and small business owners leave their business for a year, chances are there may be no business left to work again.

- Financial IQ is 90% emotional IQ and 10% technical information about finance or money.

- The world is filled with talented poor people. The reason for the lack of financial success is that many people play safe.

- For most people, the reason they don't win financially is that the pain of losing money is far greater than the joy of being rich.

- Workers work hard enough to not be fired, and owners pay just enough so that workers won't quit.

- Job Security meant everything to my educated dad. Learning meant everything to my rich dad.

- Many people are focused too much on money and not their greatest wealth, which is their education.

- Schools were designed to produce good employees instead of employers. The schooling process actually discourages creativity.

- We are living in the information age that offers more opportunities for financial rewards than ever before. In the Information Age, quality information is our most important asset.

- It is communication skills such as writing, speaking, and negotiating that are crucial to a life of success.

- The hardest part of running a company is managing people.

- The most important specialized skills are sales and understanding marketing.

I read *Think and Grow Rich* and *Rich Dad Poor Dad* series in my late 20s. But I think the right age to start reading such books is 15-18 because, at that time, a person is very confused about what to do in life.

Coming to the third book that surprised the world with its theory of working less for just a few hours a week has again influenced millions of people, especially today's generation, who want to become rich as well as enjoy life.

It's called *The 4-Hour Work Week,* written by Tim Ferris.

The book talks about the **New Rich** people who don't work whole life to retire and enjoy old age. And they don't work for long hours, don't believe in hard work, and are not restricted to one place.

Instead, they start living like a retired person at a young age by working less and smart, and from anywhere in the world.

For example, a New Rich person (Mr. A) maybe earning half of the other person (Mr. B), but if he is spending only one-fifth of the time used by Mr. B, then it's actually Mr. A who is richer among the two.

How?

By calculating the hourly rate.

For example, let's say Mr. A earns $ 100,000, and Mr. B earns $ 200,000.

Now, if we compare the absolute income of two people, Mr. B is twice as rich as Mr. A.

But the book says to find out who is richer among the two; we need to compare their **relative income** and not absolute income.

To calculate the relative income, we need to find out how much time they spent in earning their income.

Let's say Mr. A spends only 100 hours in a year to earn $ 100,000.

Whereas, Mr. B spends 500 hours in a year to earn $ 200,000.

So, Mr. A makes $ 1,000 per hour.

And Mr. B makes $400 per hour.

In terms of relative income, Mr. A makes more money than Mr. B per hour and hence richer than Mr. B.

This book also talks about the **Pareto Principle**, also known as the 80/20 rule. So, if you want to work only for a few hours, then you need to eliminate or outsource all the unimportant work.

These books are not guides or courses on how to become rich. They are revolutionary books that planted an idea that any ordinary person can become rich and successful by adopting the right thinking, attitude, and working.

These books are just a first step towards your goal of becoming rich. I refer to such books as "Awareness Books." Such books help you to know what successful and rich people do differently from others.

Remember, I told you about the four stages of Mastery in one of my previous issues. These books are written for people who are in the first stage, "Unconsciously Incompetent," so that they can move towards the second stage, "Consciously Incompetent."

In short, books like *Think and Grow Rich*, *Rich Dad Poor Dad*, and *The 4-Hour Workweek* help people realize and identify in which areas they are incompetent to master the game of becoming Rich.

The word "Rich" is very subjective. It has different meanings to different people. Let me tell you what the word "Rich" means to me.

For me, "Rich" means having sufficient money to retire today without any compulsion to work in the future. And this is possible only when I'm getting some money every month to take care of all my expenses.

No, I'm not talking about pension as most of us are not eligible for it.

I'm talking about PASSIVE INCOME.

Generally, there are two types of income:

a) Active Income – It's the money you earn whenever you do some work. For example, salary, consultancy fees, commission on sales, etc.

b) Passive Income – It's the money you earn even if you're not working. For example: rental income, royalties, subscription fees, interest on savings, dividend stocks, etc.

If you want to become Rich, Passive Income plays a very important role.

Even the greatest investor on this planet, Warren Buffett, says, "Make money while you sleep or work until you die."

A long time back, I watched an interview where a celebrity said, "I work because I don't want to work."

On the same note, I also work today in such a way that I don't want to spend my time, my energy, my mental and physical work in making Active Income tomorrow.

In simple words, I have to work smartly today so that tomorrow my Passive Income takes care of my expenses. And I can enjoy my life as I want. Even if I want to do the same work that I'm doing now, it will be considered as my hobby and not compulsion.

Q) Why it's not easy to become rich, working for someone else?

It's because your boss can't make you rich. He is busy making himself rich.

You see, unless you're getting royalties for your work or possessing stocks of your company, it's not possible to become rich while working for someone else.

You may counter my point by saying:

- a) What if I'm getting a good salary or commissions or both every month?

- b) What if I'm making much more money as an employee than most of the self-employed and small business owners?

- c) What if I'm investing my money in stocks, real estate, mutual funds, insurance, etc.?

Well, to answer, first and second questions, you're getting so much money simply because you're putting in your time, energy, knowledge, skills, mental and physical efforts.

My questions are:

What if you reduce your work or want to take a long vacation due to health or family issues?

What if you met an accident which has affected your physical abilities?

What if you're bored with your work and want to do something different?

Now coming to the third question, yes, it's a good thing that you're investing your money somewhere else that can act as security at difficult times as well as bring you passive income.

Still, I don't think it can make you rich unless you've thorough knowledge about that industry where you've invested your money. Also, it depends upon your willingness to take risks considering that you could lose your money in that investment.

Sadly, many people, particularly employees and self-employed, are so much consumed in their daily work that they make their investment decisions based on the advice of family, relatives, and friends.

Well, I'm not an expert on managing and investing money, but I would like to say that even if you hire professionals and consultants, then also it's critical to learn about the industry where you're investing your hard-earned money.

Many rich people invest money in real estate, stocks, bonds, businesses, movies, etc. but they either learn everything about that industry or hire the best people to take care of their investments.

Moreover, they have a lot of time and energy to learn about different investments because they are not working as an employee in their business. They have hired others to take care of their main business.

So, becoming rich through investments depends upon your willingness to learn, and the time and energy you devote to learning how to make money from money. And it also depends upon your financial capability to hire the best people available in the market who can take care of your investments.

But if you're investing your hard-earned money just because your friend or relative recommended you, then it's a gamble you're playing with your money.

Q) Why it's not easy to become rich by working as a Freelancer or Self-Employed Professional?

I've seen many professionals quit their job and start freelancing because of the following reasons:

- They want to be their own boss.

- They are a victim of office politics.

- They think they can earn much more if they start their own practice.

- They are good at networking. If they have many contacts, they assume they can keep getting business from them.

Of course, there are many advantages of becoming self-employed, especially for those who are highly competent and expert in their fields.

But there are a few disadvantages as well that could make them financially broke if they don't pay serious attention to problems faced by self-employed people.

As a matter of fact, a large number of people become self-employed because they have no jobs. This is the reason some self-employed people always remain underemployed.

It means they earn less than what they could have earned in a job.

The second reason is office politics because of which many innocent people get fired and become self-employed as they have no other option left.

As per my personal experience, I can say without any doubt that office politics has the power to destroy the whole business. I've seen many people quit jobs not because they are incompetent, but they are victims of office politics.

If you're a business owner and worry about outside competition, let me tell you that first, you need to be worried about inside politics, especially if you have a big staff.

A long time back, I created my own theory related to office politics:

Incompetence leads to Insecurity.

Insecurity leads to Politics.

And Politics leads to Incompetence.

The point is people who are dependent on politics for their survival are actually incompetent.

Unfortunately, I've seen some cases where competent people who ignored politics inside their company and just focused on their work had to pay a big price.

That's why it's important to not only become excellent in your work but to save yourself from incompetent, insecure people who will go to any level to stop you from progressing.

So, people become self-employed not only because they want to, but they have no other choice.

But living the life of a self-employed professional is not so easy.

Here are some disadvantages of being self-employed:

- Initially, you have to be a jack-of-all-trades, even if you consider yourself as an expert in your domain.

- For the first few years, you have to work day and night. You can't afford to take leaves even if it's urgent. There are no vacations, paid leaves, or any other employee benefits. This is quite normal for visionary entrepreneurs and people who are doing business right from the beginning. But not easy for people who were employees before.

- There are no incorporation benefits.

- Since the whole business depends on you, so the more you work… the more clients you serve… the more you involve yourself physically… then only you can make more money.

- And most important… you can't afford to get sick for a long time… you can't afford to lose any body part in an accident… And you can't afford to die.

- Some people become self-employed because they consider themselves super-experts in their area of work. For example: architect, lawyer, doctor, musician, accountant, artist, player, actor, author, etc. However, they are not good at selling. They start their own practice because it's quite common in their profession. Another reason some people become self-employed is they easily get assignments from their old relationships. But things change when sooner or later, they start struggling to get new clients.

Self-employed is like a daily job. You have to work every day. Only the difference is, instead of working for a single boss, you are working for multiple clients.

However, it's always good working for more than one person. At least, your job is not dependent on a single person. So, more job security as compared to a company employee who keeps checking the mood of the boss.

I have tremendous respect for self-employed professionals, especially for those who are experts and providing excellent service to their clients.

But I'm equally concerned about their lack of understanding to run a system-based business, and more importantly, their lack of sales & marketing skills.

If you like to work alone… if you're good at networking and building relationships… if you're good at dealing with clients… if you have super confidence in your expertise… if you don't want to be bothered about the nitty-gritty of running a big business… then it's good for you to be self-employed.

However, if you're struggling to get new clients… if you're good in persuasion but poor in maintaining relationships… if you're not so expert as compared to your competitors… if you can manage customers, employees, investors... then I would suggest turning your self-employed job into a business so that you can hire the best people in the areas where you're weak.

Besides, the biggest advantage of turning your full-time job into a system-based business is that you're getting cash flow without getting physically involved all time.

Q) What do you mean by a system-based business? Why owning a system-based business give more job security as well as the opportunity to become Rich?

To answer this question, let me share a story that I read in Robert Kiyosaki's *Cashflow Quadrant*.

The story was about a small village that was facing a water crisis. The village hired two people to bring clean water into the village.

The first person carried two buckets to bring water from the lake to the village. This process of going back and forth was repeated several times a day. Each time this person brought water to the village was compensated for service.

On the contrary, the second person took the time to make a plan to build a pipeline from the lake to the village. Although it took a lot of time to build the pipeline, once it was completed, the village had water 24 hours a day, 7 days a week.

Unlike the first person, the second person didn't choose a manual approach to bring water. Instead of thinking about making money right from the first day, the second person created the system-based business where the pipeline began to deliver water on a consistent basis, and in return, money also began to flow regularly.

By creating a system-based business, the second person built a cashflow machine.

A system-based business is not dependent on people. It works on auto-pilot. It's just like what you see in a manufacturing plant where robots are producing automobiles. And managers and engineers are sitting in a control room, keeping an eye on everything.

But it doesn't mean you need high-end technology to build a system-based business.

What you need is a template, clearly written steps based on your experimentation and experience so that low skilled people can run the entire operations without your direct involvement.

A system-based business is like an automatic machine which is producing continuous cashflow to you even if you're not working.

For any business, the most important thing is cashflow. Cashflow helps you in expanding your business. Cashflow helps you in becoming self-reliant. Cashflow helps you in paying all your debts.

In order to get a consistent cash flow, you need to build a system-based business. For this, you need to work on your business; and not in your business. When you work on your business, you can standardize it as much you want... you can replicate it wherever you want... and you can sell it whenever you want...

Q) What is your favourite business model?

Every business model has its own pros and cons. No business model is perfect. It all depends upon your personality what kind of work you enjoy the most.

In my case, I like two business models just because I find them quite suitable for my lifestyle. Both of them are generally used in selling B2C products. Ironically, most of my work experience is in B2B… first, selling very expensive softwares to big corporates… and second, selling my training programs to all kinds of businesses. But now I've shifted into subscription selling.

The **Subscription model** is one of my favourite business models.

You can sell low-priced items like newspapers and cable TV subscriptions. And you can sell high-priced services like club membership and investment newsletter subscriptions.

I found the subscription model a bit easy to start and manage.

If you're good at direct response marketing, then you can market and sell directly to customers.

And you can build a long-term relationship with your subscribers.

If you're a small business owner or self-employed professional, adopting a subscription model in your business can do wonders for you.

One of the best examples of subscription models is OTT streaming media service, like Netflix and Amazon Prime Video.

As you know, they have a huge library of old and new movies, documentaries, web series.

By paying monthly subscription fees, you can watch movies from wherever you want. What is required is a smart TV or a laptop or a smartphone.

Moreover, they keep adding new stuff to attract new subscribers.

Streaming media is a disruptive technology that is gradually going to destroy movie theaters, movie rental, and DVD business.

These days technology is playing a huge role in a subscription model business.

Another good example of a subscription model is the Tata Sky cable TV service in India because of its super lucrative offers.

Once you install Tata Sky, you will see so many advertisements on its home channel persuading you to subscribe to different channels. So, you're not only paying the subscription fees to keep your service active, but you're also paying additional fees to subscribe to fitness, beauty, comedy, food, music, classroom, and celebrity channels.

This is a great example of upselling services to existing customers.

Another good example of a subscription model is newsletter publishing, where an expert can share his or her knowledge to hundreds and thousands of subscribers all over the world.

One of the big disadvantages of self-help books is that generally 60-80% part of the book is full of motivation, philosophy, stories… and only a small part talks about the real thing, which is, teaching an income-generating skill.

Whereas, a newsletter could be all meat & potatoes info. I mean, a paid newsletter could talk about every technique in detail like a subscriber is directly learning from the expert.

Unlike books, which are one-sided communication, a newsletter may cover the latest research, new and universal applications of old principles & techniques, latest news & updates, questions & answers, advanced topics, powerful exercises, and hot tips.

A book develops a one-time relationship with the reader, but a newsletter develops a long-lasting relationship with the subscriber.

The other business model that I like is the **Franchise model**. I'm not talking about buying a franchise. That anybody can do who has money and resources.

I'm talking about building a new franchise and selling it globally. It requires your real talent.

Mc Donald's is one of the finest examples.

McDonald's doesn't make the best burgers, but they have one of the best systems to make and sell identical burgers without hiring expensive people.

Do you remember, in one of the old issues I talked about Ray Kroc, the man who built McDonald's? *The Founder* movie is based on his life.

Instead of going to his old business friends, Ray Kroc persuaded ordinary young people to buy and run their own franchise of McDonald's.

The best thing about the franchise model is that once you build a perfect prototype, you can easily replicate the same in different areas of the city, state, and even countries.

However, you've to be extremely persuasive, like Ray Kroc, to sell your concept to franchise buyers and investors.

Like Ray Kroc, who was a small businessman without any big qualifications, there were other ordinary people who started the global franchise business. For example:

Dominos Pizza was founded by Tom Monaghan, a college student.

Kentucky Fried Chicken was founded by Colonel Harland Sanders, who did various jobs throughout his life and later franchised his secret recipe at the age of 62.

Subway was founded by Fred DeLuca, again a college student.

Although most of the famous and successful franchises are in the food and hospitality industry, what's important to learn from the franchise model is how to build a system-based business that could be run by low-skilled people and easily replicate all over the world.

One of the best things about the franchise model is that **everything is scripted**. I mean all operations are run based on the operation manual - right from how to prepare the product to what to wear to how to communicate with the customer.

I recommend reading *The E-Myth Revisited*, written by Michael E. Gerber, which talks about the franchise model in detail.

Q) What is the difference between Influence and Persuasion?

Influence is used to change people's thoughts. It may work gradually but has a long-lasting effect.

For example,

Political party propagandists use influence tactics to make people like the leader and dislike opposition.

PR (Public Relations) agencies and media use influence tactics to make people like movie stars, sportspeople, politicians, and celebrity businesspeople.

Advertising agencies use influence tactics to make people like brands.

Whereas, Persuasion is used to make people take action. It works fast but has a short-term effect. It means you need to keep applying persuasion tactics to the same person whenever you want him or her to take action.

For example,

Politicians use persuasion to get votes.

Salespeople use persuasion to get orders.

Parents use persuasion to make children do the homework.

Managers use persuasion to get things done.

Both Influence and Persuasion can be used together to increase the effectiveness of your selling power. For example, if a person is highly influenced by your thoughts, it becomes easier for you to persuade and sell your products and services to that person.

Q) Which industries are heavily dependent on Influence and Persuasion?

Influence and Persuasion are used daily in both personal and professional lives to get things done. But there are some professions and industries which are heavily dependent on these skills.

Here are some of them:

Advertising

Advertising can be broadly classified into two types:

Image Advertising: It's also called General Advertising or Brand Advertising. It's used by companies to influence people's minds to like their products.

Generally, big companies use Image Advertising to build their brands. Their primary job is to influence people's minds and position their products. Or it can be said their job is to buy some space in people's minds so that people remember them and prefer their products whenever they decide to buy.

Image advertising is heavily used in traditional media like TV, radio, newspapers, magazines, and billboards.

The biggest disadvantage of Image Advertising is that it is not accountable. It's difficult to measure which advertisement brought sales; and which advertisement destroyed sales.

That's why you will find many advertising agencies (both traditional and digital) generally work on brand building activities instead of creating ads that could directly bring sales to clients.

Instead of presenting a strong sales argument, General Advertising agencies are more interested in creating highly emotional entertaining ads.

They hire celebrities to increase the power of their ads.

They want people to like and appreciate their ads, which could help them in getting more clients and awards.

Direct Response Advertising: Being a hard-core salesperson, I'm biased towards Direct Response Advertising. Direct Response uses Persuasion principles and techniques to bring immediate sales.

Direct Response can be further categorized as:

- Mail Order Advertising – It is the process of running advertisements in newspapers and magazines with a coupon or a phone number or a website address to place the order.

- Direct Mail Advertising – It's the process of mailing Sales Letters to different lists.

- Infomercials – Long-form advertisements that you see on TV.

- Internet Marketing – It includes SEO, display advertisements, landing page, sales page, video sales letters, emails, and social media posts that are persuading people to take any kind of action.

Unlike General Advertising, in Direct Response, you will find Call to Action in every ad.

Direct Response is mostly used by small businesses that are more interested in increasing sales and not in brand building. These companies can't afford to spend money on an advertisement that does not bring sales.

Direct Selling

It is also called One-to-One or Face-to-Face Selling. It includes:

- Institutional Sales (selling to corporations and institutions as a whole rather than selling to individual parts of the company)

- One-to-one demonstrations

- Telemarketing

- Inside sales

A large number of traditional businesses adopt this method to market and sell their product. They either build their own sales team or hire individual agents or a Direct Sales Agency to sell their products. For example: Distributors, Dealers, Resellers, Wholesalers, Retailers, Affiliates, and Insurance Agents.

Direct Sales Agencies are into hard-core selling. Generally, they do all of the work, right from generating inquires to closing the sale to providing training and support. And in return, they get commissions on selling other companies' products.

In cases where manufacturers don't want to pay money to the middlemen and want to have full control over their sales & marketing operations, build their own sales team.

In Direct Selling, salespeople play a very important role. They have to continuously build their funnel (pipeline). They have to be good at prospecting, presenting, relationship building, and most importantly, closing.

This is what a traditional sales cycle looks like:

1. Prospecting: Hunting for new customers

2. Gathering information about your prospects

3. Start building rapport with your prospects

4. Identifying the wants and needs of your prospects

5. Qualifying your prospects

6. Presenting your solution

7. Overcoming objections of your prospects

8. Closing the deal

9. Bonding to build a long-term relationship with your customer

10. Getting referrals from your customers

Multi Level Marketing (MLM)

Multi Level Marketing has become a huge industry but has also gained a bad reputation.

Like Direct Sales agencies, MLM also uses Direct Selling methods to sell their products. However, there are some differences...

First, many MLM companies are selling their own products.

Second, instead of hiring salespeople on their payroll, they build a chain of people to sell their products. This is called Network Marketing.

These people can be employees, business owners, housewives, or students. They start selling MLM products to make some extra money, but gradually some of them get so much involved in the MLM business that they leave their full-time job.

This industry is heavily dependent on Persuasion tactics to make new members.

Sadly, this industry has earned a bad reputation because many MLM companies are involved in completely unethical Pyramid selling.

The companies show big dreams of becoming rich... financially independent... be your own boss... because of which many people become their members without understanding the real purpose.

Members of MLM are told to approach their near and dear ones to sell their products. The reason is the people who are closed to us have no or low resistance towards us. MLM members can easily enter their house, pitch their products, and get referrals.

By approaching near and dear ones reduces the chances of facing rejections, which is very common in Direct Sales.

However, the real problem starts when these members, instead of selling products to end-users, start selling their products to new members so that they can become eligible for higher positions and commissions.

The focus shifts from selling products to recruiting more and more members and then persuading these new members to buy enough stock from them to become eligible for higher commissions. This is what the Pyramid Selling is.

In this way, many unethical MLM companies survive and grow by selling their products to their own members instead of selling to customers.

Cults

Cults are another bad example where Persuasion is used heavily but unethically.

A cult is a closed-door organization, a social group that is formed on some ideology, beliefs, cause, or religious, spiritual, traditional practices.

Generally, cults are founded by charismatic leaders who create their own rules, culture, and duties to be performed by followers regularly.

Cults can be local groups with a few members to international organizations with millions of members.

One of the main functions of cults is to recruit new members without any pay and make them so much devoted towards the leader and organization that they give all their time, money, and energy to the organization.

Cults create such an environment that it's become difficult for people to leave the organization.

Just like MLM, cults become powerful and rich by recruiting more and more members.

And just like businesses employ their best salespeople to bring new sales, cults also use their best people in recruiting new members.

The cult leader is considered a God figure inside the organization.

No member dares to question the leader's ideology.

No member dares to argue with the leader.

No member dares to leave meetings, lectures, and daily rituals.

When you meet their old members, you'll feel like they are brainwashed to the extent that they cannot listen to anything against their organization, beliefs, and leader.

Many members, along with their family, spent their whole life serving cults without expecting anything in return.

Members live together at a place far from the general public so that they don't get influenced by outsiders. But their highly trained recruiters keep roaming in cities, towns, and villages looking for people who can match the psychographic profile of their members.

Once recruited, these members go through a rigorous influence and persuasion process, after which they work day and night without expecting any payment in return.

Q) Who are your favourite Master Persuaders who have also written great books?

Before I tell about some of my favourite Master Persuaders who have also written great books, I would like to share one of my experiences that could save you a lot of time that you invest in reading.

When I started reading books, I used to read business, motivational, self-improvement books... whatever recommended by top business people, celebrities, great performers, friends, and colleagues.

Though it helped me in increasing my knowledge in various areas, it reduces my productivity drastically.

On the one side, I became a voracious reader and considered intelligent among my peer group, but on the other side, I became a poor practitioner when it comes to selling skills.

So, the big lesson that I learned after spending years reading is... **Masters are not great readers; they are great practitioners.**

Just like in the case of Martial Arts. You need to learn a new technique and then practice it daily to become better at it.

There is a Japanese management philosophy called *Kaizen*. It says small continuous improvements in all functions and by all people can improve the overall productivity.

So, I adopted the same philosophy in my life to become better in my skills.

Instead of reading various subjects, I started re-reading only classic books.

Instead of becoming a voracious reader, I become a deep thinker.

Instead of reading, I started studying books.

This philosophy changed my life completely. I started getting better results, though gradually.

Earlier I used to get anxiety to not miss even a single book on a subject I was interested in. But when I changed my approach from a reader to a deep thinker to a practitioner, that anxiety disappeared.

Still, I'm an old-school guy, devoted to learning from Masters. Here are some of my favourite Master Persuaders who also wrote some great books.

Claude C. Hopkins

If you're from the advertising industry, then I'm sure you've heard of Claude Hopkins. He is considered the granddaddy of advertising, perhaps the most successful copywriter of all time. A copywriter is a person who writes advertisements.

Claude Hopkins was responsible for turning small businesses into huge through his very persuasive ads.

Some of the top brands could have never become a household name if this man was not there. For example:

Palmolive – The owner of Palmolive approached Claude Hopkins and his colleagues with a different product, Galvanic Soap – a laundry soap. Hopkins team suggested the soap maker to not go for advertising of this product.

The team asked the owner if they had any other product. The soap-maker said they had a toilet soap called Palmolive made with Palm and Olive oils. But they didn't consider it as an advertising opportunity.

Hopkins team spotted an advertising opportunity in this product. They argued that since Roman beauties used palm and olive oils, this soap could strongly appeal to women. And the rest is history.

Another example of Claude Hopkins's greatness is the way he created the toothbrushing habit in Americans.

At that time, less than 10% of Americans used to brush their teeth every day. When the promoter of Pepsodent approached Claude Hopkins to create promotions for their toothpaste, he realized he needed to find a trigger for its daily use.

Hopkins found that most of the advertisements that time were talking about the preventive measures as the primary function of toothpaste.

But Hopkins knew that talking about preventive measures would not help in persuading customers to use toothpaste.

These advertisements failed to understand the important aspect of human nature.

People would do anything to solve a problem but very little to prevent it.

So, Hopkins sat down with a pile of dental textbooks to find out the problem.

Hopkins read book after book by dental authorities on the theory on which Pepsodent was based. In the middle of one book, he found a reference to the mucin plaques on teeth, which he afterward called the FILM.

Hopkins decided to advertise Pepsodent as a creator of beauty that deals with that cloudy film.

Hopkins created persuasive advertisements based on his findings that not only changed the habit of more than half of the American population to brush their teeth every day but also made Pepsodent the No.1 choice to remove this film. Here is one of the ads:

Why That Tartar?

If You Keep Teeth Clean?

All Statements Approved by High Dental Authorities

It is Due to Film

TARTAR shows that teeth are not kept clean. The basis is a slimy film. If you removed it daily tartar would not form.

That film on your teeth causes most tooth troubles. It is ever present, ever forming. You can feel it with your tongue.

The film is what discolours, not the teeth. It holds food substance which ferments, and form acid. It holds the acid in contact with the teeth to cause decay.

Millions of germs breed in it. They, with tartar, are the chief cause of pyorrhoea.

The film is viscous, so it clings. It gets into crevices and stays. The ordinary dentifrice does not dissolve it. The toothbrush leaves much of it intact. That is why the best-brushed teeth so often discolour and decay.

Every dentist knows this. Dental science has for years sought a way to combat that film. That way has now been found. And, for daily use, it is embodied in a dentifrice called Pepsodent.

We ask you to write for a free 10-day Tube and learn what it means to your teeth.

Watch It Disappear

Get this free tube of Pepsodent and use like any toothpaste. Note how clean the teeth feel after using. Mark the absence of the slimy film. See how the teeth whiten as the fixed film disappears. You will know in a few days what clean teeth mean.

Pepsodent is based on pepsin, the digestant of albumin. The film is albuminous matter. The object of Pepsodent is to dissolve it, then to constantly combat it.

The way seems simple but for long it seemed impossible.

Pepsin must be activated, and the usual method is an acid harmful to the teeth.

Then the invention of a harmless activating method made this application impossible. And it seems to solve the problem of this tooth-destroying film.

Pepsodent has been proved under able authorities by many clinical tests. Leading dentists all over America have come to endorse and adopt it. Now we urge you to try it.

....

This is an approximately 100 years old advertisement but much more effective than ads we see today.

Claude Hopkins is considered the highest-paid copywriter of all time. In 1907, at the age of 41, Hopkins was hired by an advertising agency at a salary of $185,000 a year. That's around $5 million with inflation.

Another example of Claude Hopkins's advertising acumen is how he used a story to sell carpet cleaner at the beginning of his advertising career.

Hopkins was looking for wood used in carpet cleaners.

He came to know about Vermillion wood that had an interesting story about how the wood came from the forests in India that were owned by the British Government at that time. The wood was cut by convicts and then hauled to the Ganges river by elephants. Since the vermillion wood was heavy than water, so a log of ordinary wood was placed on either side of each vermillion log to float it down the river.

Hopkins decided to use vermillion wood in carpet cleaners and pitch this story in his campaigns.

It was difficult for him to convince his employers because they believed sweeper users had no interest in wood. What they want in carpet cleaners is broom action, efficient dumping devices, and pure bristle brushes.

However, Hopkins didn't give up and persuaded his employers to order vermillion wood.

For the campaign, Hopkins used letterheads lithographed in vermillion colour. His envelopes were vermillion addressed in white ink.

Hopkins printed two million pamphlets with vermillion covers and a rajah's head on the front. The pamphlet had a story and pictures of forests, convicts, the elephants, Ganges river, etc. which aroused curiosity to bring women to see that wood.

As a result, the carpet sweeper company made more money in the next six weeks than they had made in any year before.

The point is story sells even if it has nothing to do with the functioning of the product.

The greatest contribution of Claude Hopkins is his two classic books:

1)   Scientific Advertising

2)   My Life in Advertising

Scientific Advertising is considered the Bible of advertising. David Ogilvy, the founder of Ogilvy & Mather, said, "Nobody should be allowed to have anything to do with advertising until he has read this book seven times. It changed the course of my life."

Here are some key ideas Hopkins discussed in these books:

- Advertising is just salesmanship. It is not meant for awareness or entertainment. The people you entertain are not the same people that will buy from you.

- Advertising is effective because instead of reaching one person, you can reach thousands or even millions of people.

- An ad should be informative. It should contain enough information for a consumer to make a decision. No more, no less.

- Doing anything blindly is madness.

- Understanding psychology and the science behind why customers purchase products is necessary to be a great advertiser.

- An advertisement should be judged on the basis of results only.

- Small changes in headlines and the copy can create a drastic change in results. Spend a lot of time writing out headline ideas until you find the winner.

- Create split tests to find the best performing headlines, images, call to action, and other elements that make up ads.

What Claude Hopkins wrote around 100 years back has become much more applicable nowadays because of internet marketing. Today advertisement has taken various forms. For example: landing page, sales page, social media post, email, webinar, etc.

Many people think Copywriter's job is just to write ads and sales letters. It's a mistake if you consider a good copywriter a master of words only. A good copywriter is a person full of crazy ideas.

I keep suggesting business owners hire or consult a good sales copywriter regularly, even if these business owners have nothing to do with advertising.

There are many reasons why you need a copywriter to grow your business.

If you want to study the needs and desires of your market, you need a copywriter.

If you're launching a new product, you need a copywriter.

If you want to change the name of existing products, you need a copywriter.

If you want to build a marketing system, you need a copywriter.

If you're launching a political campaign, you need a copywriter.

If you want to make press releases, you need a copywriter.

If you want to run PR campaigns, you need a copywriter.

If you want to create a website, you need a copywriter.

If you're running an e-commerce store, you need a copywriter.

If you want to make a movie, you need a copywriter.

If you want to give a political or corporate speech, you need a copywriter.

If you want to run a fundraising campaign, you need a copywriter.

If you want to pitch an investor, you need a copywriter.

In short, a copywriter is an ideas man who can help in many ways to influence and persuade your target market.

David Ogilvy

Another legendary Master Persuader whom I admire a lot is again from the advertising industry. I'm talking about David Ogilvy, popularly known as Father of Advertising.

David Ogilvy is considered one of the greatest persuaders of all time.

Ogilvy created some great campaigns like Come to Britain, Come to France, Come to the United States, and Come to Puerto Rico that helped these countries in becoming a popular tourist destination.

Some of his clients were Rolls Royce, Mercedes, Shell, IBM, American Express, Sears Roebuck.

Ogilvy, who started as an apprentice chef in Paris and then worked as a door-to-door salesman in Scotland selling cooking stoves, became enormously successful in advertising because he always studied his market. He knew the hot buttons of people.

Trained at the Gallup research organization, Ogilvy attributed the success of his campaigns to meticulous research into consumer habits.

Here are headlines of some of his famous ads:

- At 60 miles an hour the loudest noise In the new Rolls-Royce comes from the electric clock

- The man in the Hathaway shirt

- How to create advertising that sells

- Reward your top executives with a sabbatical
  year in Britain – on half pay

- How 3 of Super Shell's 9 ingredients fight
  engine noise – including one hard-to-hear
  form of knock that could lead to real damage

- Darling, I'm having the most extraordinary
  experience... I'm head over heels in DOVE!

- Should every corporation buy its president a
  Rolls-Royce?

- Now Puerto Rico offers 100% tax exemption
  to new industry

- How women over 35 can look younger

- How direct response advertising can increase
  your sales and profits?

- How to tour the U.S.A. for £35 a week

- What's under the bonnet of a Rolls-Royce?

David Ogilvy is the author of two famous books:

1) *Confessions of an Advertising Man*

2)   *Ogilvy on Advertising*

Here are some key points discussed in these books:

- The consumer isn't a moron; she is your wife.

- 99% of advertising doesn't sell much of anything at all.

- If it doesn't sell, it isn't creative. In the modern world of business, it is useless to be a creative, original thinker unless you can also sell what you create.

- Products, like people, have personalities, and they can make or break them in the market place.

- It takes a big idea to attract the attention of consumers and get them to buy your product. Unless your advertising contains a big idea, it will pass like a ship in the night. I doubt if more than one campaign in a hundred contains a big idea.

- Advertising people who ignore research are as dangerous as generals who ignore decodes of enemy signals.

- The best ideas come as jokes. Make your thinking as funny as possible.

- What you say is more important than how you say it. What really decides consumers to buy or not to buy is the content of your advertising, not its form.

- Never write an advertisement which you wouldn't want your family to read. You wouldn't tell lies to your own wife.

- The more informative your advertising, the more persuasive it will be.

- There is no need for advertisements to look like advertisements. If you make them look like editorials pages, you will attract about 50% more readers.

- I don't know the rules of grammar... If you're trying to persuade people to do something, it seems to me you should use their language, the language they use every day, the language in which they think. We try to write in the vernacular.

- Never stop testing, and your advertising will never stop improving.

Tony Robbins

The third Master Persuader, whom I admire, is a famous motivational speaker who has influenced millions of lives in the last three decades. I'm talking about *Anthony Robbins*.

Robbins never attended college and started his career as a salesman, selling tickets for seminars on motivation.

Later he got the chance to learn *Neuro Linguistic Programming* (NLP) from John Grinder.

....

NLP is the science and art of modeling other people in order to produce similar behavior & results in the self or other people.

It is generally used in personal development, communication, and even psychotherapy (in treating problems like depression and phobias).

NLP was created by *Richard Bandler* and *John Grinder* in the 1970s. They claim that NLP methodology can model the skills of exceptional people allowing anyone to acquire those skills.

....

Tony Robbins also learned how to firewalk and incorporated it in his seminars. Firewalk became one of the most striking features of his seminars.

In the late 1980s, Robbins started promoting his services as a "Peak Performance Coach" through infomercials that made him immensely popular in America.

Robbins has coached some of the most powerful people like Bill Clinton, Princess Diana, Oprah Winfrey, Nelson Mandela, Mother Theresa, Mikhail Gorbachev, Margaret Thatcher, Leonardo Di Caprio, Serena Williams, Hugh Jackman, Larry King, and Mike Tyson.

Two of his famous books are:

1) Unlimited Power

2) Awaken the Giant Within

Here are some important points covered in these two books:

- You become what you do most of the time.

- If you do what you've always done, you'll get what you've always gotten.

- All persuasion is an altering of perception.

- You shape your perceptions, or someone shapes them for you.

- Greatest fears and limitations are self-imposed.

- It's not the events of our lives that shape us, but our beliefs as to what those events mean.

- Many people are passionate, but because of their limiting beliefs about who they are and what they can do, they never take the action that could make their dream a reality.

- All human problems are behavioural problems.

- Your behaviour is the result of the state you're in. The state is the result of your internal representations and your physiology. If you can change a state, you can change your behaviour.

- The way we communicate with others and the way we communicate with ourselves ultimately determine the quality of our lives.

- To effectively communicate, we must realize that we are all different in the way we perceive the world and use this understanding as a guide to our communication with others.

- People feel uncomfortable and suspicious of those who have values very different from their own.

- The secret of success is learning how to use pain and pleasure instead of having pain and pleasure use you. If you do that, you're in control of your life. If you don't, life controls you.

- It is your decisions... not the environment that controls your destiny.

- Consciously decide who you want to be.

- Decision without Action is pointless.

- Define precisely what you want. And then take action. If you don't take action, your desires will always be dreams.

- Anything done by successful people can be easily modelled. Modelling is the pathway to excellence.

- If you have an excellent model of how to produce a result, discover specifically, what the model does and duplicate it. It helps you to produce similar results in a much shorter period than you may have thought possible.

- Don't major in minor things.

My list of favourite Master Persuaders doesn't end here. I'll keep talking about them whenever I get a chance.

But from the next volume, I'll go back to teaching Persuasion principles and techniques.

Digital Courses

Become A Master of Closing Sales: The ultimate course on Closing Deals

Decoding Your Customer's Mind: Why your customer chooses you over your competitors?

Persuade and Grow Rich: A streetsmart for small businesses to convert NOs into YESes

Turn Your Business into Cashflow Machine: A proven automatic method to bring new customers and repeated sales from existing customers

LIVE Online Trainings

Types of Trainings

Public Workshop

In-house Training

One-to-One Coaching

Topics

Mastering Persuasion in Business: Learn science & art of persuasion in converting NOs into YESes

Become A Master of Closing Deals: Learn how to deal with objections and the most powerful closing techniques.